WordPerfect® 12

FOR

DUMMIES®

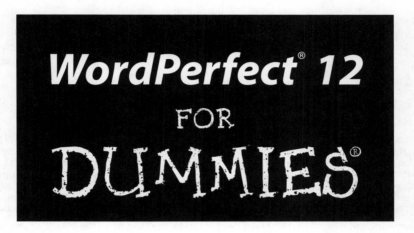

WordPerfect® 12
FOR
DUMMIES®

by Margaret Levine Young, David Kay,
and Richard Wagner

WILEY

Wiley Publishing, Inc.

WordPerfect® 12 For Dummies®

Published by
Wiley Publishing, Inc.
111 River Street
Hoboken, NJ 07030-5774

For general information on our other products and services or to obtain technical support, please contact our Customer Care Department within the U.S. at 800-762-2974, outside the U.S. at 317-572-3993, or fax 317-572-4002.

Wiley also publishes its books in a variety of electronic formats. Some content that appears in print may not be available in electronic books.

Library of Congress Control Number: 2004110663

ISBN: 0-7645-7808-1

Manufactured in the United States of America

10 9 8 7 6 5 4 3 2 1

1O/SU/QZ/QU/IN

WILEY

About the Authors

In high school, **Margaret Levine Young** was in a computer club before there were high school computer clubs. She stayed in the field throughout college, graduated from Yale, and went on to become one of the first PC managers in the early 1980s at Columbia Pictures, where she rode the elevator with big stars whose names she wouldn't dream of dropping here.

Since then, Margy has co-authored more than 25 computer books about the topics of the Internet, UNIX, WordPerfect, Microsoft Access, and (stab from the past) PC-File and Javelin, including *Access 2003 All-in-One Desk Reference For Dummies, Dummies 101: The Internet For Windows 98, UNIX For Dummies,* and *WordPerfect for Linux For Dummies* (all published by Wiley Publishing, Inc.), *Poor Richard's Building Online Communities* (published by Top Floor Publishing), and *Windows XP: The Complete Reference and Internet: The Complete Reference* (published by Osborne/McGraw-Hill). Aside from explaining computers to anyone who will listen, her other passion is her children, along with music, Unitarian Universalism (www.uua.org), reading, and anything to do with eating. She lives in Vermont (see www.gurus.com/margy for some scenery).

David C. Kay is a writer, engineer, artist, and naturalist, combining disparate occupations with the same effectiveness as his favorite business establishment, Acton Muffler, Brake, and Ice Cream (now defunct). Dave has written or contributed to more than a dozen computer books, including various editions of *WordPerfect 11 For Dummies, Graphics File Formats,* and *The Complete Reference, Millennium Edition.*

Besides writing computer books, Dave consults and writes for high-tech firms, and also teaches about wildlife and edible plants. For recreation, he paints theatrical sets, makes strange blobs from molten glass, sings Gilbert and Sullivan choruses in public, and hikes in whatever mountains he can get to. He longs for the Rocky Mountains of Canada, pines for the fjords of New Zealand, and dreams of tracking kiwis and hedgehogs in Wanaka. He feels silly writing about himself in the third person like this and will stop now.

Richard Wagner is an experienced *For Dummies* author whose writings span both technical and non-technical worlds. His tech books include *WordPerfect 11 For Dummies, XML All-in-One Desk Reference For Dummies, XSLT For Dummies,* as well as 15 other computer books. He also invented and architected the award-winning NetObjects ScriptBuilder software product. In his non-tech life, Richard is author of *Christianity For Dummies* and *Christian Prayer For Dummies* and editor of the Digitalwalk.com e-zine.

Dedication

I dedicate this book to Kimberly and the entire team at Jeta Workshop.

Acknowledgments

Special thanks go to Susan Pink, who kept the project on track and shepherded the book throughout the editorial process, to Lee Musick for his keen attention to detail and helpful technical suggestions, and to Tiffany Franklin for getting this project off the ground and rolling.

Publisher's Acknowledgments

We're proud of this book; please send us your comments through our online registration form located at www.dummies.com/register/.

Some of the people who helped bring this book to market include the following:

Acquisitions, Editorial, and Media Development

Project Editor: Susan Pink

Acquisitions Editor: Tiffany Franklin

Technical Editor: Lee Musick

Editorial Manager: Carol Sheehan

Media Development Supervisor: Richard Graves

Editorial Assistant: Amanda Foxworth

Cartoons: Rich Tennant (www.the5thwave.com)

Production

Project Coordinator: Adrienne Martinez, Maridee Ennis

Layout and Graphics: Lauren Goddard, Denny Hager, Joyce Haughey, Michael Kruzil, Melanee Prendergast

Proofreaders: John Greenough, Carl Pierce, TECHBOOKS Production Services

Indexer: TECHBOOKS Production Services

Publishing and Editorial for Technology Dummies

Richard Swadley, Vice President and Executive Group Publisher

Andy Cummings, Vice President and Publisher

Mary Bednarek, Executive Acquisitions Director

Mary C. Corder, Editorial Director

Publishing for Consumer Dummies

Diane Graves Steele, Vice President and Publisher

Joyce Pepple, Acquisitions Director

Composition Services

Gerry Fahey, Vice President of Production Services

Debbie Stailey, Director of Composition Services

Contents at a Glance

Table of Contents

Part IV: All the World's a Page: Going Beyond Your Desktop 253

Chapter 13: Publishing for the Web 255

Chapter 14: Using WordPerfect in a Microsoft Office World 267

Introduction

*1*f you thought that the purpose of word processing was to write, not to do amazing things on a computer . . . If you ever secretly wondered who in the world actually uses *all* those features advertised on the box your software came in . . . If you'd rather create nice-looking, readable documents, not try to use every possible feature in WordPerfect in 90 seconds flat . . . If you're smart enough to say, "Call me what you will — I just want to get some work done, please!" . . . Congratulations — you've come to the right place.

How to Use This Book

This book is a reference book, so when some feature in WordPerfect has you tying knots in your mouse cord, you can just look up what you want in the table of contents or the index.

If your brow is already furrowed from merely looking at the pictures of Word-Perfect on the box, check out the early chapters first. These chapters are written for beginners; they speak of mice and menus and similar basics. They help you get used to the what, why, and how of giving commands to WordPerfect. After you understand the basics, though, you don't have to read the chapters in any sequence.

Conventions Used in This Book

We try to avoid conventions (too many long lines to the restroom). Mostly, you find full, robust sentences, not cryptic abbreviations or other so-called conventions. On the other hand, if we always used instructions such as

> Move the mouse so that the mouse pointer covers the word Edit on the menu bar and then press the left mouse button. A menu appears, containing the word Cut. Move the mouse so that the mouse pointer covers the word Cut. . .

you'd be comatose by Chapter 2, and this book would take on encyclopedic dimensions. When we want you to choose a command from the menu bar and then choose another command from the submenu that appears, we use this cute little arrow: ⇨. So, instead of the long drawn-out instructions just presented, we write "Choose Edit⇨Cut" instead.

We also use a few other conventions to make things more readable. When we want you to type something, it appears in **bold** type. Internet addresses look `like this`. When we suggest pressing two keys at the same time, such as the Ctrl key and the C key, we use a plus sign, like this: Ctrl+C.

Foolish Assumptions

This section explains what we assume about you, our esteemed (and, thanks to the joy of software, occasionally steamed) reader:

- ✔ You use a PC with Windows and WordPerfect Office 12 installed.
- ✔ You want to create text documents that look nice.
- ✔ You know some basics of working in Microsoft Windows, probably enough to at least browse the Web or check your e-mail.
- ✔ If you're lucky, you have a guru available — an expert, like one of those infuriatingly clever 10-year-olds born with a computer cable for an umbilical cord — for the really tough stuff.
- ✔ You have a typical installation of WordPerfect Office 12. WordPerfect is accommodating almost to a fault and lets itself be twisted and restructured like a ball of Silly Putty. If buttons and things on your screen don't look like the buttons in the figures in this book or if your keyboard doesn't work as this book describes, be suspicious that someone got clever and changed things. The differences might be small enough that you can figure out what to do anyway. If not, go find the person who changed things and ask for help.

Although we assume that lucky readers have a computer guru at their disposal, we also know that gurus can be hard to coax down from the top of the mountain. So we teach you a few of the important guru-type tricks where it's practical.

How This Book Is Organized

Unlike computer manuals, which often seem to be organized alphabetically by height, this book is organized by what you may be trying to do. For example, we don't explain all the commands on the Edit menu in one chapter. Our reasoning is that the Edit commands don't necessarily have anything to do with editing and that Edit is a foolish category because isn't almost everything you do in a word processor a sort of edit anyway? No, what this book does is break things down into the following six useful categories.

Part I: Exploring the Essentials

Part I gets you up and running by showing you how to use the essential features of WordPerfect. This part is the place to go for the basics of using menus and toolbars to navigate your document and control WordPerfect. You also explore how to create a document, edit it, check the spelling, and make it come out of your printer.

Part II: Formatting Your Text

A few holdouts from the 1960s probably still love to create documents that look like they were typed on an old manual typewriter — monospaced text with double-spaced paragraphs. But we suspect that you've probably moved into the 21st century and would like to create some snazzy-looking documents that include fancy fonts, page numbers, and text styles. If so, check out Part II. It's all there.

Part III: Making Your Documents Come Alive

In this era of digital cameras, scanners, and ink jet printers, creating a document often involves more than just typing plain old text, no matter how nice the font looks. Part III enables you to "get with the program" as you discover how to make your documents come alive with pictures, tables, borders, and other types of cool formatting.

Part IV: All The World's a Page: Going Beyond Your Desktop

WordPerfect is a popular software program, but you can't be sure that everyone who reads your document also has WordPerfect on their machine. Good thing the folks at Corel realized that too, because they developed an arsenal of tools you can use to get your documents in just the right format, whatever the occasion. Part IV focuses on how to use WordPerfect to publish Web pages, Adobe Acrobat (PDF) documents, and XML files. And, because most everyone and their brother use Microsoft Office, you'll discover how Word Perfect can work "perfectly" with Microsoft Office documents.

Part V: More Stuff You Can Do with Your Documents

Nestled in WordPerfect are some nifty features that allow you to manage and work with multiple documents. Check out Part V to find out about these capabilities. What's more, if you ever wanted to put on a trench coat and do some sleuthing, now's your chance. This part also explores how to work with reveal codes, WordPerfect's secret coding language behind your documents.

Part VI: The Part of Tens

In honor of the decimal system, the Ten Commandments, and the fact that humans have ten fingers, Part V is where we stick other useful stuff. We would have made this part an appendix, but appendixes have no fingers and . . . look, just check it out, okay?

Icons Used in This Book

Icons are pictures that are far more interesting than the actual words they represent. They also take up less space than words, which is why they're used on computer screens in such blinding profusion.

This icon alerts you to the sort of stuff that appeals to people who secretly like software. It's not required reading unless you're trying to date a person like that (or are married to one).

This icon flags useful tips or shortcuts.

This icon suggests that we're presenting something useful to remember so that you don't wear out your book by looking it up all the time.

This icon cheerfully denotes things that can cause trouble. (Why doesn't life come with these icons?)

Where to Go from Here

If WordPerfect is installed on your computer, you may have already tried to do something in the program and are likely intrigued, perplexed, or annoyed. Flip to the section of the book that meets your present needs:

- If you're just getting your feet wet with WordPerfect or Microsoft Windows, turn to Chapter 2.

- If you're ready to dive into the basics of text editing, check out Chapter 3.

- If you've already created documents that you want to look great, see Chapters 6 through 9.

- If you just got a new digital camera and want to show off your pictures in your documents, check out Chapter 11.

- If you want to publish Web pages using WordPerfect, turn to Chapter 13.

- If you're a WordPerfect user in a place filled with Microsoft Office, flip the page to Chapter 14.

Part I
Exploring the Essentials

In this part . . .

You're ready to employ the state-of-the-art in word processing technology. You have the power to create tables, graphics, columns, fonts, borders, tables of contents, illustrations, sidebars, envelopes, junk mail — you name it! In short, you're ready to launch yourself into the blazing, glorious world of word processing — except for one teensy little problem. You were wondering, perhaps: How do you start the silly thing? Or type a basic document? And, um, how do you print something? Or delete a sentence? Or save your work? Good questions, pilgrim — questions that deserve answers. And here's where to find them: Part I of *WordPerfect 12 For Dummies*. Read on.

Chapter 1

WordPerfect Basics: Out of the Box and Raring to Go

*W*hen you're discovering something new, whether it's driving a car or using WordPerfect, the best advice has always been: Start with the basics and build from there. We show you how to perform the Big Five word-processing operations: get the program (WordPerfect) running, type some text, save the text in a file on disk, open the file again later, and print the file. By reading this chapter, you find out how to coax WordPerfect into performing these five operations. Then, in later chapters, we get into some refinements, such as editing the text after you type it (Chapters 3 and 4) and making it look spiffier (Chapters 6 through 9).

Starting WordPerfect

To begin using WordPerfect, you have to start the program. You don't need to step on the clutch, but you do need to follow these steps:

1. **Choose Start⇨All Programs (or Start⇨Programs if you're using Windows ME).**

   A list of all the programs installed on your computer appears.

2. **Choose WordPerfect Office 12.**

   Another list appears, showing all the programs that are part of WordPerfect Office 12.

3. **Choose WordPerfect.**

   WordPerfect fires up, and the WordPerfect window appears. Or, if this is the first time you've run WordPerfect 12, a dialog box appears, asking you what mode you want to work in.

4. **If you see a dialog box, asking what mode you want to work in, click the OK button to select WordPerfect mode.**

   WordPerfect 12 allows you to work in different modes. For now, just click OK to select WordPerfect mode. (See Chapter 18 for details on modes.) And if you'd prefer not to see this dialog box when you start WordPerfect, uncheck the Show at startup box.

A Perfectly Good Window

After WordPerfect is running, you see the WordPerfect window, as shown in Figure 1-1. The wide expanse of white screen is a digital version of that plain old piece of white paper you can hold in your hand.

The following list describes in more detail what you see in Figure 1-1:

✔ **Title bar:** The title bar is at the top of the window, displaying the words `WordPerfect 12 - [Document1 (unmodified)]`. This line tells you the name of the document you're editing (more about documents later) and reminds you that you are, in fact, running WordPerfect. The `(unmodified)` part tells you that you haven't typed anything yet.

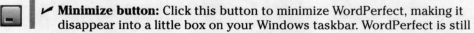 ✔ **Minimize button:** Click this button to minimize WordPerfect, making it disappear into a little box on your Windows taskbar. WordPerfect is still

running when you minimize it. You can return the program to the way it was by clicking the WordPerfect 12 button on the taskbar.

 ✔ **Maximize/Restore button:** The middle button lets you switch back and forth between having WordPerfect fill the whole screen (maximized) and filling just a part of it. Click it once to *maximize* the document. Click it again, and you restore WordPerfect to its original size. The button changes its name and appearance from Maximize to Restore.

 ✔ **Close button:** To put things simply, this button makes WordPerfect go away. It exits, disappears, terminates, goes poof! This button is useful, but it's also kind of dangerous if you're in the middle of working on a document. Not to fear, however, because WordPerfect asks you to save changes before going bye-bye. For more information, see the section called "Leaving WordPerfect," later in this chapter.

✔ **Document window controls:** You can use these three buttons to do the same thing as the WordPerfect window controls, only for your document. Minimize, maximize (or restore), or close a document. We talk all about editing many documents at the same time in Chapter 16.

✔ **Menu bar:** The row of words just below the title bar is WordPerfect's main menu bar. We talk more about commands in Chapter 2.

✔ **WordPerfect 12 toolbar:** Below the menu bar is a row of buttons that make up the WordPerfect 12 toolbar, which from here on we call, simply, "the toolbar." The buttons usually have little pictures on them. Later in this chapter, we show you how to use some of these buttons to save and print a document.

✔ **Property bar:** The property bar has a bunch of controls that let you change how things look in your document. Whatever you're doing in WordPerfect, the property bar changes to let you control all the characteristics, or properties, of what you're working with. It's pretty neat, actually.

✔ **Application bar:** The bottom line of the WordPerfect window shows you which documents you're working with in WordPerfect (we discuss using multiple documents more in Chapter 16) and status information about what's happening in WordPerfect right now. Several controls are also on the application bar, and we talk about them in Chapter 2.

✔ **Scroll bars:** Along the right side of the window is a gray strip that helps you move around the document; you find out how to use it in Chapter 2. If your document is too wide to fit across the screen, WordPerfect displays a scroll bar along the bottom of the window, too, right above the application bar.

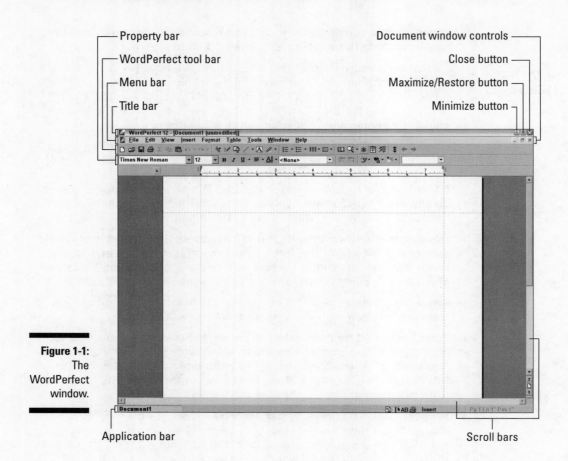

Property bar

WordPerfect tool bar

Menu bar

Title bar

Document window controls

Close button

Maximize/Restore button

Minimize button

Figure 1-1:
The
WordPerfect
window.

Application bar

Scroll bars

Typing Something

As a word processor, WordPerfect is designed for assembling pieces of text into something meaningful. As a result, the task of typing all those letters, words, phrases, and sentences seems like a rather important part of using WordPerfect.

Whatever you type appears at the cursor's location. You can use the mouse or the keyboard to move that cursor (as Chapter 2 explains). By default, you're in *insert mode,* which means that whatever you type is inserted into the text. If your cursor is between two letters and you type a new letter, the new one is inserted between the two original letters.

To undo text you've just typed, click the Undo button on the toolbar. (The Undo button looks like a left arrow.) Or you can press Ctrl+Z, or click Edit on the menu bar and then click Undo. (See Chapter 2 for more details.) To fix an earlier mistake, first move the cursor to the text that you want to change. If you want to delete just a letter or two, you can move the cursor just after the letters and then press the Backspace key a couple of times to wipe them out. Or you can move the cursor right before the letters and press the Delete key. Same difference — the letters disappear. See Chapter 3 to find out how to delete larger amounts of text.

Wrapping Your Text for You

After you begin typing, you can go ahead and say what you have to say. But what happens when you get to the end of the line? Unlike a typewriter, WordPerfect doesn't go "Ding!" to tell you that you're about to type off the edge of the paper and get ink on the platen. Instead, WordPerfect (like all word processors) does something called *word wrap*. It figures out that you are almost at the right margin and moves down to the next line *all by itself*.

Not pressing the Enter key at the end of each line is important. WordPerfect, like all word processors, assumes that when you press Enter, you're at the end of a paragraph. If you press Enter at the end of each line, you'll have a hard time making formatting changes to your document later on.

If you change the margins later or use a different font, WordPerfect adjusts the formatting so that your paragraphs fit within the new margins.

If you want to split one paragraph into two, simply position your cursor just before the letter where you want the new paragraph to begin and press Enter. Voilà! WordPerfect moves the rest of the line down to a new line and reformats the rest of the paragraph to fit.

Saving Documents

Every time you type in WordPerfect, whether it's a love letter to your secret admirer, a huffy memo to your boss, a to-do list for your spouse, or the next great American novel, you create a *document*. WordPerfect calls your unsaved documents `Document1` (or `Document2`, `Document3`, and so on, depending on how many unsaved documents you have open).

Saving a document for the first time

You can save a document in at least three ways. We're sure that your insatiable curiosity will drive you to find out all three, but the following method is our favorite:

1. **Click the Save button on the toolbar.**

   The toolbar is the row of little buttons just below the title bar. If you don't like clicking tiny buttons, choose File⇨Save. Or, if you love pressing key combinations, press the Ctrl+S. The Save File dialog box appears, as shown in Figure 1-2. (Check out Chapter 2 to find out more than you ever wanted to know about working with dialog boxes.)

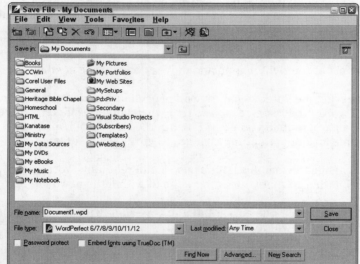

Figure 1-2:
The
WordPerfect
Save File
dialog box.

2. **In the File Name box, type a name for the document.**

   When the Save File dialog box first appears, WordPerfect tries its best to supply a name for your document by putting the first line, sentence, or series of words into the File Name box, followed by a .wpd extension tacked on the end.

   The text is highlighted so you can type a new name if you don't like the one WordPerfect gave you. Feel free to name your document (almost) anything you want. (You don't have to type the .wpd part, although you may if you really, really want to.)

   You can press the Esc key at any time to cancel saving the file.

3. **If you want, choose a different folder or disk drive for your document file:**

   - To save your document in some other folder in My Documents, double-click any folder shown in the dialog box.

   - To create a new folder, choose File⇨New⇨Folder; type a name for the new folder that appears, and then press the Enter key.

   - To save somewhere outside My Documents (or on another disk drive), click the down arrow next to My Documents. In the list that appears, click to choose any other folder or drive (such as A: for your floppy disk drive).

   If you've used other Windows programs before, you might be surprised to see a menu bar in the Save File dialog box. Enjoy the added functionality — on the house!

4. **Press the Enter key on your keyboard or click the Save button.**

   WordPerfect saves the document in the file that you chose. You can tell that this procedure worked because the document's title bar changes from `Document1` to whatever you named your file.

Saving a file for the second time

If you make changes to a file after you've saved it, you need to save your changes. If you want to keep two versions of the document (the original and the revised version, for example), you can do that, too. What you can't do is have two documents with the same name in the same folder; WordPerfect overwrites the old version of the file with the new version — after warning you.

When you try to save a file for a second time but you don't change the name slightly, a Save As dialog box appears, telling you that the file already exists and asking whether you really want to replace it (irrevocably deleting the existing file in the process). You have two, count 'em, two options here:

✔ Yes, to replace the existing file

✔ No, to enter a different name for your new file

From there, saving the file is the same as described in the preceding section, "Saving a document for the first time." Press the Esc key if you have second thoughts about saving the file. The dialog box disappears.

Chapter 16 describes useful things to know about files, including how to delete, move, and copy them.

Saving a document the third, fourth, and fifth times

When you want to save the contents of the document without renaming it, you can simply click the Save button. WordPerfect assumes you want the document saved with the same filename and folder as before.

WordPerfect automatically saves a backup of your document every ten minutes. See Chapter 19 for details on how you can change the setting to another interval.

Filename rules

Whether you were the teacher's pet or the rebel at the back of the class, you must follow certain rules for naming files in WordPerfect (and in other Windows programs for that matter). There's no way around them. Here they are:

- Filenames can be as long as 255 characters. Try to rein it in, now!

- Most filenames contain a period (.). What follows the period is called an extension, is usually three letters, and usually describes the type of the file. WordPerfect documents use the extensions .wpd (which stands for word-processing document), .frm (which stands, obscurely, for mail merge forms, covered in Chapter 15), and .dat (mail merge data files, also in Chapter 15).

- You can omit the period and the extension if you want. (WordPerfect adds them by default.)

- Although you can use any extension you want for your document, we strongly recommend sticking with the standard .wpd extension. Windows looks at the extension to determine what kind of file it is and allows you to perform certain actions based on the file type. If you don't use a standard extension, Windows won't know what to do with the document.

- You can use letters, numbers, spaces, and almost all punctuation in the name and extension. However, certain characters are no-no's to use in the filename, including the following: \, /, :, *, ?, and <>|. If you try to use one of these characters, WordPerfect politely tells you about the problem and allows you to change the name.

- You can use either capital or small letters; neither Windows nor Word-Perfect much cares. In fact, the programs don't even distinguish between caps and lowercase letters (they're not *case sensitive*). PIQUED MEMO.WPD, piqued memo.wpd, and Piqued Memo.wpd all are the same filename, as far as Windows is concerned. (The .wpd extension may or may not show up, depending on your Windows settings.)

Opening and Editing Files

Sometimes you make a brand-new document from scratch. But often, you want to edit a document that's already stored on your computer. It may be a document that you made earlier and saved, a document created by someone else, or a love note left for you by a secret admirer. (Hmmm, secret admirers are getting more high-tech these days, aren't they?) Whatever the document is, you can look at it in WordPerfect. This process is called *opening,* or *loading,* the document.

Here's how to open a saved document:

1. **Click the Open button on the toolbar.**

   This button is the one with a tiny yellow folder on it — usually, the second button from the left. If you don't like clicking little buttons, choose File⇨Open, or press Ctrl+O.

   WordPerfect displays the Open File dialog box, as shown in Figure 1-3. Displaying this dialog box is the program's subtle way of saying that it wants to know which file you want to open. The Open File dialog box can show you the files in only one folder at a time; the name of the folder you're currently looking in appears in the Look In box.

2. **Choose a file from the list.**

   To choose a file, click a name in the list of displayed names. WordPerfect highlights the name by displaying it in another color to show that it knows the one you want.

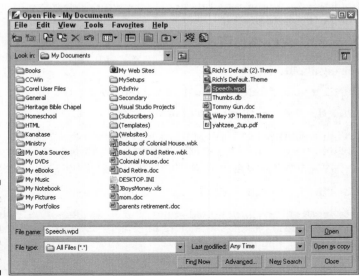

Figure 1-3:
Opening a file you made earlier.

Can't see your file? To look for it in any folder shown in the dialog box, double-click the folder. To look in other disk drives or folders on your PC, click the down arrow next to the Look In box. Double-click any folder or disk drive that appears. The place WordPerfect usually keeps its files is in your My Documents folder.

3. Click the Open button (or press the Enter key).

WordPerfect opens the file, reads the document, and displays it on-screen. Now you can make changes in the document, save it again, print it, or whatever. You can also just double-click the filename to open the document.

When you open a document created in another software program, you briefly see a little box with the message that a conversion is in progress. For more details, see the discussion of file types in Chapters 13 and 14.

Printing Your Document

After you type a document or edit it until it looks the way you want it to look, you'll probably want to print it. After all, the goal of most word processing is to produce — on paper — a letter, memo, report, or what have you. If you work in the Paperless Office of the Future (just down the hall from the Paperless Bathroom of the Future), you may be able to send your memo or letter electronically at the touch of a button. For the rest of us, though, paper works well.

These steps show a fast way to print your document:

1. Save the document first, just in case something goes wacky while you're trying to print it.

To save, click the Save button on the toolbar. (Refer to "Saving Documents," earlier in this chapter, if you don't know what we're talking about.)

2. Turn on your printer and make sure the printer has paper.

3. Click the Print button on the toolbar.

The Print button has a little printer with a piece of paper sticking out of the top — it's usually the fourth button from the left.

A big Print To *(your printer name here)* dialog box appears.

4. Click the Print button in the Print To dialog box.

WordPerfect then prints the document in all its glory. Pretty simple, huh? Chapter 5 contains lots more information about printing, including the care and feeding of your printer.

If you don't like the way your polished prose looks on the page, go to Chapter 6 to find out how to choose which typeface (or typefaces) to use for the text. Chapter 8 tells you how to center and justify text, number pages, and print page headers and footers.

Leaving WordPerfect

Because Windows allows you to run multiple programs at the same time, you don't have to leave WordPerfect every time you want to check your e-mail, browse Amazon.com, or play a little game of Solitaire. In fact, you may choose to leave WordPerfect running all day so that you can switch back to it in a jiffy. But sooner or later, you may want to close WordPerfect.

To shut down WordPerfect, choose File➪Exit. (We talk more about how to use commands in Chapter 2.) If you've created or changed a document but haven't saved the document in a file, WordPerfect asks whether you want to save the document now. Click Yes to save the document, click No to skip saving it, or click Cancel to return to WordPerfect without exiting.

Choose No only if you're sure that the document doesn't contain anything you ever want to see again.

You can leave WordPerfect also by clicking the shiny red Close button at the top of the WordPerfect window.

Never turn off the computer without exiting WordPerfect and Windows; you may catch these programs unawares (with their digital pants down, as it were) before they could save your documents. If something unexpected happens and your computer chokes before you can exit WordPerfect, you may get some complaints the next time you start the computer. (See Chapter 19 for information about what to do if you see them.)

Getting Some Help

Calling for help in a Windows program such as WordPerfect is a little like calling for help at the Arnold Schwarzenegger School of Lifeguard Training: Prepare to be a overwhelmed. You don't just get information — you get an entire, muscle-bound, information-retrieval-and-management system designed to meet your assistance requirements.

We're not even going to try to explain everything that this Dream Team of life-savers can do. Instead, we just give you the simplest way to use Help. For the fancy stuff, we recommend that you play around in Help to your heart's content.

Using the Help menu

The simplest part is calling for Help. Click Help on the menu bar (or press Alt+H). At this point, it's a good thing that you're not literally drowning when you call for help in WordPerfect, because now you must decide precisely *how* you're going to ask for help. The Help Topics option is reasonable and straightforward. The Ask the PerfectExpert option is so cool that we talk about it in its own section (see "Asking PerfectExpert," later in this chapter).

If you select Help Topics, you see a Help window with several tabs at the top, the first three of which are found in the Help windows of many programs:

- **Contents:** This option is associated with an icon that looks like a closed book. You can see a list of topics or you can click one of the question marks to see the Help information for a particular topic.

- **Index:** WordPerfect Help displays a list of all topics, arranged alphabetically. As you type the first few letters of the topic you're interested in, WordPerfect displays the index entry that starts with what you typed.

- **Find:** Okay, what you were looking for wasn't in the index. That's okay; WordPerfect Help can flip through the entire Help file, looking for any word you want. But wait — this is Windows. The first time you try to find something, a Find Setup Wizard asks you technical questions about how you want to search the Help file. Just click the Next button and the Finish button, and then go get a cup of coffee while Windows creates a word list. When it's finished, you see a screen very much like the one on the Index tab. As you type your word, WordPerfect Help shows you which words match what you typed. Click a matching word, and WordPerfect Help shows you some Help topics.

- **Corel Knowledge Base:** If you can't find the information you're looking for in the first three tabs, the Corel Knowledge Base serves as the last line of help for answers to common questions. To use the Knowledge Base, type a term you want information about (such as *thesaurus*) and click the Search button. If you're connected to the Internet, your Web browser launches, takes you directly to the Corel Web site (`www.corel.com`), and looks up the answer for you. The results of your search are displayed in your default Web browser.

You get the same information about a topic (and the info is displayed in the same window) whether you choose the Contents, Index, or Find method to search for it. Often, several areas of text are highlighted in green; each of these areas is itself a topic. When you click one of these areas, you get information on that topic. If you get lost in this labyrinthine Hall of Help and want to find your way back, look for a Back button at the top of the Help window and click it. To make the Help window go away, the easiest thing to do is click the button with the *X* in it (the Close button) in the upper-right corner.

Getting context-sensitive help

If you want the Help feature to pare down the list of topics to things that are related to whatever you're doing right now, you can get context-sensitive Help by pressing F1. When you're in the middle of using a menu or a dialog box, press F1. Zap! WordPerfect figures out exactly which topic you ought to be interested in. If you press F1 with the pointer in the middle of your text, you see the same Help window that appears when you choose Help➪Help Topics on the menu bar.

Another form of context-sensitive help is available. In the upper-right corner of almost all dialog boxes, you find a button with a question mark on it. Click that button, and your mouse pointer turns into a little cartoon "thought balloon" with a question mark on it. Click something in the dialog box, and a little yellow Help box pops up with a description of the thing you clicked.

These steps show you how to ask for help with menu commands and buttons:

1. **Press Shift+F1.**

   Or, if you're in a dialog box, click the question mark button at the top of the dialog box. The mouse pointer turns into a little pointer with a cartoon thought balloon attached to it.

2. **Point to a menu command or button, and click it.**

3. **If you're looking in a menu, scroll through the menu until you find the topic you want help with.**

4. **Release the mouse button.**

   The context-sensitive Help for that command appears.

Asking PerfectExpert

Another tool to help you along the way is PerfectExpert. PerfectExpert can sit by your side and guide you step-by-step through the process of creating a document. To access PerfectExpert, choose Help➪PerfectExpert. The Perfect-Expert pane (see Figure 1-4) appears on the left side of the screen. This pane contains a bunch of buttons corresponding to the steps in a writing project — at least what Corel thinks the steps in a writing project should be.

Figure 1-4:
Perfect-
Expert at
your side.

Here are some tips for using PerfectExpert:

- ✔ **Begin with the Start button and end with the Finish button.** The buttons you click in between Start and Finish are up to you.

- ✔ **Each time you click a button, you get more buttons to click; or you can just write a document in the document window, as usual.** PerfectExpert's buttons simply step you through the same features you could access through WordPerfect's commands and buttons.

- ✔ **To begin a new document, click Start.** You can then click the Blank Document button that's displayed to create a new, blank document. If you choose the New Project/Existing Document button instead, a PerfectExpert dialog box appears — the same one that appears if you choose File⇨New from Project on the menu bar.

  To see a Help screen, click the More Help On button, at the bottom of the PerfectExpert panel.

See Chapter 12 for more on how to use PerfectExpert to create a variety of documents.

Chapter 2

Cruising Your Document

● ●

In This Chapter

▶ Choosing commands from menus

▶ Making WordPerfect behave with the toolbar, the property bar, and the application bar

▶ Working with dialog boxes

▶ Using QuickMenus for even more ways to choose commands

▶ Ruling your document

▶ Moving around in the document with your mouse and keyboard

▶ Scrolling the document using your mouse wheel

▶ Navigating with the Go To dialog box

● ●

*Y*ou've figured out the basics of starting WordPerfect. Now it's time to have some fun and go cruising through WordPerfect and your documents. That reminds me of a song I once heard from an obscure group called the Wordsmith Boys:

> *Well, she got her daddy's 'puter*
>
> *And she cruised through the document text, now*
>
> *Seems she forgot all about the spreadsheet*
>
> *Like she told her old man, now*
>
> *And, with the autoscroll scrolling*
>
> *She goes cruising just as fast as she can, now*
>
> *And she'll have fun, fun, fun*
>
> *Till her daddy takes WordPerfect away*
>
> *Fun, fun, fun, till her daddy takes WordPerfect away*

Cruising your document involves being able to move the cursor around your document to the exact location you're looking for and then doing something when you get there. In this chapter, we show you how to do that using the menu, toolbar, and some nifty commands. In other chapters, we tell you what to do when you get there, such as deleting things and moving text around (Chapter 3) and making the text look different (Chapters 6 and 7). We guarantee that this'll be fun, fun, fun . . .

Telling WordPerfect What to Do

Have you ever traveled overseas and dined at a restaurant where no one spoke your native tongue? To order a meal, you can communicate with the waiter in one of three ways:

- ✔ The difficult but highly impressive way: *Speak the lingua franca.*
- ✔ Order by number, if you're lucky enough to get a restaurant with numbered entrées.
- ✔ Point at the entrée on the menu and murmur, hoping the waiter is able to figure out what you want to order.

Over the years, using a computer has involved similar communication options. In the days before Windows, you had to "speak the language" by knowing which commands to type. That technique worked great if you knew the commands, but it stunk if you were clueless about what to type next. Next, software started allowing you to give commands reminiscent of "ordering by number" using special keys and menus. Today, software applications are all equipped with toolbars, dialog boxes, and pop-up menus that enable you to just point and murmur — and WordPerfect figures out the rest.

The result of all this highly obliging, verging-on-sycophantic user-friendliness is that you now have three more-or-less alternative ways to order WordPerfect around:

- ✔ Using the menu
- ✔ Typing commands from the keyboard
- ✔ Clicking toolbars, dialog boxes, and QuickMenus

Each of these options are discussed in the following sections.

Choosing commands from menus

Taking its cue from fine-dining establishments everywhere, WordPerfect has more than one menu of commands. Of course, instead of offering a list of aperitifs, the menu bar offers word-processing-specific options and commands, as shown in Figure 2-1. Table 2-1 gives you a quick look at the menus offered on the menu bar.

Figure 2-1:
The menu
bar.

`File   Edit   View   Insert   Format   Table   Tools   Window   Help`

Table 2-1	WordPerfect Menus	
Menu	*Description*	*Cross-Reference*
File	Basic file and document operations (open, save, print)	Chapters 1, 5, and 12
Edit	Common document editing functions	Chapters 3 and 4
View	Options and functions for viewing a document and WordPerfect	Chapter 17
Insert	Functions to add text, graphics, or special formatting to your document	Chapters 10 and 11
Format	Formatting operations	Chapters 6, 7, 8, and 9
Tools	Commands that support your word processing	Chapter 4
Table	Operations for creating and formatting a table	Chapter 10
Window	Functions for managing your open files	Chapter 16
Help	Commands for accessing Help	Chapter 1

Clicking the menu bar

To see what's in a menu, click the name of the menu in the menu bar. The menu name becomes highlighted, and a *drop-down menu* (sometimes called a *pull-down menu*) appears. For example, choose File⇨New, and the New menu option is highlighted.

If you don't find anything that you like, close the menu by clicking the menu name again or by clicking elsewhere in the WordPerfect window.

What do all those keys with Fs on them do?

Back in the days before mice, WordPerfect users did everything with function keys. *Function keys* are the keys with Fs on them in the top row of your keyboard; their jobs change with every program you run. Although most people who use WordPerfect point and click with the mouse to perform a command, those with a penchant for function keys use them instead. Here are some that you might find useful:

F1	Help (we discuss Help at the end of this chapter)
F2	Find and Replace (see Chapter 4)
Shift+F2	Find Next (to search for a specific item in a document)
F3	Save As (to change the filename before saving)
Shift+F3	Save (to save a file that already has a filename)
F4	Open File (this one's self-explanatory)
F5	Print (same with this one)
F9	Fonts (to see a list of font types)

Choosing a command

To choose a command from a menu, simply click the command. Related commands are clumped together and separated from other command clumps by a line.

In addition to the commands, you may find other suggestive symbols — sort of like the little red dots next to the hot stuff on a Chinese menu. This list shows what a few of those symbols mean:

- **A right arrow after the command:** The arrow indicates that the menu has a submenu. Click the arrow to see more.

- **A check mark next to the command:** The check mark means that a menu option is already turned on. You can turn off the option by clicking the command.

- **An ellipsis (. . .) after the command:** The ellipsis tells you that the command has more to say, if you ask. If you click the command, the command gift-wraps its thoughts in attractive little dialog boxes, which we discuss in the following section.

Avoiding toil by using toolbars

The WordPerfect window features several bars containing buttons and controls, which WordPerfect calls, loosely, *toolbars*. We focus on the three most prominent of them:

✔ **The WordPerfect 12 toolbar (alias "the toolbar"):** This is the Mother of All Toolbars, a collection of buttons for some of the most common tasks people do in WordPerfect. You can start here if you want to open, save, and print documents, among other tasks.

✔ **The property bar:** In WordPerfect, the property bar is the spot where you can modify the properties (such as **boldness**) of text in your documents.

✔ **The application bar:** The application bar is the bar at the very bottom of the WordPerfect window. Its buttons perform a hodgepodge of tasks.

We explain these toolbars in detail in the following sections.

Your very own toolbar primer

Here are some general facts to know about toolbars and their buttons:

✔ **A toolbar button provides hints.** If you want an explanation of a button, just move your pointer above it (don't click). A little yellow box delivers a brief one-liner about the button and lists its keyboard shortcut, if there is one.

✔ **You can turn some toolbar buttons off and on.** A few of the buttons, such as the Bold, Italic, and Underline buttons, remain "on" and look like they're pressed down when you click them. To turn them off, click them again.

✔ **Some toolbar buttons contain drop-down menus.** To the right of some toolbar buttons are little down arrows. Click an arrow to see a drop-down menu of choices.

✔ **You can hide toolbars from view.** To display or remove a particular toolbar from your screen, choose View➪Toolbars. In the Toolbars dialog box, click to add or remove

a check mark in the box next to the toolbar you want to show or hide, respectively. Click OK to close the Toolbars dialog box.

✔ **You can move toolbars.** Except for the application bar, you can move toolbars to different areas of the WordPerfect window. To do so, move the mouse pointer to the gray area around the buttons. The pointer turns into a little four-headed arrow. Drag the toolbar to its new location.

You can attach the toolbar to any of the four sides of the WordPerfect window. As you drag the toolbar, its outline changes to the same size as the side of the window. When you release the mouse button, the toolbar docks onto the new location and stays there until you decide to move it again. If you want to let the toolbar float, simply drag it toward the center of the screen.

✔ **You can customize toolbars.** You may add and remove buttons from toolbars. To add or change buttons, see Chapter 18.

Working with the WordPerfect 12 toolbar

The toolbar (whose formal name is the WordPerfect 12 toolbar) is a collection of buttons for some of the most common WordPerfect tasks, such as opening, saving, and printing documents. You can also find buttons for cutting, copying, and pasting text. And if you want to add bullets or numbers to your text, look no further than the toolbar. Figure 2-2 shows the toolbar and some of the most common buttons you'll use on it.

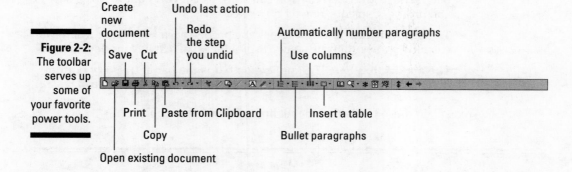

Figure 2-2: The toolbar serves up some of your favorite power tools.

Create new document
Undo last action
Redo the step you undid
Automatically number paragraphs
Save   Cut
Use columns
Print   Paste from Clipboard
Insert a table
Copy
Bullet paragraphs
Open existing document

Producing results with the property bar

Any object you can hold in your hand has certain characteristics, or *properties,* associated with it. There's nothing magical about this fact; it's just the way things are. Take, for instance, a blue coffee mug filled with the hot, beany liquid. If you were asked to describe the cup's properties, you might answer that it has several traits: a pretty indigo blue color, a 12-ounce capacity, burning hot sides due to its contents, and so on.

Each piece of a document — whether it's a single word, a chunk of text, a paragraph, a picture, or a table — has similar characteristics. A word, for example, has a font typeface, color, and style attributes (**bold,** *italic,* or underlined). In WordPerfect, boldface text is said to have a bold *property.*

You can change properties in WordPerfect by using menu bar commands, but that approach takes longer. Like the toolbar, the property bar is a convenience, meant to keep the important text style options a single click away.

Because the property bar is all about the properties of whatever you're typing, the bar changes on its own, depending on where your cursor is! When you start typing, your property bar looks like the one shown in Figure 2-3. But say, for example, that you decide to add a little table to your document.

(You've been reading Chapter 10, haven't you?) Suddenly, the property bar includes buttons that offer information about your table, as well as telling you about the text in the table's columns, as shown in Figure 2-4.

Figure 2-3:
The default property bar.

Figure 2-4:
The property bar when you're working with a table.

If you're a control freak, you may not like all this change going on around you without your permission. But take our word for it; this feature is quite useful. It means that you don't have to go searching through WordPerfect's menus to find out exactly which commands might be relevant to what you're working on. Instead, WordPerfect puts the things it thinks you might be interested in right there on the property bar.

Some buttons on the property bar (the Bold, Italic, and Underline buttons, for instance) appear to be on (pressed) whenever your cursor (insertion point) is among text that has that button's property. If your cursor is among bold text, for instance, the B button appears pressed.

Some of the property bar buttons are really drop-down lists more than they are buttons. Click the arrow on the far-left side of the property bar in Figure 2-3, for example, to see a list of fonts. Then click a font to choose it. (We talk more about fonts in Chapter 6.)

Applying yourself to the application bar

The application bar is kind of a gray area — both literally (it's the gray area at the bottom of the WordPerfect window) and figuratively (its purpose in life is kind of murky, filled with a hodgepodge of tasks). Figure 2-5 shows you what's on this bar.

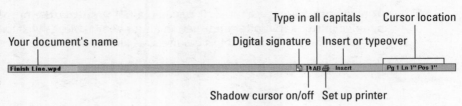

Figure 2-5:
The application bar hosts a bunch of stuff.

The WordPerfect application bar displays buttons that reveal or control various aspects of WordPerfect or your document. These buttons are as follows:

- ✔ **Document buttons:** The left side of the application bar displays the name of the document you're working on. As we discuss in Chapter 12, this feature comes in handy when you're working with more than one document. Clicking the name of the document activates it in the window.

- ✔ **Digital signature:** Clicking the icon with the pad and pen displays a dialog box that allows you to digitally sign a document for security purposes. You may not really need this kind of security. If so, *ignore this button unless you're James Bond!*

- ✔ **Shadow cursor:** The button that has a kind of blurry-looking capital I enables you to switch the shadow cursor on or off. While the regular cursor is the blinking vertical line after which text appears when you type, the *shadow cursor* shows you where the cursor or insertion point *would* go if you were to click the mouse button. Click the blurry picture once or twice, move your mouse around the document, and you'll get the idea. (See Chapter 4 for more information on the cursor.)

- ✔ **All Caps:** The button labeled AB enables you to switch between typing normally and typing in all uppercase. It does the same thing as the Caps Lock key on your keyboard, but it's more helpful: You know All Caps is turned on because the button has a pressed-in state.

- ✔ **Print:** The printer icon takes you to the Print To dialog box. From there, you can set up your printer or print your document. See Chapter 6 for more on printing.

- ✔ **Insert/typeover mode:** The button where the word Insert appears in Figure 2-5 controls whether you're typing in insert or typeover mode. This button does the same thing as the Insert key on your keyboard. (See Chapter 4 for more on insert and typeover modes.)

If you use styles (see Chapter 9), a style name will appear in this space instead of Insert.

When you're editing something fancy, such as a table or a merge file, other information may appear in this box.

✔ **Text cursor position:** At the far right, the application bar tells you where you are in your document, including the page number (Pg), how far down the page you are (Ln), and where you are across the page (Pos).

Using dialog boxes

If you click a menu command that has an ellipsis (. . .) after it, a *dialog box* appears. The dialog box is charged with gathering specific information from you to perform a command. For example, you use the Font Properties dialog box (choose Format⇨Font) to specify the font you want to use, and the Print dialog box (choose File⇨Print) enables you to specify how you want your document printed.

Each dialog box has various doohickeys that take various shapes and sizes, such as check boxes, lists, and buttons. These items are properly called *controls,* but we think *doohickeys* sounds a whole lot more fun.

The two most common and important doohickeys you'll see in almost every dialog box are the OK and Cancel buttons. Clicking OK means "Do it — and do it the way this box says to do it." Clicking Cancel means "Forget it — I didn't really want to do this. Get me outta here, and ignore everything I said in this box."

You could say that some WordPerfect dialog boxes have a mutt of a button — Close. The Close mutton . . . er . . . button is a cross between the OK and Cancel buttons. Like Cancel, it exits the dialog box without performing the primary dialog box action. However, like OK, any settings you changed while you were in the dialog box are processed and can't be canceled.

Using QuickMenus

Another standard, though less obvious, way of performing a task is through QuickMenus, sometimes referred to in other Windows programs as *pop-up menus* or *right-click menus.* A QuickMenu appears when you right-click a button or menu item.

To illustrate, select a word in a document and perform these steps to see a QuickMenu:

1. **Move your mouse pointer over text in your document or any part of the WordPerfect window.**

2. **Right-click anywhere.**

   A little box pops up and displays a menu right where your mouse pointer is.

Voilà! The QuickMenu displays several commands that you can perform on that selected word. For example, you can center the text by choosing Center or paste the contents of the Clipboard by choosing Paste.

QuickMenus are context-sensitive and hidden all over the place. Each Quick-Menu contains commands that have something to do with the particular thing that you're pointing at.

You can find QuickMenu options associated with buttons on the application bar at the bottom of every WordPerfect window.

To choose a command from a QuickMenu, simply click it (with either the left *or* the right mouse button). WordPerfect leaps into action and performs the command.

Controlling Your Document with the Ruler

This must be familiar ground — everybody knows what a ruler is, right? Ummm . . . maybe. The WordPerfect ruler is not your ordinary tick-marks-along-the-edge sort of thing (although it has those, too). It's a behavior-controlling ruler (like the ones your grade school teachers had), except that this ruler controls the behavior of your paragraphs. Specifically, it controls the indents and tabs of whatever paragraph you're working in.

Like the various other bars, you can hide or display the ruler depending on your preference. If you can't find the ruler, which appears in Figure 2-6, don't rush out to get new glasses — yet. Choose View from the menu bar, and if no check mark appears beside the word Ruler, click it to make the ruler appear.

Figure 2-6:
Pay homage
to your ruler.
He's picking
up your tab.

The top of the ruler shows your left and right margins, as well as your para-graph indents. In the little strip below the actual ruler, the little triangles show tab settings. The triangles take different shapes, according to which kind of tab they represent. Some tabs are already set, but you can change these default tabs if you want. You can add tabs, remove tabs, or move tabs around.

We discuss all this stuff in Chapter 8, but the quick tour goes like this:

- ✔ To move a tab or paragraph margin around, you *drag* it.
- ✔ To change the type of tabs you're adding, *right*-click the tab you want to change and select the kind of tab you want from the menu.
- ✔ To delete a tab you no longer need, drag the triangle off the ruler.

Make sure that the blinking cursor is in the correct paragraph before you set tab stops or indents with the ruler.

Navigating Your Document

You have, two primary ways of navigating around your document. (Computer people like to talk about *navigation* rather than just *moving;* we must be a group of frustrated sailors.) As you use WordPerfect, you find that two is the absolute minimum number of ways to do anything, and in many cases, WordPerfect provides four or five ways.

You can move the cursor by

- ✔ Pointing and clicking the mouse
- ✔ Using keys on the keyboard

In WordPerfect, as in most Windows programs, two cursor-like things appear on the screen:

- ✔ **The mouse pointer:** The *mouse pointer* can change shape depending on what WordPerfect thinks it's pointing at. In WordPerfect, the pointer is usually a little white arrow. If WordPerfect is busy, the pointer turns into an hourglass. And if your mouse is pointing to a place in WordPerfect where you can type, you see a gray blinking line in the location in the document where you would be typing if you clicked the mouse.

  If you don't see the mouse pointer on-screen, just move the mouse a little to make it appear.

- ✔ **The cursor:** Also called the *insertion point,* the cursor tells you where your typing will appear. The cursor is a slowly blinking vertical bar; you can't miss it.

In the following sections, we help you get the cursor into firing position so that you can take aim at some text. First, we talk about using the mouse. Next, we talk about using the boring old keyboard. Finally, we throw in a few other ways in which WordPerfect lets you cruise your document.

Mousing around

Like any Windows application, WordPerfect uses the mouse for just about everything except typing text.

Moving nearby

If the place in the document where you want to go to is displayed on-screen, just position the mouse pointer there and click. Follow these steps:

1. **Move the mouse pointer to the position where you want to work.**

   If you move the mouse pointer off your text into some white space, you see the *shadow cursor* (see the sidebar "The shadow knows," for information on how to use the shadow cursor).

2. **Click the mouse button.**

   This action tells WordPerfect to put the cursor right where the mouse pointer is.

3. **You may want to move the mouse pointer out of the way so that it doesn't obscure the text you're going to edit.**

   You don't really have to, though, because as soon as you begin typing, the mouse pointer disappears, in an effort to stay out of the way.

Moving to the far reaches of the document

If you can't see the text you want to edit, don't panic — it's still there, but it has fallen off the edge of the screen. WordPerfect displays your document as though it were written on a long scroll (imagine medieval monks or Egyptian

TIP

The shadow knows

When you move your mouse pointer into the white space in your document, a gray symbol, called the *shadow cursor,* appears on the same line as your mouse pointer. The shadow cursor tells you where your cursor will appear if you click the mouse.

The exact appearance of the shadow cursor also tells you how the text you type will be formatted. For example, if you move your mouse pointer to a blank area an inch or so in from the left margin, the shadow cursor looks like a vertical line and a right arrow. This symbol tells you that unlike most word processors, WordPerfect is happy to have you click white space, and that if you do, WordPerfect will obligingly stick in a tab character or two so that your cursor will appear where you clicked. If your mouse pointer is near the center of the line, a vertical line with *two* arrows appears, indicating that WordPerfect will center the text that you type there. Nice!

scribes). The beginning and ending portions of the document are rolled up, and only the middle part is visible. If you want to see a different section of the text, WordPerfect unrolls the scroll for you and displays it on-screen.

Scrolling with the scroll bar

You may have noticed a vertical gray bar running along the right side of the WordPerfect window. Figure 2-7 shows this *scroll bar*. You use it to tell Word-Perfect to roll and unroll the metaphorical scroll that contains your document.

The scroll bar is similar to a little map of your document, with the full length of the scroll bar representing your entire document: The top end is the beginning of the document, and the bottom end is the end of it. The gray box on the scroll bar (the *scroll box,* in Windows parlance) represents the part of the document you can see on-screen right now. The scroll box moves up and down the scroll bar the way an elevator moves up and down a shaft. By looking at the position of the scroll box in the scroll bar, you can tell where you are in the document — at the beginning, middle, or end.

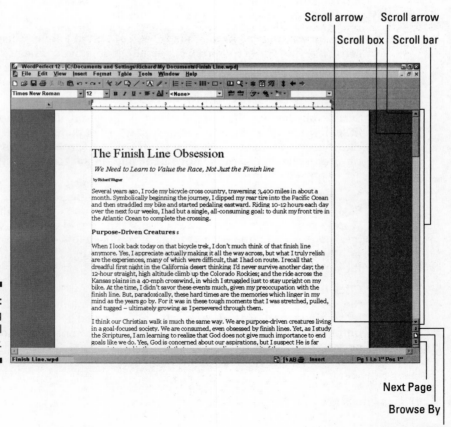

Scroll arrow   Scroll arrow

Scroll box | Scroll bar

Figure 2-7:
Unrolling
the scroll
bar.

Next Page

Browse By

Previous Page

This list shows the things you can do to the scroll bar with your mouse (most of these options are labeled in Figure 2-7):

✔ **Move anywhere in the document in a big hurry:** Use the mouse to drag the scroll box up and down the scroll bar. As you move the scroll box, thus scrolleth the text of the document. To drag the scroll box, point to it with your mouse pointer, press and hold down the mouse button, and move the mouse pointer up or down. The scroll box moves with the mouse pointer as long as you hold down the mouse button. When you release the button, the scroll box stays where you left it, and the document scrolls to match. If you let your mouse pointer stray too far into the text (that is, if you move the mouse to the left while you're trying to scroll up or down), the scroll box pops back to where it was when you started. This can be annoying, but don't panic; continue to hold down the mouse button and move back to the right so that the mouse pointer is on the scroll bar again. The scroll box pops back to where it was before you made the mouse pointer wander into your text.

✔ **Move to the beginning or end of your document:** Drag the scroll box down to the bottom of its elevator shaft. Then do the reverse — drag the scroll box up to the tippy-top.

✔ **Move forward or backward one screen of text at a time:** Click the scroll bar (not the scroll box). For example, to move to the next screen of text in the document, click the scroll bar below the scroll box. To move to the preceding screen, click above the scroll box. The scroll box moves, and the document scrolls up (or down) one screen.

✔ **Scroll your text one line at a time:** Click the scroll arrow button — the little button with a single arrow on it at either end of the scroll bar. The button with the up arrow (at the top of the scroll bar) moves you toward the beginning of the document, and the button with the down arrow moves you toward the end.

✔ **Move (browse) through the document page by page:** Click the Next Page or Previous Page buttons. When you click one of these buttons, WordPerfect scrolls the document so that the top of the next (or previous) page is at the top of the screen. If you have lots of tables, footnotes, or other things in your document, you can use these buttons to move to the next table, next footnote, or next whatever.

✔ **Click the Browse By button:** This action brings forth a little yellow tag that offers you Browse By options. If you want to look at the document by scrolling from page to page, table to table, and so forth, this is the option for you. Simply click until the object you want is mentioned. Then click the Next Page or Previous Page (actually Next Table, Previous Table, or other object) button.

✔ **Display a window full of scary-looking codes:** If you click the tiny little bar-like button at the very top or very bottom of the scroll bar, you may accidentally display the WordPerfect Reveal Codes window, which we describe in gory detail in Chapter 8. Yikes! Click that bar-like button again to make the window go away.

Clicking the scroll box displays a tiny yellow sticker with the current page number. If you right-click the scroll bar, a QuickMenu pops up. We talk about this menu at the end of this chapter (see the section "Going anywhere and getting back again").

If your document is too wide to fit across the WordPerfect window, another scroll bar runs across the bottom of the window, right above the application bar. This scroll bar works just like the vertical scroll bar we've been talking about, except that it moves sideways and has no Next Page and Previous Page buttons.

Scrolling with your mouse wheel

Most newer mouse models have a little wheel nestled comfortably between the left and right buttons. If you have one, you can use it to scroll up and down a document.

To use the mouse wheel to scroll a document, follow these steps:

1. **Click the document with your mouse to make sure that the WordPerfect window is active.**

2. **Roll the wheel with your forefinger in the direction you want to scroll.**

   Moving the wheel in a downward direction scrolls down the document. Moving the wheel upwards scrolls the document up.

If many technological advances these days seem to be more novel than they are truly useful, the mouse wheel is one exception. It's one of those innovations that make you say, "Why didn't they think of that before?" In fact, after you get used to "wheeling it," we think you'll never cruise your document in another way again.

Scrolling the speedy autoscroll way

WordPerfect 12 gives you another speedy way to scroll your document: autoscroll (like the Autobahn, but faster). The Autoscroll button appears in the toolbar, on the near-right side (see Figure 2-8).

Figure 2-8:
Zipping
around your
document
with the
Autoscroll
button.

Autoscroll

To use autoscroll, follow these steps:

1. **Click the Autoscroll button — but don't move your mouse.**

   Note that a special, two-headed Autoscroll mouse pointer has appeared in the middle of your WordPerfect window. The pointer looks like the picture on the Autoscroll button.

2. **Move the pointer just slightly down (or up) from center by moving your mouse toward you (or away from you).**

   At some point, your document begins to scroll, slowly. If you leave the pointer where it is, the scrolling continues at that speed.

3. **To speed up autoscroll, move the pointer to a position farther up or down from center.**

   The document scrolls more quickly.

4. **To stop autoscroll, return the pointer to the center of the window or click the mouse button.**

   Clicking anywhere in your document (or on the Autoscroll button) turns off autoscrolling and returns your mouse pointer to normal.

If you don't own a mouse with a wheel, you may find autoscroll to be an effective tool. However, if you have a mouse wheel, we recommend using it instead. The mouse wheel is a more natural, intuitive way to scroll a document and frees you from extra clicks of the mouse.

Using the keyboard: Staying close to home

We've concluded that there tend to be two sorts of computer people in the world:

- ✔ *The mousies*, who would much rather point-and-click their way around the screen than use something as arcane as a keyboard.

- ✔ *The punchies*, who much prefer the speed of punching keys on their keyboard than being forced to do all sorts of gyrations with their mouse to move around a document.

If you consider yourself a punchie, you're probably thinking, "Okay, that mouse is cute to move around a document, but it slows me down. I don't want to have to lift my hand, grope around for my mouse, and knock over my coffee cup just to see the next page of my letter." For you, dear friend, WordPerfect has navigation keys. You can forget about using the mouse; just press keys to get where you want to go.

The main keys you use are the *cursor-control keys,* consisting of the left, right, up, and down arrow keys, and the Home, End, PgUp (Page Up), and PgDn (Page Down) keys.

To move your cursor up or down one line or to move left or right one character, use the arrow keys: These keys are great for positioning the cursor in an exact spot.

This list describes some of the finer points of using cursor-control keys:

- ✔ If the cursor is on the top line of the WordPerfect window and you press the up-arrow key, WordPerfect does your bidding. To move up a line, WordPerfect must display that line, so it scrolls the document down a tad. (If the cursor is already at the tippy-top of the document, it can't move upward, so nothing happens.)

- ✔ Ditto if the cursor is on the bottom line of the screen and you press the down-arrow key.

- ✔ Don't confuse the left-arrow key with the Backspace key, which usually also has a left arrow on it. The Backspace key *eats* your text as it moves leftward. The left-arrow key just moves the cursor to the left and slides around below the letters like a hot knife through ice cream. Also, watch out for the Delete key, which eats text going to the right.

- ✔ As you move the cursor, it moves from letter to letter in your text. When you move to the right off the end of a line, the cursor moves to the left end of the next line. Unlike the mouse pointer, the cursor can go only where there is text. The cursor must have text to walk around on, as it were; you can't move it off the text into the white void of the blank page.

Using Ctrl with the arrow keys

By pressing the Ctrl key while you press an arrow key, you can make the cursor move farther, as shown by the key combinations in the following list:

- ✔ **Ctrl+up arrow:** Moves the cursor to the beginning of the current paragraph; if you are already there, Ctrl+up arrow moves the cursor to the beginning of the preceding paragraph.

- ✔ **Ctrl+down arrow:** Moves the cursor down to the beginning of the next paragraph.

- ✔ **Ctrl+left arrow:** Moves the cursor left one word.

- ✔ **Ctrl+right arrow:** Moves the cursor right one word.

To use the Ctrl key, press it while you press another key, as though it were the Shift key. Don't release it until you have released the other key.

Moving farther and faster

How about those other keys we mentioned earlier — the Home, End, PgDn (Page Down), and PgUp (Page Up) keys? You can use them to range farther afield in your documents — an especially useful capability as they get larger (the documents, not the keys).

You can move to the beginning or end of the line by pressing one of these keys:

- **Home:** Moves the cursor to the beginning of the current line.
- **End:** Moves the cursor to the end of the current line.

We use the End key all the time to get back to the end of the line we are typing so that we can type some more.

You can move up or down one screen of information by pressing one of these keys:

- **PgUp:** Moves the cursor to the top of the screen. If you are already there, the PgUp key moves up one screen's worth of text and scrolls the document as it does so.
- **PgDn:** Moves the cursor to the bottom of the screen. If you are already there, the PgDn key moves down one screen's worth of text and scrolls the document as it does so.

To move to the beginning or end of the document, press one of these keys:

- **Ctrl+Home:** Moves the cursor to the beginning of the document.
- **Ctrl+End:** Moves the cursor to the end of the document.

If you are wondering how long a document is, press Ctrl+End to get to the end of it. Then look at the application bar to see what page you're on (the number after Pg).

Going anywhere and getting back again

WordPerfect has a Go To dialog box that you can use to tell it where to go. Unfortunately, you can't tell WordPerfect to go where you occasionally *want* to tell it to go, but this option is better than nothing. And it's useful for moving around in really large documents.

There are four — count 'em, four — ways to display the Go To dialog box:

- ✔ Choose Edit➪Go To from the menu.
- ✔ Press Ctrl+G.
- ✔ Use the scroll bar's QuickMenu — that is, point to the scroll bar and click the *right* mouse button to display the QuickMenu; then choose the Go To command.
- ✔ Click the location section of the application bar (the part that shows you the page, line, and cursor position).

When you perform one of these commands, the Go To dialog box is displayed, as shown in Figure 2-9.

Figure 2-9:
Use the Go
To dialog
box to tell
WordPerfect
where to go.

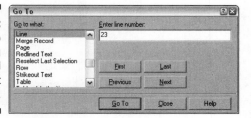

The Go To dialog lists several choices to tell WordPerfect where to go! Here's how to use just the basic choices in the list:

- ✔ **To move the cursor to the top (or bottom) of the current page:** Click Top of Current Page from the list (or Bottom of Current Page) and then click Go To or press Enter.
- ✔ **To move the cursor to the top of a different page:** Click Page from the list, click the Enter Page Number box, and then type the number of the page you want to go to. Then click Go To or press Enter.

You can just jump around from page to page and make edits without closing the Go To dialog box. (Just click in the document to make edits.) When you're ready to close the dialog box, click the Close button.

For those times when you're jumping around in the document and making edits, the Go To dialog box has a helpful "go back to where I was" feature. To return the cursor to its most recent location, select Edit Position in the Go to What list, and then click the Previous button in the Go To dialog box. Your cursor flies back to its earlier location like a well-trained homing pigeon. Keep clicking Previous to return to even earlier locations. Click the Next button to return to later editing locations.

Chapter 3

Discovering "Perfect" Text Editing

• •

In This Chapter

▶ Selecting text with the mouse

▶ Selecting text with the keyboard

▶ Extending a selection

▶ Deleting, moving, and copying selected text

▶ Using insert and typeover modes

▶ Undoing and redoing

▶ Finding text

▶ Searching and replacing text

• •

You've probably seen those house fix-it-up programs on TV in which the host works to restore a wreck of a house and change it into something beautiful. Not every home featured on these shows is transformed into a king's mansion, but each house is fundamentally improved, bringing out the best of the structure and getting rid of the ugly stuff in the process.

You can think of WordPerfect as the host of a program like that, perhaps one we'd call *This Old Document.* In fact, much of your time spent in WordPerfect is to perform similar tasks — starting with some rough text, you edit and refine it, and ultimately transform the document you started with into something that would make Norm Abram proud. Not that WordPerfect by itself can change your document into the next Grisham novel, but it can assist you to bring out the best of what you've written and get rid of the mistakes.

In this chapter, you discover the nuts and bolts of text editing in WordPerfect. You start off "hammering" text blocks, selecting and moving them around. You also find out how to "drill" for text in your document and replace it with something else. So, get on your trusty WordPerfect tool belt and let's continue.

Selecting Text: The Point-and-Shoot Approach

Before you can edit text, you need to know how to select the text you want to work with. To select an arbitrary block of text (from any point to any other point), just follow these steps:

1. **Put the mouse pointer at the beginning of the stuff you want to select.**

2. **Press the mouse button and drag the mouse pointer to the end of what you want to select.**

   The text is highlighted as you drag, as shown in Figure 3-1.

3. **Release the mouse button.**

   The selected text remains highlighted, and you can do stuff to it (see the section "Doing Stuff with Selected Text," later in this chapter).

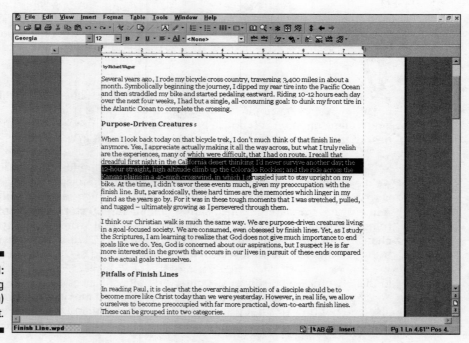

Figure 3-1:
Selecting
(highlighting)
text.

This clicking-and-dragging stuff makes perfect sense if all the text you want to select is on the screen. But what if the text you want to select starts, say, three lines from the bottom of the screen and extends off the bottom for another couple of lines? Dragging that mouse pointer off the bottom of the screen could take some doing, but that's exactly what you need to do! To select text beyond the bottom of the screen (or the top, for that matter), *slowly* move the cursor toward the bottom of the screen. At some point, the text on the screen begins to move upwards, bringing new text onto the screen at the bottom. This new text is highlighted because WordPerfect figures you're trying to select it.

Unless your reflexes are a lot better than ours (a depressingly real possibility), this text will shoot by so fast that you'll end up highlighting more text than you wanted. *Don't panic!* More important, *keep holding down the mouse button.* Just move the mouse pointer up a little, and the text will stop streaming by. Then continue moving the mouse pointer up until you reach the end of the text you wanted to select. After you find it, release the mouse button.

Of course, if the text whizzed by really fast, the *end* of what you want to highlight has now disappeared off the *top* of the screen. You guessed it: *Don't panic!* More important, *keep holding down the mouse button.* This time, ever so gently move toward the top of the screen. Soon, text will begin flowing onto the screen from the top. When you see the place where you want to stop highlighting, move the cursor back down into the WordPerfect window. Now you can find the end of the text you wanted to highlight. At last, you can give your index finger a rest and let go of the mouse button.

If all this sounds too involved (and for selecting large amounts of text, it definitely is), you'll probably want to check out the faster ways to select words, sentences, and paragraphs or even the QuickMenu approach. All these methods are described shortly.

Highlighting: Chunky or smooth?

Just as peanut butter comes in two varieties — chunky and smooth — so too does text selection in WordPerfect. By default, WordPerfect prevents you from selecting just a portion of the word.

We find this auto-select feature sort of chunky and incredibly annoying. If you also find automatic word selection to be annoying, you can turn it off. To do so, choose Tools⇨Settings. In the Settings dialog box, double-click Environment. Clear the "Automatically select whole words when dragging to select text" check box, which appears near the bottom of the Environment Settings dialog box. Click OK and then click Close, and you'll be able to select any characters you want with the mouse.

If you're new to selecting text with your mouse, it can look weird at times. Here are a couple of tips:

✔ If the text you want covers several lines, don't bother dragging the mouse pointer to the end of the line and then back to the beginning of the next line, and so on. This method wastes effort and looks funny. Pretend like you're driving in Boston, and simply close your eyes and go. Move boldly and directly toward your destination.

✔ You can go backward as well as forward (and up as well as down) — it makes no difference — but you can't expand the selection in both directions. The place where you begin must be either a beginning point or an ending point.

Using the Mouse to Select Words, Sentences, and More

Here are some fast ways to select words, sentences, and paragraphs:

✔ **To select a word:** Double-click the word (position the mouse pointer anywhere in the word and then double-click the left mouse button).

✔ **To select a group of words:** Double-click the first word in the group, holding down the mouse button on the second click. Drag the edge of the highlighting (in either direction) to the other end of the group that you want to select. This method works even if you turned off automatic word selection (see the "Highlighting: Chunky or smooth?" sidebar). If you complete this maneuver successfully, you're eligible to receive your advanced mouse driver's license.

✔ **To select a sentence:** Triple-click the sentence (move the mouse pointer anywhere in the sentence and triple-click the mouse button — it's similar to a double-click, but with one more click).

The WordPerfect idea of a sentence is anything that ends with a period and has a space before the next character. Therefore, the sentence "i write like e. e. cummings." contains three sentences, as far as WordPerfect is concerned.

If you find triple-clicks to be a bit daunting, you can use another convenient way to select a sentence: Click in the left margin, next to the sentence. (Note that your mouse pointer arrow now slants to the right.)

✔ **To select a group of sentences:** This procedure is similar to selecting a group of words. Do the triple-click described in the preceding item (like the samba, but faster), and hold down the mouse button on the last click. Then drag the highlight where you want it.

If you like the click-in-the-margin approach to selecting sentences, you can select a bunch of sentences by clicking in the left margin and then dragging the mouse pointer up or down.

✔ **To select a paragraph:** Quadruple-click the paragraph (move the mouse pointer anywhere in the paragraph and click four times in succession). Yes, the latté consumption in WordPerfect's engineering department must be at record levels if those people believe that you can quadruple-click without stuttering, but there it is: Four quick clicks of the mouse button nab you a paragraph.

If you drink only decaf (such as Decaf Sumatra — our favorite), you may find the Alternative Paragraph Selection method to be easier. Move your mouse pointer into the margin, to the left of the paragraph (where the mouse pointer turns into a right-slanting arrow), and double-click.

✔ **To select a group of paragraphs:** You guessed it: Hold down the mouse button on the fourth click and drag. Or click twice in the left margin and drag.

Table 3-1 summarizes all of these point-and-click actions for you.

Table 3-1	Selecting Text with Your Mouse
To Select	*Perform This Action*
Word	Double-click the word
Group of words	Double-click the first word, and then drag to the last word you want to highlight
Sentence	Triple-click anywhere in the sentence
Group of sentences	Triple-click the sentence, and then drag to the last sentence you want to highlight
Paragraph	Quadruple-click anywhere in the paragraph
Group of paragraphs	Quadruple-click anywhere in the paragraph, and then drag to the last paragraph you want to highlight

What about selecting a page? Logically, this procedure should consist of five clicks, but even the highly wired WordPerfect engineers decided that five clicks were beyond their motor skills. Instead, to select a page, try the QuickMenu approach, described in the next section.

The QuickMenu approach

You can select sentences, paragraphs, and pages by using the QuickMenu (or pop-up menu). First, click anywhere in the sentence, paragraph, or page you want to select. Then move your mouse pointer to the left margin. (The shadow cursor goes away, and the mouse pointer turns into a mouse pointer tipped to the right.) With a quick right-click, you get the QuickMenu shown in Figure 3-2.

Now you get a chance to select a sentence, a paragraph, a page, or even the All option. Click your choice (using either mouse button), and the sentence, paragraph, or page you originally clicked is highlighted. Notice that the menu has no option to select a word. You have to point and shoot with the mouse to select a word or group of words.

The Menu bar approach

You can also select a sentence, a paragraph, a page, or the entire document by using the main menu. Just as you do with the QuickMenu, you begin by clicking anywhere in the text you want. Then you choose Edit⇨Select. You'll see most of the same options as those in the QuickMenu.

Figure 3-2:
The left
margin
QuickMenu
for selecting
text and
other cool
stuff.

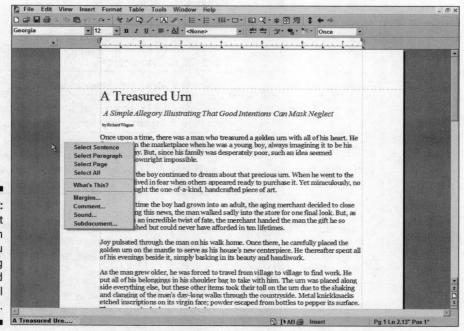

TECHNICAL STUFF

Selecting a rectangle of text

Edit⇨Select has an option that's easy to overlook, but we think it's pretty cool — and a timesaver. When you select text that extends over more than one line, your selection goes to the end of the first line and then starts at the beginning of the second line, and so on until you get to the end of the selection.

But what if you just wanted to select a rectangular selection of text? For example, suppose you have a bunch of asterisks at the start of a series of lines that you'd like to remove. Rather than removing the first two characters on each of ten contiguous lines, you could choose Edit⇨Select⇨Rectangle to do it in one quick swoop.

To select a rectangle of text, follow these steps:

1. **Position the cursor at the beginning of the text you want to select.**

   The column you are on serves as the top-left corner of the rectangle.

2. **Move the cursor to the last column of the text you want to select.**

   The text selection wraps around as normal for now. Don't worry about that. Just find the column that serves as the bottom-right corner of the rectangle.

3. **Choose Edit⇨Select⇨Rectangle.**

   The rectangular area of text is now selected.

Selecting Text with the Keyboard

Most people prefer to use the mouse for text selection because point-and-click is second nature and often seems easier than remembering all sorts of key combinations. Still, some people prefer to keep their hands on the keyboard. Fortunately, many alternatives are available for the rodent-averse among us, whom we prefer to call Speedy Typists. All these alternatives involve the navigation keys, which are the arrow keys and the associated pad of keys that have such useful-looking names as Home and End.

Here's the highly complex secret of selecting text with the navigation keys: Hold down the Shift key and press the navigation key. That's it — really. To be painstakingly specific, these steps show you what to do:

1. **Position the cursor at the beginning or end of the text you want to select.**

   Click the mouse at that position or press the navigation keys to move the cursor.

2. **Hold down the Shift key.**

3. **While you hold down the Shift key, use the navigation keys to stretch the selection area to the other end of the text.**

   The selected text is highlighted, and you can do stuff to it (see the section "Doing Stuff with Selected Text," later in this chapter).

Table 3-2 shows you how to select text from where the cursor is positioned.

Table 3-2	Key Combinations for Selecting Text
To Select Text Up To	*Press*
Next character	Shift+→
Preceding character	Shift+←
Beginning of next word	Shift+Ctrl+→
Beginning of current word	Shift+Ctrl+←
Same position, down one line	Shift+↓
Same position, up one line	Shift+↑
End of line	Shift+End
Beginning of line	Shift+Home
Beginning of next paragraph	Shift+Ctrl+↓
Beginning of current paragraph	Shift+Ctrl+↑
End of document	Shift+Ctrl+End
Beginning of document	Shift+Ctrl+Home
Bottom of screen	Shift+PgDn
Top of screen	Shift+PgUp
Bottom of document	Shift+Ctrl+PgDn
Top of document	Shift+Ctrl+PgUp
End of street	Accelerator pedal
Beginning of tape	Rewind button

Extending Selections

Suppose that you just finished carefully selecting text. With sudden shock, you see that you really should have selected more than you actually did. You are consumed by regret and self-recrimination. Ah, how much like life itself is word processing. Unlike real life, however, WordPerfect gladly lets you select more text — or less, for that matter. You don't even have to make the selection over again; simply extend your selection.

To extend a selection you've already made, follow these steps:

1. **Hold down the Shift key.**
2. **With the mouse pointer anywhere in the selected text, hold down the left mouse button.**

   The endpoint of the selection shrinks back to the point where you clicked.

3. **Click where you would like the selection to end.**

Of course, you can do the same thing from the keyboard. Follow these steps:

1. **Hold down the Shift key.**
2. **Press any of the navigation keys to move the endpoint.**

   Press the keys just as you did to make the original selection.

WordPerfect doesn't allow you to change the original starting point of a selection; you can move only the endpoint.

Doing Stuff with Selected Text

This section might as well be called "Doing Stuff with Molecules," for the breadth of discussion it opens. After all, you can cut, copy, paste, move, delete, replace, search, spell check, grammar check, or typeset the text. You can also turn selected text into a bulleted or numbered list. Oh, and when you get bored with those actions, you can always change the font, paragraph style, indention, position, and orientation. We could go on, but our heads start to spin just thinking about all the things you can do with selected text. The rest of the book explores those topics. In this section, we point out four essential operations that you'll constantly find yourself doing with selected text:

- ✔ Copying and pasting text with the Clipboard
- ✔ Cutting and pasting text with the Clipboard
- ✔ Copying and moving text around with your mouse
- ✔ Deleting text

Copying and pasting with the Clipboard

Microsoft Windows sports a handy utility called the *Clipboard*, which is a temporary haven for selected text, a graphic, or another thingamajig that you cut or copy into it. You can then paste the thing that's on the Clipboard into your WordPerfect document or, for that matter, into another Windows program.

Keep in mind that the Clipboard can contain only one thing at a time. If you copy or cut out something new, the old contents of the Clipboard are wiped out. In addition, the Clipboard is only a temporary storage facility, so when you close or log out of Windows, the contents of the Clipboard are wiped out, too.

Suppose that you're writing a contract for Dingelhausen-Schneitzenbaum Furniture Prefabrication Company and you are oddly averse to typing Dingelhausen-Schneitzenbaum Furniture Prefabrication Company more than once. Copying and pasting saves your fingers and your sanity by enabling you to make multiple copies of Dingelhausen-Schneitzenbaum Furniture Prefabrication Company all over your contract. (Guess which feature was useful in writing this paragraph?)

To copy some text, follow these steps:

1. **Select the text.**

2. **Click the Copy button on the toolbar or press Ctrl+C.**

3. **Click where you want the new copy.**

4. **Click the Paste button on the toolbar or press Ctrl+V.**

When you click the Copy button (or press Ctrl+C), WordPerfect copies your selection to the Windows Clipboard. The text stays in the Clipboard until something else replaces it, so you can paste as many copies as you want. If you were to switch to another Windows program, you could typically copy text there, too, as long it knows what to do with text.

WordPerfect is smart about including spaces after periods and commas when you cut or paste words and phrases. You may notice that it removes extra spaces after a comma and inserts a space, if needed, after a period. Wicked cool!

Keyboard skills to last a lifetime

The keyboard commands that are used for cutting, copying, and pasting in WordPerfect (Ctrl+X, Ctrl+C, and Ctrl+V, respectively) are used in nearly every other Windows program. For this reason, it's slightly to your advantage to remember and use these commands rather than the WordPerfect menu commands. True, the keyboard names are not particularly mnemonic. We keep track of them by remembering that the X, C, and V keys form a cute little row on the bottom row of the keyboard in this order: cut, copy, and paste. Here's another handy way to remember these three keyboard commands: The X key for cut resembles a pair of scissors; C stands for *copy,* and the V key for paste looks like a funnel where you drop something to a specific place.

A QuickMenu approach to Clipboarding

If you have trouble remembering Ctrl+C, Ctrl+X, and Ctrl+V, or where the Copy, Cut, and Paste buttons are on the toolbar, the QuickMenu is just your cup of (instant) tea. To order from the QuickMenu, follow these steps:

1. **Select something.**

   Make sure that your mouse pointer is somewhere in the text area — not on a menu or in the margins.

2. **Right-click the selected text.**

   A QuickMenu appears.

3. **Choose Cut, Copy, or Paste from the QuickMenu.**

The Clipboard usually copies any character formatting, such as font, size, or color, along with the text. If you don't want to copy the formatting, choose Paste Without Font/ Attributes from the QuickMenu.

4. **Depending on the option you chose from the QuickMenu, do one of the following:**

   ✔ If you chose Cut, move the cut text and click the Paste button.

   ✔ If you chose Copy, click the location where you want to paste the copied text. Then click the Paste button, or press Ctrl+V, or right-click and choose Paste.

   ✔ If you chose Paste, the selected text will be replaced with the contents of the Clipboard.

Cutting and pasting with the Clipboard

Cutting and pasting aren't much different from copying and pasting. The only difference is that the original selection gets removed as soon as you cut it.

To cut and paste some text, follow these steps:

1. **Select the text.**
2. **Click the Cut button on the toolbar or press Ctrl+X.**

   The selected text vanishes, but a copy is kept in the Clipboard.
3. **Click in the location where you want to paste the text.**
4. **Click the Paste button on the toolbar or press Ctrl+V.**

Just as with copying and pasting, you can paste as many copies as you want. As with copying, if you cut something new, it replaces the old stuff in the Clipboard.

Copying and moving text with your mouse

You can use cut and paste to move text around in a document. However, an even quicker way is to eliminate the "middleman" and use your mouse to directly move the selected text.

To do so, select what you want to move and then drag the highlighted text where you want it. The text doesn't actually move, however; only the cursor (or shadow cursor) moves. The text is moved *after* you release the mouse button.

If you move your mouse pointer into white space, the shadow cursor shows you where your text will actually end up. On the other hand, if you're just dragging some words around in your text, the regular cursor moves around in that text to tell you where all this dragging will take your words. When you release the mouse button, the move is complete.

You can also copy text by using almost exactly the same technique you use to move it. To copy, hold down the Ctrl key while you drag. A copy of the selected text is placed in the new location. The original selected text stays put, just where it was.

Deleting text

We often wonder how writers in the pre-computer era ever managed to write long documents, let alone books. In the woebegone quill-and-ink and typewriter days, deleting a chunk of text smack dab in the middle of a document was a major deal, involving many late nights of rewriting just to get the printed text right. In fact, we believe you can trace the long, sordid relationship of writers and their caffeine to this age-old deletion problem.

But as S.E. Hinton once wrote, "That was then, this is now." In the digital, high-tech world, deleting text in a document is a breeze. In fact, you might have so much giggly fun deleting text in WordPerfect that you start typing gibberish just so you have an excuse to remove it later.

The simplest way to delete a block of text is to *select,* or highlight, it with your mouse or keyboard and press the Delete or Backspace key. You can delete one character at a time in these two ways:

   ✔ The Delete key deletes the character *after* the cursor.
   ✔ The Backspace key deletes the character *before* the cursor.

Copying between documents with the Clipboard

The Clipboard is particularly useful for copying between documents. Because WordPerfect allows you to have more than one document open at a time, you can copy text in document A and paste it in document B. See Chapter 16 for information about having more than one document open at a time.

Deleting secret codes

If the formatting of a block of text changes while you're deleting, you probably deleted one of WordPerfect's secret codes. You can undelete the deleted code using the Undo command; see the section "Just (Un)Do It," later in this chapter. Or just reformat text back to the way you want it to look. We discuss secret codes in detail in Chapter 17.

In either case, the text closes up behind you as you go. Surgery without scars.

Make sure that you don't have any text selected if you want to delete just one character at a time. If you press the Backspace or Delete key when text is selected, all the selected text is deleted all at once.

If you would rather not take your hand off the mouse to delete, just select your text, right-click, and then choose Delete from the QuickMenu.

After you select text, just press the Delete key (or the Backspace key). The text goes away, never to return. It doesn't utterly, completely go away, however; it passes on to the next dimension, from which you can recall it with the Undo command. See the "Just Un(Do) It" section later in the chapter.

If you think that you may be able to reuse the text you're deleting, you can cut the chunk out (choose Edit⇨Cut) rather than delete it, and then paste it later (choose Edit⇨Paste). However, because the Clipboard stores only a single chunk of text at a time, it's best to use the Clipboard right away before you go on and do something else. Otherwise, you may forget all about the text fragment and accidentally replace it with something else you're cutting or copying.

A much safer alternative is to move the questionable block of text to the very end of your document. Then, as you work to refine your text, you can return to this fragment later to make a final decision on its use. However, if you do choose this option, make sure to clean out the questionable text blocks before you finish your document!

Using Insert and Typeover Modes

By default, WordPerfect is set up in *insert mode,* which means that when you enter text, WordPerfect inserts the letters wherever the cursor is positioned. However when you're replacing existing text, one of the simplest ways to delete the old stuff is to type right over it. To do that, you use *typeover mode,* in which the letters you type replace (or type over) the characters to the right of the cursor.

You can switch between insert and typeover modes by pressing the Insert (or Ins) key on your keyboard or by clicking the Insert/Typeover button on the application bar (see Chapter 2 for more on the application bar).

When you're in typeover mode, position the cursor where you want to begin; anything you type then overwrites the old text as though it had never been there.

A ghost of the former text does remain, however, in the form of character formatting, such as italics. For example, if the original text included 20 characters in italics, the new text also has 20 characters in italics. Hmm. This situation may not be what you had in mind. (See Chapter 6 to find out how to format text in italics or how to get rid of this type of formatting.)

WordPerfect has a way to replace text without changing to typeover mode. Just select the text you want to replace and then begin typing. WordPerfect deletes the original text and puts in your new text.

If you find that you appear to be typing over text when you want to be inserting text, check out the application bar at the bottom of the WordPerfect window. If you're in typeover mode, you'll see an indicator that says Typeover. Switch back to insert mode by pressing the Insert key or by clicking the Insert/ Typeover button on the application bar.

Just (Un)Do It

Unfortunately, in real life, people have to live with the slipups they've made in their lives. Bummer, eh? The cool thing about WordPerfect is that you don't need to ever say to yourself *what could have been* when writing a document, because of a remarkably clever command called Undo. Delete a sentence and suddenly wish you hadn't? No problem; simply undo your mistake. Or perhaps you pasted text from the Clipboard into the wrong location. No problem, just undo.

To undo something, simply click the Undo button on the toolbar (or press Ctrl+Z or choose Edit➪Undo).

WordPerfect can usually undo whatever the last command did to your document, including deleting text, adding a new sentence, and adding a table. After WordPerfect undoes your last action, it positions the cursor at the scene of the crime in your document (that is, at the place where that last action took place).

And for those times when you say "I wish I could undo my undo," WordPerfect hands you the Redo command. To redo an action you just undid, click the Redo button on the toolbar (or press Ctrl+Shift+Z or choose Edit⇨Redo).

Using Undo and Redo effectively

Keep in mind the following tips when using Undo and Redo:

✔ **Multiple steps of Undo and Redo:** WordPerfect keeps track of the last ten actions you perform on your documents and allows you to undo each of them, one at a time. So, when you click Undo once, the last action you performed is undone. If you click it again, the second-to-last action is undone as well. And so on. (See the section "Tweaking the way Undo behaves," for details on how to increase the number of actions to keep track of.)

✔ **Undo and Redo lists:** The Undo button on the toolbar has a down arrow beside it. If you click the arrow, a list of the last ten actions that you've taken on your document appears. If you'd like to undo several of these actions at once (rather than clicking the Undo button multiple times), you can select the last action in the list you want to undo. WordPerfect then returns the document to the state it was at before the last action you selected was taken. The Redo button has a similar list.

✔ **Not every action is undoable:** Although nearly all add, delete, or formatting operations you perform can be undone, not *every* WordPerfect command can be backtracked using Undo. For example, saving a file is a permanent action and can't be undone. As a general rule, anything that involves just the current state of your WordPerfect document can be undone. But if the action involves writing the file to disk, that action is beyond what undo can take you back from.

✔ **Saving a file wipes the slate clean:** When you save a file, the Undo list is usually cleaned out, never to return; so make sure everything is exactly as you want it before saving your document. (See the section, "Tweaking the way Undo behaves," for instructions on how to tell WordPerfect to save the Undo/Redo list with your document.)

Undo can get you out of many a tight spot when you're writing documents in WordPerfect. Now, if only computer engineers could figure out a way to add that Undo button to real-life. . . .

Tweaking the way Undo behaves

WordPerfect gives you the ability to customize how Undo behaves for you. Choose Edit⇨Undo/Redo History and click the Options button in the dialog box that is displayed. In the Undo/Redo Options dialog box, you can adjust the following options:

✔ **Number of Undo/Redo items:** Usually, WordPerfect lets you undo the last 10 things you've done by using the Undo/Redo History dialog box. But heck, if you find that WordPerfect isn't remembering quite enough, you can go crazy and crank up the number of items in the Undo list all the way to 300 (that's the limit). To change the number of actions WordPerfect remembers, set the number to whatever you need in the Number of Undo/Redo items box.

In general, if you have a slower computer, keep this number small to avoid bogging WordPerfect down. But if you have a relatively new and powerful computer, you'll be just fine no matter the setting.

✔ **Save Undo/Redo items with document:** If you'd like to save your Undo/Redo history with your document, click the Save Undo/Redo Items with Document Text check box. This option enables you to preserve your history as part of the document. You can even close the document and reopen it — your Undo list will still be there.

The Search for Sanity — Finding Text in a Document

If you have lost your marbles, your cool, or your sense of values, you have come to the right place. WordPerfect's Find and Replace command can help you find them. (WordPerfect can also help you replace them with something better — such as *cottage cheese* for *marbles*. You find out about replacing text in the section called "Finding and Replacing Text," later in this chapter.)

In the normal scheme of things, the search for the word *sanity* requires a journey of only two, or perhaps three, steps in a WordPerfect dialog box:

1. Choose Edit⇨Find and Replace or press F2.

The Find and Replace dialog box, shown in Figure 3-3, springs to your aid.

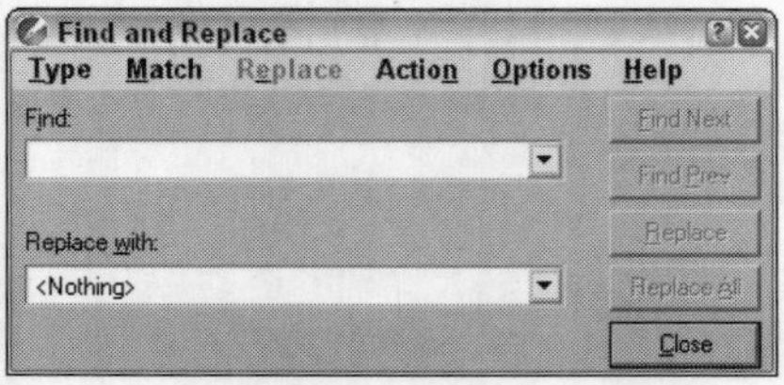

Figure 3-3:
The Find and Replace dialog box.

Find and Replace	? ☒
Type Match Replace Action Options Help	
Find:	Find Next
[ ] ▼	Find Prev
	Replace
Replace with:	Replace All
<Nothing> ▼	
	Close

2. In the Find box, type the text you're looking for.

You can edit the text if you want by moving the cursor around using the Backspace key, Delete key, and so on.

3. **Search toward the end or beginning of the document as follows:**

  • To search toward the end, click the Find Next button (or press Enter).

  • To search toward the beginning, click the Find Prev button.

If the text you're looking for exists, it appears highlighted in the document window. If the text that WordPerfect found is not the precise instance of the text you want, just click the Find Next or Find Prev button again until you get it.

If your quest is futile, WordPerfect displays a window saying that it can't find the text. Reassure it that you're not mad by clicking the OK button.

TIP

If you want to search for something you looked for recently, click the down arrow to the right of the Find box. WordPerfect displays a list of recent searches you've performed.

Changing the way you search

The Find and Replace dialog box has its own little menu bar. If the Find and Replace option is working the way you want it to, we recommend that you skip this menu altogether. But if Find and Replace is driving you crazy, look here to see whether you can get it to behave a little more to your liking.

The Find and Replace function has five options, which you can check out by choosing Options from the menu bar in the Find and Replace dialog box. Those options are as follows:

✓ **Begin Find at Top of Document:** Unless this option is checked, Word-Perfect starts looking for what you're trying to find at your current location in the document. Usually, this is what you want, but if you want to make sure you've found the *first* place your text appears in your document, click Begin Find at Top of Document.

✓ **Wrap Text at Beg/End of Document:** This is what WordPerfect usually does. It searches starting at your current location and, when it gets to the end, it continues searching from the beginning. That way, if what you're looking for appears *before* your current location, you'll find it anyway. WordPerfect is even smart enough to know where it started, so that after it loops around to the beginning of your document again, it stops when it finds the last occurrence of your text before the place where you started searching.

✓ **Limit Find Within Selection:** Often you're interested in looking for text in only a particular part of your document. For example, if you're looking for a bit of text in the paragraph you're currently working on, you can select the text you want to look in and use the Limit Find Within Selection option to force WordPerfect to focus its search. This is particularly useful if you have a really long document.

If you select text before entering the Find and Replace dialog box, the Limit Find Within Selection option is automatically selected for you.

✔ **Include Headers, Footers, and so on in Find:** By default, WordPerfect searches everything, including headers, footers, footnotes, and other stuff that doesn't exactly appear in the body of your document when it's searching for text. If for some reason you don't want WordPerfect to look at that stuff, you know what to do: Click this option to turn it off. (Take a peek at Chapter 8 for more info on using headers and footers.)

✔ **Limit Number of Changes:** This option enables you to limit the number of instances that WordPerfect automatically changes text that you ask it to find and modify. We discuss finding and replacing text later in this chapter.

In your document, you can select the text for which you want to look before you use Edit⇨Find and Replace (or press F2). When you do that, the text appears automatically in the Find box as the text to search for.

Searching for sanity and finding insanity

By default, WordPerfect assumes that you're just looking for a set of characters, even within a word. As a result, finding the wrong word — for example, finding the word *insanity* when you're searching for the word *sanity* — is a common problem. Good news — this condition is quite treatable. Your therapy is on the Find and Replace dialog box's menu bar. We prescribe choosing Match⇨Whole Word. The phrase `Whole Word` appears below the Find text box to remind you.

Certain things you select in the Find and Replace dialog box, such as Whole Word mode, are *sticky,* which means that they stay selected until you change them or until you close the dialog box. You see a check mark next to these commands if they're on. The words you type for Find and for Replace With are also sticky.

The capability to find a set of characters, even within words, is a useful feature. If you're searching a document for discussions of *reliability,* for example, you may also want to find *unreliability, reliable,* or *unreliable.* You can find any of these words by typing **reliab** (with the Whole Word option turned off) as your search text.

Getting picky about what you find

Most of the time, you don't much care what kind of *sanity* you find. Anything will do: *Sanity, sanity, sanIty,* or *SANITY.* Obligingly, the Edit⇨Find and Replace command ignores the fine points, such as what's uppercase and what's lowercase, by default.

If you're picky about which typeface, size, style, or case you want to search, don't give up — just put a Match to it. That is, you choose Match from the Find and Replace dialog box's menu bar. When you choose Match⇨Case, Find pays attention to the uppercase or lowercase letters you type in the Find box, and it finds only versions of the text that are identically typed. WordPerfect reminds you about this feature by displaying `Case Sensitive` below the Find text box.

When you choose Match⇨Font, WordPerfect displays the Match Font dialog box, which enables you to look for *sanity* in, for example, Arial bold font. Check off what you want by pointing and clicking. Click OK when you finish.

If you're among the WordPerfect secret-code cognoscenti, be aware that you can also find codes. You can look for specific codes, such as `Lft Mar` and `Bot Mar`, by choosing Match⇨Codes in the Find and Replace dialog box. If you would rather type a specific code, choose Type⇨Specific Codes in the Find and Replace dialog box. (See Chapter 17 for full details on how to become like James Bond and read these secret codes.)

Finding and Replacing Text

If your forthcoming best-seller, *The Search for Sanity,* just isn't working out, don't go crazy. Just replace *sanity* with *chocolate,* for example, and see how it hangs together. To accomplish this literary feat, use the same Edit⇨Find and Replace command (or press F2) that we describe in the preceding section. But now you get to explore the further reaches of the dialog box in Figure 3-3: the Replace With box and the Replace and Replace All buttons. In the normal scheme of things, replacing *sanity* with *chocolate* is simple. Follow these steps:

1. **Choose Edit⇨Find and Replace (or press F2).**

2. **In the Find box, type the text that you want WordPerfect to find and replace.**

   If you select *sanity* in your document before issuing the command, the word appears automatically in the Find text box.

3. **Click in the Replace With box and type the replacement word or phrase.**

   To follow along with our example, you'd type *chocolate.*

4. **Click either Find Next or Find Prev.**

   WordPerfect goes in search of your search text — *sanity,* in our example. If it finds *sanity,* WordPerfect highlights it; if WordPerfect doesn't find it, it tells you so.

5. If your text has been found, you can do the following:

- If you want to replace the text, click Replace. The ever-eager Find and Replace goes in search of any additional instances of your search text.

- If you want to skip by this instance of word without replacing it, click Find Next.

- If you want to look for the previous instance of the word earlier in your document, click the Find Prev button.

Find and replace tips

This list shows some general tips for replacing text:

- ✔ The quickest way to find or replace text is to press F2.

- ✔ The commands in the Type, Match, and Options menus work the same way for replacing text as they do for finding text.

- ✔ When you type something in the Replace With box, the Replace command appears on the Find and Replace dialog box's menu bar (until now, it's been a barely visible, pale gray).

- ✔ To replace every instance of the text in your search, click Replace All rather than Replace. WordPerfect changes all instances at the same time, without asking for you to review and approve the changes. You can achieve fast results, but you also can do a lot of damage very quickly. For example, unless you turn on Whole Word mode (from the Match menu), you can end up replacing not only *sanity* with *chocolate,* but also *insanity* with *inchocolate.*

Before we scare you away from ever using the Replace All option, let us remind you of that nifty Undo command you read about earlier in the chapter. You can undo an entire Replace All operation with a single click of the Undo button. Whew!

- ✔ To delete every instance of the text in the Find box, first put a space in front of the text in the Find box; then put nothing at all (not even a space) in the Replace With text box. This step makes sure that you don't end up with two spaces where the deleted word used to be.

- ✔ You can leave the Find and Replace dialog box displayed while you work on your document, which can be helpful if you do a great deal of searching. To edit your document while the dialog box is visible, simply click your document and begin typing.

- ✔ To replace only a limited number of instances of your Find text, choose Options⇨Limit Number of Changes in the dialog box's menu bar. The Limit Number of Changes dialog box appears, in which you can specify the maximum number of changes you want to make. For example, if you want to make only five changes, type 5 in the dialog box. When used with Replace All, WordPerfect replaces only the first five instances of the text.

Finding and replacing all forms of a word

Here's a cool feature: WordPerfect can search for not only a specific word but also *all forms of that word,* including plurals and past tenses. If you write a short story about skiing in Colorado, for example, and later decide to change the setting to Bermuda, you can replace all forms of the word *ski* with the equivalent forms of the word *surf. Skiing* becomes *surfing, skied* becomes *surfed* — the whole shebang.

To tell WordPerfect to find or replace all forms of a word, choose Type➪Word Forms from the menu bar in the Find and Replace dialog box. WordPerfect tells you that it will now look for word forms by displaying Word Forms of below the Find and Replace With boxes.

To search for all forms of a word, type the simplest form (singular, present tense) of the word you want to search for (such as *ski*) in the Find box, and click the Find Next or Find Prev button. WordPerfect finds the next occurrence of the word in any of its forms.

To replace all forms of one word with the matching forms of another word, type the simplest forms of the two words (such as *ski* and *surf*) in the Find and Replace With boxes and then click the Find Next or Find Prev button. Word-Perfect finds the first occurrence of the word you're looking for; displays the word in the Find box; and displays, in the Replace With box, the word with which it plans to replace the original word. If WordPerfect found *skied,* for example, it displays surfed in the Replace With box. If you want to make the change, click the Replace button; if not, click the Find Next or Find Prev button again. Either way, WordPerfect searches for the next occurrence of the word.

Using the Replace All button when you replace word forms is not always a great idea. You can get into trouble if the word you're searching for has other meanings, if it can be used both as a verb and a noun, or if it can be used in noun phrases. (Do you really want WordPerfect to change *ski poles* to *surf poles,* for example?) It's a good idea to eyeball the replacements WordPerfect suggests as they go by.

Chapter 4

Working with the Spelling and Grammar Tools

*W*e sure are attracted to new features, aren't we? Whether you're looking for a new automobile or a new mattress, you can count on the manufacturer providing more and more bells and whistles to entice you to buy. Sometimes these features are useful and innovative (such as a built-in GPS system in a car), but other times they're pure fluff (such as a built-in GPS system in a mattress). WordPerfect and other software applications are no exception. To persuade you to upgrade, software developers have been known to throw in everything, even the kitchen sink. (We have enough problems keeping our dishes clean as it is, so we avoided that recent Kitchen Sink for Windows XP upgrade.)

WordPerfect, however, sports a set of features that are anything but fluff — its amazingly useful spelling and grammar tools. After you understand how to use these writing assistants, you can significantly improve the writing quality of your documents.

In this chapter, you explore how WordPerfect makes the job of proofing and tweaking your documents easier than ever. You can check for misspellings with Spell Checker; improve your grammar with Grammatik; locate a synonym that will really impress your boss with the Thesaurus; and discover what the heck that impressive word means with the Dictionary.

Proofreading as You Type

Given that the name of the software you're using is WordPerfect, you might think that you *can't* type anything but perfect words. Perhaps version 13 will introduce that feature, but for now the software designers are getting close with their as-you-go automatic proofreading tools.

As you type along, you may notice that a few different things are going on, besides having words appear on your screen. Some of your words have a wavy red underline. Some of your words have a wavy blue underline. (Wavy green underlines mean you've been staring at the screen too long!) In addition, WordPerfect's property bar politely suggests words that perhaps you *meant* to type, but didn't because you undoubtedly were distracted.

If you can type while you're looking at the screen instead of looking at your fingers, you'll find that WordPerfect also changes some of your words as you type by using its QuickCorrect feature. Are these features the last word in convenience or just plain meddlesome? Well, perhaps both. Read on.

Spell-As-You-Go makes you see red

As you do your work, WordPerfect looks over your shoulder, and it feels compelled to point out words it can't find in its dictionaries (more accurately called *word lists*). It does this by underlining those words with a red, wavy line. Thoughtfully, WordPerfect usually has a suggestion about what you may mean instead of what you typed. This feature is called Spell-As-You-Go, and you turn it off and on from the Proofread selection on the Tools menu. (See the section "Turning on and off Spell- and Grammar-As-You-Go," for details.)

To find out what WordPerfect thinks you should have typed, right-click the underlined word. WordPerfect displays a list of suggested words or actions (such as Delete Duplicate for duplicated words), along with a few other options:

- ✔ **Correct the spelling mistake:** If the word you want is in the displayed list, you're in luck — just click the word, and WordPerfect automatically substitutes that word for the original. (If the word *More* appears in the list, click *More* for additional words.)

- ✔ **Add the word to the WordPerfect Dictionary:** If the word you want is not in the list, you have another choice: You can tell WordPerfect that what you typed really *is* a word and should be considered one from now on.

- ✔ **Ignore questionable words:** If the word you typed really isn't a word (or at least not a word that WordPerfect recognizes), but you'll be using it a lot in this document anyway, you may want to tell WordPerfect to ignore it. You may want WordPerfect to ignore product names, company names, and town names you're using in just one document. You may get tired of seeing *SoVerNet* (the Sovereign Vermont Internet provider) underlined as you write a review of rural Internet service companies. On the other hand, when you're finished with this study, you'll probably never write about those companies again. If so, add *SoVerNet* to the word list for this document by clicking the Skip in Document menu option when you right-click *SoVerNet*.

You may see other words underlined as well, usually when two of them are in a row. Every once in a while, you'll be forced to write something awkward, such as "I had had a thought that that might be a good idea." WordPerfect (and your high school English teacher) would really rather that you didn't do this, and it tells you so by underlining the repeated words. However, you can tell WordPerfect to ignore the situation by choosing Ignore from the QuickMenu.

Grammar-As-You-Go says that you blue it!

Always keeping your best interests at heart, WordPerfect is happy to point out words you perhaps didn't actually mean to type. If Grammar-As-You-Go checking is turned on, WordPerfect both spell checks and grammar checks as you type. To turn it on, choose Tools⇨Proofread⇨Grammar-As-You-Go. Grammar checking puts a blue, wavy underline under words commonly used incorrectly, such as hear and here, or their, there, and they're. Just as for a spelling error, right-click the underlined word, and WordPerfect tells you what kind of error it suspects you may have made and gives you a list of possible corrections.

Turning on and off Spell- and Grammar-As-You-Go

If you're feeling paranoid by having WordPerfect look over your shoulder as you type, you can turn off these "as-you-go" features. Just choose Tools⇨ Proofread. You have four options: Off turns off Spell-As-You-Go and Grammar-As-You-Go; Spell-As-You-Go underlines your spelling errors in red; Grammar-As-You-Go underlines grammar error in blue; and Prompt-As-You-Go suggests replacements for misspelled words as you type. Click to clear the check mark next to Prompt-As-You-Go to turn off that feature.

But beware! You may decide that your file is all ready to print just because it doesn't have any wavy underlines in it. We wish we could tell you that we've never *cent* files to the printer with *there* wrong words in them, but as you can probably *sell* from *his* sentence, WordPerfect's spelling tool can't tell whether you used the *write* word in your document; it can tell only whether the words you did use are spelled correctly. (However, WordPerfect's Grammatik grammar checker, described later in this chapter, does check for that sort of problem.)

Prompt-As-You-Go suggests perfect words

WordPerfect is not content simply to correct your misspellings. No, it wants to help you choose the perfect word for the job. (If it didn't, it wouldn't be called WordPerfect, now would it?) As you type along, you may notice a little box (called the Prompt-As-You-Go box) at the right end of the property bar, as shown in Figure 4-1. The Prompt-As-You-Go box is blank or contains the last word you typed, in red, blue, or black. Prompt-As-You-Go combines spelling, thesaurus, and grammar functions all in one feature.

Figure 4-1:
The Prompt-As-You-Go box displays the "correct-ness" of the word you're typing.

Prompt-As-You-Go box

If the Prompt-As-You-Go box is white but empty, WordPerfect has no suggestions for improving your word. If the box is gray, the feature is turned off. Choose Tools➪Proofread; in the menu that appears, click the blank area just to the left of Prompt-As-You-Go to turn the feature on. (A check mark appears if the feature is already on.)

If your original word appears in that box and is colored red, WordPerfect thinks that the word may be misspelled; if blue, that it is ungrammatical. If the word is in black, the word is okay, but WordPerfect lists alternative words you might prefer. Click the little down arrow beside your word in the Prompt-As-You-Go box, and WordPerfect gives you a list of possible replacements. To choose a replacement from the list, click the replacement word. To check other words in your document with Prompt-As-You-Go, just click them.

QuickCorrect changes your words even as you type them

Welcome to the magic world of QuickCorrect. This is another terrific feature that we love: You don't have to know anything about it, and it usually does just what you want it to. As your high school typing teacher could tell you in an instant, most typing mistakes fall into a few general categories: reversing two letters, putting the space *after* the first letter of a word rather than before, capitalization errors, and really dumb spelling errors we wouldn't make if we weren't typing so fast.

The folks at WordPerfect figured that if these were such simple common errors, why not have WordPerfect correct them for you? That's exactly what Quick-Correct does. For example, try to type *teh* as a word in your WordPerfect document. No matter how hard you try, WordPerfect changes it to *the*. WordPerfect figures (correctly, we suspect) that you meant to type *the*.

If for some reason you really did want to type *teh* (maybe *teh* is the name you've chosen for your newly discovered subatomic particle), you have to be clever. To keep WordPerfect from QuickCorrecting something, add an extra letter to the end so that WordPerfect doesn't recognize it. For example, you could type *tehh*. Then type a space after it to tell WordPerfect you're finished with this word. Now you can go back and get rid of the extra *h*. This is a quick, if clumsy, way to work around QuickCorrect in a pinch. For a more permanent solution, there's a better way.

If you find that WordPerfect is constantly correcting you in ways you don't want (like substituting *the* for *teh*) — or failing to correct errors you make often — you need to take a look at the QuickCorrect dialog box, shown in Figure 4-2. Choose Tools⇨QuickCorrect.

Figure 4-2: The QuickCorrect dialog box, where WordPerfect tells you about a lot of favors it would like to do for you.

What's going on in QuickCorrect is quite simple: You type the stuff in the left column, and QuickCorrect replaces it with the stuff in the right column.

So you want to type *teh* all the time? No problem. Just delete the *teh* correction line in QuickCorrect by using the following steps:

1. **Scroll down until you see the word you want to be able to type in the left column.**

   You can do this by using the scroll bar on the right side of the dialog box or by clicking in the Replace column and pressing the Page Down key on the keyboard. In this case, you're looking for *teh* in the left column.

2. **Click the word in the left column.**

   In this case, click *teh*.

3. **Click the Delete Entry button.**

Has QuickCorrect failed to correct something you usually mistype? No problem. Just add your typo, misspelled word, or miscapitalized word to Quick-Correct, along with the correction. For instance, to have QuickCorrect correct the misspelling *hte,* do this:

1. **In the Replace box, type the misspelling of the word.**

   In this case, type **hte**.

2. **In the With box, type the correct spelling of the word.**

   In this case, type **the**.

3. **Click the Add Entry button.**

4. **When you're finished with the QuickCorrect list, click OK.**

There are a few very useful QuickCorrect entries, such as (R), which turns into ®, (c), which turns into ©, and 1/2, which turns into ½.

QuickCorrect can be annoying if you legitimately need to use a lot of words that QuickCorrect thinks are errors. If you encounter this problem, you can turn off the option by clearing the Replace Words As You Type check box at the bottom of the QuickCorrect dialog box. Then click OK.

Flying Spell Checker Yourself

The WordPerfect Spell-As-You-Go feature (the one that puts underlines under your misspellings) is kind of like flying Spell Checker on autopilot: It looks around your document while you're doing something else and finds the misspelled words. You can, if you want, also fly Spell Checker by hand.

Take a reality check here, however. Although one of the great joys of today's word processing is that you no longer really have to be able to spell, you shouldn't get too excited. WordPerfect doesn't really know how to spell either. What WordPerfect *does* know how to do is check a word against a list to see whether it's there.

Spell Checker looks for spelling errors and other common problems, such as duplicated words, words that contain numbers, and strange capitalization. You can turn these features off if they get in the way. Just click Options in the Spell Checker dialog box to see a list of what is turned on or off. Click a feature to change its on or off status.

To check the spelling of words in your entire document, follow these steps:

1. Display the Spell Checker tool.

Any of the following actions activates the Spell Checker dialog box:

- Choose Tools⇔Spell Checker.

- Press Ctrl+F1.

- Click the open-book icon near the right end of the toolbar.

- With your cursor located anywhere in the text area of your document, click the right mouse button and then click Spell Checker in the QuickMenu that appears.

The Spell Checker tool, shown in Figure 4-3, pops up, and the spelling check begins.

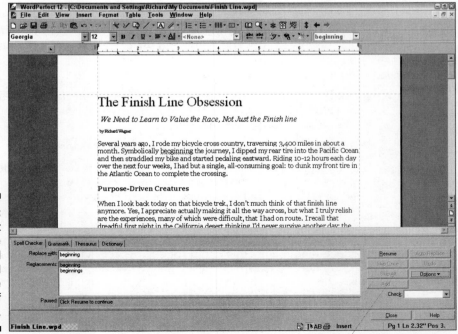

Figure 4-3:
WordPerfect with the Spell Checker tool at the bottom of the screen.

It doesn't matter where you're working in the document — Spell Checker checks the whole thing, from top to bottom. You can change this arrangement by clicking the down-arrow in the Check section of the Spell Checker tool; choose To End of Document if you want to check starting from where you are now.

If Spell Checker finds a word that's not in its word list, it highlights the word in your document and displays it in the Not Found box in the Spell Checker tool.

2. **Skip or replace the highlighted word in your document.**

   If the highlighted word is okay, you have two options (or three, if you count adding the word to WordPerfect's word list, which we cover in the next section):

   - Click the Skip Once button. This action means "Don't worry about it — get on with the spell checking!"

   - Click Skip All. This action means the same thing, but it adds "And don't bother me again about this word!" (until the next time you use Spell Checker).

   If you believe that the highlighted word is indeed misspelled, you have three options:

   - If you know the correct spelling, just double-click the Replace With box, type the correct word, and click the Replace button.

   - If Spell Checker displays the correct spelling in the Replace With box, click Replace.

   - If you're not sure of the correct spelling, scroll through the Replacements box. If you find the correct spelling, double-click it.

3. **Repeat Step 2 for every misspelled word.**

   WordPerfect continues until every word has been checked. When the spell check is complete, WordPerfect tells you so and asks you whether you want to close Spell Checker.

4. **Tell Spell Checker whether or not you want to close it.**

   If you click Yes, Spell Checker closes. If you click No, you can leave the Spell Checker tool on-screen while you work on your document as usual. If it's in the way, you can drag it around just as you would a toolbar. You can always click Close to get rid of it.

If you have a large document, you might want to spell check less than your entire document. Click Check in the Spell Checker dialog box; then choose Word, Sentence, Paragraph, Page, To End of Document, or Selected Text. You can also check a specified number of pages from the current insertion point by choosing Number of Pages. Whatever you check remains selected until you put Spell Checker away again.

Dealing with Real Words that WordPerfect Doesn't Know

Perhaps WordPerfect can be forgiven for not knowing uncommon names, such as *Margy* (how one of us spells her name). But it's still annoying to have to repeatedly skip names and other real words that are unknown to WordPerfect. The solution is to add these words to WordPerfect's vocabulary.

Adding words to WordPerfect's vocabulary

The simplest way to add words to WordPerfect's vocabulary is through Spell Checker. Start Spell Checker as you normally do. (What? You forgot how already? Press Ctrl+F1 or refer to the preceding section for other ways.)

When Spell Checker highlights a word you think is okay, click the Add button in the Spell Checker tool. This step adds the word to something called the *user word list.* As far as Spell Checker is concerned, the word is a real word now. Spell Checker will never bring it up again and will sincerely regret having brought it up in the first place.

You can also add a word through the Spell-As-You-Go feature. When a word that you'd like to add to WordPerfect's Dictionary is underlined in red, right-click the word to display the QuickMenu. Choose Add from the menu.

Correcting and customizing WordPerfect's vocabulary

Adding words to WordPerfect's vocabulary is easy. If you add a word by mistake or need to otherwise tailor WordPerfect's vocabulary, however, you need to understand a bit more about how WordPerfect stores its vocabulary. WordPerfect uses *word lists* — special computer files — to store its vocabulary. It refers to the following two word lists (and any other word lists you might specify) whenever you use its Spell Checker, Spell-As-You-Go, and QuickCorrect features:

- ✔ A main word list consisting of words in official, genuine English (or another language). You don't add anything to this list.
- ✔ A user word list of anything else you consider to be a word.

The reason most people need to fool with word lists is to remove words they've added accidentally. It's easy to go tripping merrily through your document, clicking Add for every word Spell Checker flags. Such glibness eventually causes you to add a word such as *klockwurst* to the word list. (The word was supposed to have been *knockwurst,* but you typed it just before quitting time and were looking at the clock.) Now *klockwurst* is considered a genuine word, so Spell Checker ignores any subsequent *klockwurst*s.

To correct this situation, you must go deeper into the labyrinthine of Spell Checker than a novice normally goes. Walk this way, please:

1. **Choose Tools⇨Spell Checker to display the Spell Checker tool.**

2. **Click the Options button, and then choose User Word Lists from the menu that appears.**

    The User Word Lists dialog box appears.

3. **In the list of User Word Lists, click the list name you want to edit.**

    You see `Document Word List` and `WT12US.UWL` — the user word list that comes with WordPerfect. Choose that user word list if you're trying to remove a word that you added by clicking Add in Spell Checker.

4. **In the lower part of the dialog box, scroll through the Word/Phrase column of the word list until you see your mistake. Select it, and then click the Delete Entry button.**

    The word is gone, gone, gone.

5. **Find your way back to the Spell Checker tool by clicking the Close button.**

Dealing with Grammatik

Spell checking is a black or white exercise: A word is spelled right, or it isn't. Because there isn't much gray area or subtlety in spelling, WordPerfect can do a great job of automating the task and making reliable suggestions. And WordPerfect gets smarter as you tell it about new words.

WordPerfect tries to perform an equivalent task with your grammar through its Grammatik feature. Grammatik means well, tries hard, and can be useful in finding obvious grammatical errors in your document. However, what's right and wrong with the grammar of a sentence is often a matter of style and is not as clear cut as the binary world of spell checking.

If you consider yourself a novice writer, Grammatik can be a helpful tool for improving obvious problems. But if you have even intermediate grammar skills, you may find that your writing style is constantly butting heads with Grammatik's suggestions.

Grammar checking itself works just the same as spell checking: It starts at the beginning of the document and gives you the option to skip suggestions you don't want to see in the future.

To start, choose Tools➪Grammatik (or Alt+Shift+F1). Grammatik shows you the word it doesn't like, an explanation of what's wrong with it, and its suggestions for improving your text. The Replace, Skip Once, Skip All, and other buttons work just as they do for spell checking.

If you want to poke around and figure out what Grammatik thinks it's doing, click Options and select Checking Styles. You'll see a list of all the collections of rules Grammatik uses to analyze your writing. Edit one of those rules, and you'll really see Grammatik's guts revealed.

Grammatik is a useful feature, but it's never a substitute for having a real, live human read your document.

Taming the Roar of the Mighty Thesaurus

If you're in search of variety in your document, the Thesaurus is surely one of the most practical and useful tools that could be integrated into a word processor. You can view the Thesaurus by choosing Tools➪Thesaurus.

To use the Thesaurus, do the following:

1. **Double-click the word in your document to highlight it.**

   For that matter, you can highlight it any one of a dozen other ways — see Chapter 3 for the gory details.

2. **Choose Tools➪Thesaurus.**

   The bottom half of the WordPerfect window displays the Thesaurus tool, as shown in Figure 4-4. The Thesaurus displays the word it's currently looking up (your selected word, to begin with) in a text box at the top of that window.

3. **To look at possible replacement words, click the + sign for that category.**

   A list of words in that category appears, indented under the category.

4. **To choose a replacement word, click it.**

   When you click a replacement word, the word appears in the text box where your original word appeared. WordPerfect then automatically looks up that word, and its synonyms appear in a second window in the Thesaurus. If you click a word in that list, you get *yet another* window of synonyms! Click a word in one of these windows and get on with it!

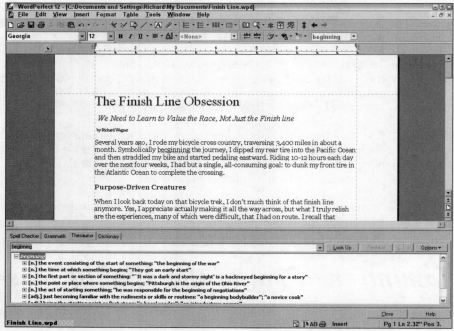

Figure 4-4:
Finding the perfect word with the WordPerfect Thesaurus.

5. **To replace the word you originally highlighted in your document with your newly chosen word, click the Replace button in the Thesaurus.**

   If you can't find the Replace button, that's because no word is selected in your document. (Maybe you clicked in the document window by mistake.) Click the Insert button, instead, to insert the new word in your document.

6. **Click the Close button to send the Thesaurus back to its cave.**

Getting Precise Definitions with the Dictionary

WordPerfect 12 sports a handy built-in Oxford Dictionary that frees you from dusting off that old six-inch thick dictionary lying dormant on your bookshelf. To access the Dictionary and look up the definition of a word, follow these steps:

1. **Double-click the word in your document to highlight it.**

2. **Choose Tools⇨Dictionary (or press Alt+Ctrl+F1).**

The bottom half of the WordPerfect window displays the Dictionary tool shown in Figure 4-5. The Dictionary shows the word you're looking up in a text box in the top-left of the window and selects the closest matching word found in the Dictionary in the list below.

You can also look up a word in the Dictionary by selecting the word (or placing the cursor in the word somewhere) and right-clicking it to display the QuickMenu. In the QuickMenu, choose Dictionary from the list.

3. **View the definition for the matching word.**

The definition for the selected word in the list is displayed in the main part of the Dictionary window. If your word is associated with a root word, the root word is displayed in the list instead. For example, *begin* is provided in the dictionary rather than *beginning*.

4. **To look up another word, click the box in the top-left corner of the window and type a new word.**

The Dictionary looks for the new term in its list of words. If the Dictionary finds it, the word is shown in the list, and its definition is shown at the right.

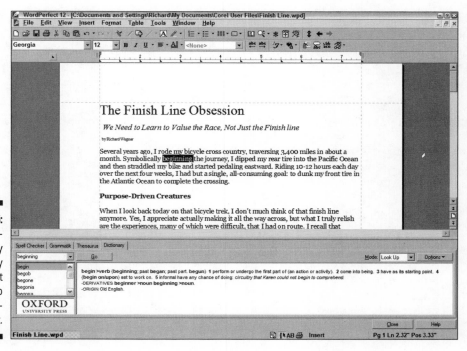

Figure 4-5:
A handy-dandy dictionary is built right into Word-Perfect.

 5. Click the Close button to close the Dictionary tool.

Unlike the other tools (Spell Checker, Grammatik, and Thesaurus), the Dictionary doesn't add or replace any words in your document. The Dictionary is used only for looking up definitions.

You can, however, copy a word or group of words from the Dictionary definition box to the Clipboard. To do so, select the word and right-click to display the QuickMenu. Choose Copy. You can then add the word or definition to your document by choosing Edit⇨Paste.

Chapter 5

On Paper at Last — Printing Stuff

Several years ago, the idea of a paperless office was all the rage as techno-geeks looked to the future. The thinking was that once everyone started using computers, who'd need to use paper? We could just communicate electronically. In hindsight, maybe that claim was slightly unrealistic, at least for now and anytime soon. Yes, e-mail and the Internet have radically changed the way everyone communicates, but you probably see as much paper around your office as you ever did. In fact, perhaps all this innovation serves to offer up *more* communication needs, making the need for printing even greater than before!

In the real world of a paper-barraged office, you need to know how to print your documents. In this chapter, you explore just how to do it. For details about creating and printing some popular documents, including mailing labels and envelopes, see Chapter 15.

Ready to Print?

You've written and formatted your document, and it looks *mahvelous*. Now you're ready to see how it looks on paper. But before you can do so, you had better be certain that your printer is ready to help.

Make sure that the printer is plugged in to both the wall and your computer. Be sure that your printer has an ink or toner cartridge — that is, unless you're interested in printing your document in white on white.

Get a sneak peek at your printed document

WordPerfect does a good job showing you what your document will look like while you're editing it in Page view. But if you're like us, you find it comforting to do a quick print preview before you send that mega-document to your printer. To preview your printed document, choose File⇨Print Preview. WordPerfect displays a view of your document similar to Page view and displays a Print Preview toolbar. A preview is worth a thousand words (or at least a thousand pieces of saved paper anyway), as shown in the figure. When you're finished previewing, choose File⇨ Print Preview again to go back to the regular editing view of your document.

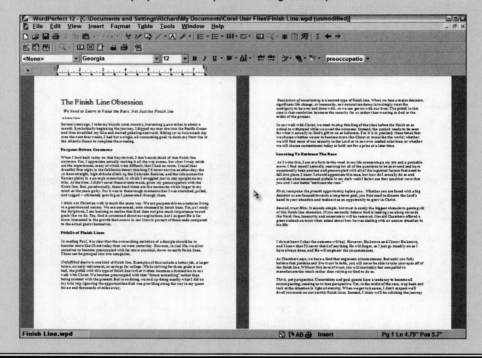

You should also make sure that your printer is paying attention to what your computer has to say. Most printers can be either on-line or off-line. These printers have an on-line light and an on-line button that you can press to switch between on-line and off-line. If your printer is off-line, it ignores any information that your computer sends to it; it's as if the printer were turned off.

If your printer uses sheets of paper, you may want to print drafts of documents on the other side of used paper. We keep a stack of paper with stuff on just one side and use it for everything except the final drafts of our documents.

Before WordPerfect 12 can print anything, Windows must know all about your printer. When you (or someone) installed Windows on your computer, you should have told Windows which printer (or printers) you have. Windows shares this information with WordPerfect. If you're not sure whether Windows knows about your printer, read *Windows XP For Dummies* or *Windows ME For Dummies* (both by Andy Rathbone and published by Wiley Publishing, Inc.). If you're not sure whether Windows knows about your printer, check out the printer's status in the Control Panel program that comes with Windows. (In Windows XP, click Start and then click the Printers and Faxes icon. In Windows ME, click Start, choose Settings, and click or double-click the Printers icon).

Printing an Entire Document

WordPerfect gives you a good idea of what your document will look like when it's printed. If you use Page view (choose View⇨Page or press Alt+F5), you can even see where your headers and footers appear, as well as the top and bottom margins of the pages. (Chapter 8 describes Page view and the other views that WordPerfect provides.) But you can't get the total effect until you see your document on paper. These steps show you how to print your document:

1. **Make sure that your printer is turned on, on-line, and ready to print.**

   Double-check that the right kind of paper is loaded — recycled paper for drafts, or nice, new, blank paper for final versions, or letterhead, or whatever.

   Before printing the final draft of a document, you may want to consider checking its spelling. See Chapter 4 for complete instructions.

2. **Save your document, just in case something bizarro happens while you're printing it.**

3. **Click the Print button on the toolbar.**

   Alternatively, you can choose File⇨Print or press F5. WordPerfect displays the large and imposing Print dialog box, shown in Figure 5-1.

   To see how your document will be printed based on the current Print settings, click the Layout Preview button, at the top-right of the dialog box. The screen shown in Figure 5-2 appears. To hide this panel, click the Layout preview button again.

   If your dialog box looks a little different than Figures 5-1 and 5-2, don't be concerned. Some of the settings may come and go depending on what kind of printer you have.

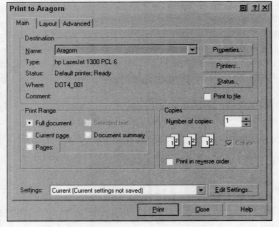

Figure 5-1:
Telling
WordPerfect
the who,
what,
where,
when, and
why of
printing your
document.

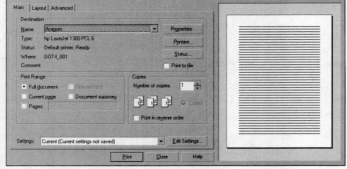

Figure 5-2:
Get a
preview of
the current
print layout
settings.

If you have some text selected when you decide to print, the Print dialog box assumes that you just want to print *only* what is selected (you'll know because the Selected Text option will be selected). If that's not what you want, no problem. Just click Full Document or Current Page or whatever you want.

4. Ignore all those settings, and just click the Print button.

WordPerfect informs you that it's preparing the document for printing. Other dialog boxes may flit across the screen as WordPerfect formats the document. At long last, the printer starts to hum and begins to print. You may also notice a small printer icon in the system tray on the taskbar. (The system tray is the box on the right side of your taskbar that displays the time and probably a bunch of other icons.)

Instant printing

If you press Ctrl+Shift+P, WordPerfect prints your entire document without showing you the Print dialog box. Slam! Bang! The document goes directly to the printer.

Be sure that you really want to print the whole thing before you press Ctrl+Shift+P. If you press Ctrl+Shift+P by mistake, see "Canceling a Print Job" near the end of this chapter. (We know what you're thinking: How could anyone *accidentally* press that convoluted key combination?)

The absolute quickest way to print a document is to open your My Documents folder (or whichever folder contains your document), right-click, and choose Print. You're off and printing, pardner, faster than you could hitch up your pants and spit.

As soon as your cursor stops looking like The Sands of Time (a tiny hourglass) and returns to its normal shape, you can continue to use WordPerfect while your printer prints. You can open another document, edit the current document, or do whatever you want.

If the printer doesn't print anything, don't just print again. Your document may still be wending its way through the bowels of Windows on its way to the printer. It may have become stuck on its way. (Intestinal distress happens even to computers.) Make sure that the printer is on and on-line. If nothing happens after a minute or two, see "Canceling a Print Job," later in this chapter.

If you're looking at the Print dialog box and decide that you don't want to print the document after all, just press the Esc key or click the Close button in the dialog box. (Clicking the *X* in the top-right corner of the dialog box works, too.)

Printing Part of a Document

When a document gets long (like some chapters in this book), you may not want to print the entire thing. What if you print a 30-page report, for example, and then find a typo on page 17? Not to worry — you can correct the typo on page 17, print the single page, and replace it without printing the rest of the document twice. For that matter, you can print any selection of text.

Printing selected text

To print a selection of text, follow these steps:

1. **Select the text that you want to print.**

   Refer to Chapter 3 to find out how to select text.

2. **Click the Print button on the toolbar.**

   Alternatively, press F5 or choose File⇨Print. The Print dialog box appears (refer to Figure 5-1). In the Print Range area of the Print dialog box is an option labeled Selected Text. If you don't have text selected, WordPerfect automatically selects the Full Document option.

3. **Click the Print button (in the Print dialog box).**

Printing a specific page

Follow these steps to print one page:

1. **Place your cursor anywhere on the page that you want to print.**

2. **Click the Print button on the toolbar.**

   Alternatively, press F5 or choose File⇨Print to display the Print dialog box.

3. **In the Print Range area, choose Current Page.**

4. **Click the Print button (in the Print dialog box).**

Printing several pages

To print a few pages, do the following:

1. **Click the Print button on the toolbar.**

   Or press F5, or choose File⇨Print. Just get that Print dialog box on-screen.

2. **In the Print Range area, click in the text box to the right of the Pages option and type the page range that you want to print.**

   Type the first page, a hyphen, and then the last page you want to print. For example, to print pages 5 through 9, you'd enter 5–9.

3. **Click the Print button (in the Print dialog box).**

When your printer prints backward

Some printers print in such a way that you're always rearranging documents so that the pages are in order. Wouldn't it be nice if you could print the last page first? Then, when the printer finished printing, everything would be in the right order. Fortunately, you can tell WordPerfect to do just that. Before you click the Print button, click the Print in Reverse Order check box in the Print dialog box. Now you're ready to print.

Printing random pages

The Multiple Pages setting enables you to print contiguous pages in your document easily. You can print noncontiguous pages, too; you just have to perform an extra step. Click the Advanced tab of the Print dialog box. Use the Page(s)/label(s) option to specify the pages that you want to print. See Table 5-1 to find out how to specify a group of pages. Click Print to print the pages.

Table 5-1	Print Range Page Numbers
Entry	*Meaning*
all	Print all the pages in the document
x	Print page *x*
x,y,z	Print pages *x*, *y*, and *z* (separate page numbers with commas or spaces)
x–y	Print pages *x* through *y*, inclusive
x–	Print page *x* through the end of the document
–x	Starting at the beginning of the document, print through page *x*
x,y–z	Print page *x* and then pages *y* through *z* (you can include as many page ranges as you want, separated by commas or spaces). If you specify a list of pages (*x,y,z*) or a list of page ranges (*x–y*, *w–z*), the list must go from lowest to highest. 5,1,3 prints only page 5; 10–15, 1–5 prints only pages 10–15

Other Cool Ways to Print

Whether you print the entire document or part of it, you also have some other options: double-sided printing, multiple copies, or enlarged printing.

Printing on both sides

If you're printing a large document, you may want to consider printing on both sides of the paper. Not only does double-sided printing save trees, it also looks impressive. Some printers allow you to print on both sides of the paper automatically. But even if your printer doesn't support this, you can always do it manually.

In the Print dialog box, WordPerfect provides an entire area full of printing settings for two-sided printing. Click the Layout tab to see the Two-Sided Printing area shown in Figure 5-3.

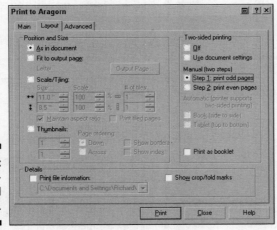

Figure 5-3:
Double-
sided
printing.

If you're lucky enough to have printer that *does* support two-sided printing, the Automatic option buttons will be clickable. If they appear dimmed, WordPerfect doesn't think your printer supports printing on both sides.

For automatic printing, you just need to specify whether you want the binding to be like a book (side-by-side binding) or a tablet (top-to-bottom binding). You'll probably want to choose book binding by clicking the Book option.

If your printer doesn't know how to print on both sides, WordPerfect can still help you do so. Use the Manual (Two Steps) options. You can print all the odd pages, put the paper back in the printer, change the option to print the even pages, and print again. Voilà — two-sided printing.

The two-sided printing options you specify on the Layout tab of the Print dialog box apply to only the current session of WordPerfect. If you know that you always want to print a certain document on both sides, you can attach two-sided printing codes to the document as follows. Click the Main tab of the Print dialog box, and then clicking the Edit Settings button. In the Edit Settings dialog box (see Figure 5-4), click the Two-Sided Printing check box under the Layout Settings folder. Click Close.

Figure 5-4:
Tweaking your printout with the Edit Settings dialog box.

Here are the general steps for two-sided printing:

1. Make sure that your printer is eager to print.

Do we need to say this? Make sure that the paper you plan to use is blank on both sides. Also, if you haven't tried two-sided printing on your printer before, try out these steps on a two-page document at first. You want to make sure that page 2 doesn't print upside down and backwards.

Other than perhaps reaching the moon by rocket, we think properly feeding the paper into your printer when manually printing double-sided pages is one of the most difficult tasks to get right the first time around. You have a one-in-four chance of getting the paper the right side up in the right direction. As a result, we strongly recommend trying a double-sided test run on a few pages before you print your 100-page tome. Otherwise, you could end up with both odd and even pages being printed on top of each other on the same side. Or maybe with the even pages appearing upside down in relation to the odd pages.

In addition, after you figure out the right way to feed paper on your printer, we recommend writing down the details so you'll have them the next time you want to print on two sides.

2. **Click the Print button on the toolbar.**

3. **Click the Layout tab.**

4. **Change the settings as necessary.**

   Refer to the Two-Sided Printing area on the right of the dialog box. If your printer knows how to print on both sides of the page, just tell it which edge you want to bind. If you're not sure, try Left first; it's probably what you want. If your printer doesn't know how to print on both sides, you can do it manually; choose Step 1: Print Odd Pages.

5. **Click the Print button.**

   WordPerfect prints according to your settings. If you're doing automatic printing, you're finished.

6. **If you're doing manual two-sided printing, you have some more steps to perform:**

   a. **Flip the paper over.**

      On most printers, after all the odd-numbered pages have been printed, you have to put them back in the paper tray so that WordPerfect can print on the other side of the paper. Exactly how you place them in the tray depends on your printer; some printers want you to place printed-side down, but others want you to do the opposite.

   b. **Repeat Steps 1–5.**

      But this time, in Step 4 choose the Step 2: Print Even Pages option.

Printing several copies

After you begin printing a document, you may want several copies. Hey, why not save yourself a trip to the copying machine? Of course, if you're printing ten copies of a 25-page document on the only printer in the office, you may not make yourself popular with your co-workers, but that's your decision. To tell WordPerfect how many copies to print, follow these steps:

1. **Click the Print button on the toolbar.**

   Also, you can press F5 or choose File⇨Print to display the Print dialog box.

2. **In the Number of Copies box, enter the number that you want.**

   You can click the little up arrow or down arrow to increase the number or decrease it, respectively. You also can tell WordPerfect how to print the multiple printouts: print the entire document before starting the next (Collate), or print however many copies of page 1 you asked for before moving to page 2 (Group Copies, or the option used when the Collate box is unchecked). The Group Copies option tends to be a little faster, especially if your printer is clever about these things, but with the Collate option you don't have to do that walking-around-the-table thing to get the documents all together.

3. **Click the Print button.**

Printing enlarged or reduced documents

To enlarge or reduce a document, you usually have to print the document, take it to a copy machine, and adjust the copy machine's enlarge and reduce settings. In WordPerfect, you can do the enlarging and reducing at your desk by adjusting settings in the Print dialog box.

To print an enlarged or reduced copy of a document, follow these steps:

1. **Click the Print button on the toolbar.**

   If you don't fancy the Toolbar, you can also press F5 or choose File⇨Print.

2. **Click the Layout tab.**

3. **Click the Scale/Tiling option, as shown in Figure 5-5.**

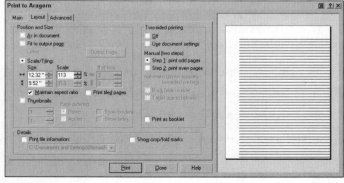

Figure 5-5:
Playing with the Enlarge/ Reduce percentage.

4. **Click the up or down arrow next to the Size box to enlarge or reduce the width or height of the page to a specific measurement.**

Printing Lilliputian style

The Layout tab of the Print dialog box contains the Position and Size area shown in Figure 5-5. The Thumbnails option allows you to print the pages of your document as itty-bitty miniatures called *thumbnails.* Using this option, you can print up to 64 thumbnails on a single 8½ x 11-inch page. Use the number boxes below the Thumbnails option and the Layout preview pane to set up the number of thumbnails you'd like to include on your printout.

You can also click the up or down arrow next to the Scale box to enlarge or reduce the page by a specific percentage.

Your document starts at 100 percent, which is the full page. Watch the preview on the right (accessible by clicking the Layout Preview button at the top right of the dialog box) as you increase and decrease the number — you'll be able to tell how much of the page won't fit when you're enlarging, or how small the page will be if you're reducing. Getting the number right may take some experimenting.

When checked, the Maintain Aspect Ratio option allows you to keep the scale dimensions between the width and height in synch. Uncheck it if you'd like to distort or contort your document.

Printing a Document from Disk

Suppose you want to print a document that isn't open. Or perhaps you wrote, saved, and printed a letter this morning, for example, and now you want to print an extra copy to show to your mother? You can open it first, admire it on-screen for a while, and then print it. But here's a faster way:

1. **Set your printer so that it's rarin' to print.**

   It doesn't matter where your cursor is or even which document is open.

2. **Click the Print button on the toolbar.**

   If you prefer, press F5 or choose File⇨Print. Either way, WordPerfect displays the Print dialog box.

3. **Click the Advanced tab in the Print dialog box.**

   Figure 5-6 shows the Advanced tab.

4. **In the bottom-left corner of the Advanced tab, click the Document on Disk option.**

Poof! A box appears in which you can type the name of the document you want to print. What, you don't want to type the whole name of the document? No problem, click the little file folder icon all the way at the right end of this new box. If the document isn't in the current folder, you must enter its full path name. If you don't know what the heck we're talking about, or if you want to know how to use that cute little file folder icon next to the Document on Disk box, see Chapter 16.

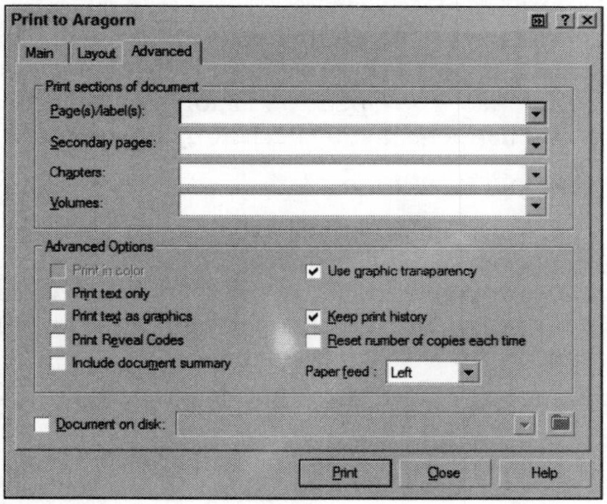

Figure 5-6:
You can
print to a
disk file and
more.

5. **Click the Print button in the Print dialog box.**

   WordPerfect prints the document without displaying it on-screen.

These steps are a good way to print a document that has already been printed and doesn't need additional editing. You can also print only selected pages from the document on disk by entering page numbers in the Print Pages boxes on the Advanced tab.

If the file doesn't exist, or if you type its name incorrectly, WordPerfect displays the message that the file was not found. Use the Folder button to browse your hard drive for the file.

Printing Several Documents

You can tell WordPerfect to print a bunch of documents, one right after the other. If you want to print ten letters, for example, and each letter is in a separate file, opening each document, printing it, and then closing it is an annoying and slow process. A slightly less annoying and slow process is to print each file from disk, as we describe in the preceding section. The best way to do it would be to select the files you want to print and then print them all in a batch, and you can do just that.

This method is a great way to get lots of printing done in a hurry, but it also wastes lots of paper, so be careful when you select the files to print. Follow these steps:

1. **Click the Open button on the toolbar.**

   Alternatively, you can press Ctrl+O or choose File⇨Open. WordPerfect displays the Open File dialog box. You can use any dialog box that enables you to select files. The Open File dialog box is our favorite because nothing bad happens if you click OK by mistake.

2. **Select the files that you want to print.**

   If the files are listed together, click the first filename and then Shift+click the last one; WordPerfect highlights all the files from the first to the last. If the files aren't listed together, click the first filename and then Ctrl+click the other filenames one by one; WordPerfect highlights the filenames that you choose but not the intervening filenames.

3. **When you have selected the files that you want to print, right-click one of the selected files and choose Print.**

   After a great deal of whirring and clicking, your documents begin emerging from the printer.

Canceling a Print Job

In most cases, printing is pretty smooth sailing. Display a dialog box or two, click some buttons, and presto — your document is on paper. Then one day, disaster strikes — you accidentally send your 150-page report to print while you're in the middle of reorganizing it. It's time to tell WordPerfect, "Stop printing!"

WordPerfect keeps track of what is going on with Print Status and History, a program that comes with WordPerfect. In the meantime, the printer is getting its directions from the Printers folder, a Windows feature. With luck, you never have to deal with the Printers folder, but we show you two ways to stop a print job: by talking to WordPerfect and by talking to Windows.

If your computer and printer are connected to a network rather than directly to each other, you may have an additional step. Your document gets passed to the network print manager, which then sends it to the printer. If the steps in this section don't help, talk with your network administrator.

WordPerfect, stop printing!

While your document is printing, you can stop the print job:

1. **Click the Print button on the toolbar.**

   If you prefer, press F5 or choose File⇨Print.

2. **Click the Status button.**

   WordPerfect displays the Print History and Status window (see Figure 5-7), which shows you the status of your current and past print jobs in more detail than you could possibly want.

Figure 5-7:
Impatient for a printout? The Print History and Status window tells you how long your print job will take.

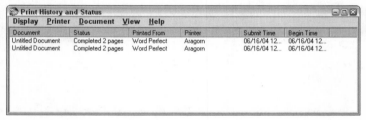

3. **Right-click the document in question and choose Cancel Printing.**

   You can also click the document and choose Document⇨Cancel Printing. The printing stops, although maybe not quite immediately.

If you decide that you don't want to cancel the print job, click the Close button (the one with the *X* in the top-right corner of the window) to make the Print History and Status window go away. You can also leave this window open if you want to check on the status of a print job. Notice that Print History and Status is a separate program and gets a separate button on your taskbar.

Windows, stop printing!

You can go to the Windows Printers folder to stop your print job:

1. **In the system tray on the taskbar, double-click the printer icon to display the Printers folder.**

You can also display the Printers folder directly from the Print History and Status window by choosing Printer⇨Open Printer. Alternatively, click the Start button on the Windows taskbar, choose Settings⇨Printers to see the Printers folder, and then double-click the icon for your printer.

The title bar is the name of your printer, and the jobs listed are being printed or need to be printed, as shown in Figure 5-8.

Figure 5-8:
Change
your mind?
You can
use the
Windows
Printers
folder for
pausing or
canceling
your print
jobs.

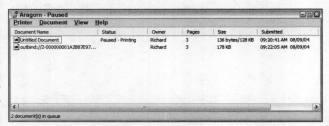

2. Cancel a print job by right-clicking it and choosing Document⇨Cancel Printing.

If your document is short (one or two pages), you have to act fast to stop the print job.

Part II
Formatting Your Text

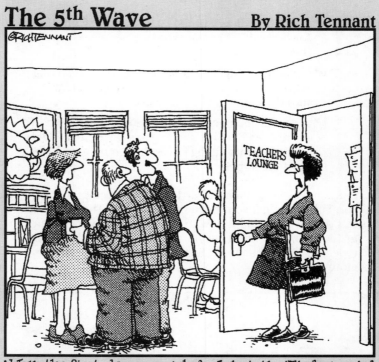

The 5th Wave   By Rich Tennant

"Well, the first day wasn't bad—I lost the 'Finder', copied a file into the 'Trash' and sat on my mouse."

In this part . . .

"I t's better to look good than to feel good." Or so the old Billy Crystal comedy skit once said. We know appearances may not be everything, but they can count for a heck of a lot when it comes to your document. The way you format a document can transform

- ✔ A bland, ordinary proposal into a totally hip "feast for the eyes" that makes your customers leap for joy.

- ✔ A skimpy 8-page term-paper-wannabe into a regulation-sized 12-page thesis that transforms you into the apple of your professor's eye.

- ✔ A dense, compact technical report that would make even Einstein's eyes glaze over into a highly readable, enthralling essay that your kids will cry out to read before bedtime.

Okay, maybe we got a little carried away, but not too much. Formatting can get your documents noticed. That's why in this part, we talk about how to jazz up, tighten up, lighten up, beef up, and spruce up your documents, with different typefaces, margin settings, line and paragraph spacing, and more good stuff.

Chapter 6

Giving Your Documents Character

· ·

In This Chapter

▶ Making text boldfaced, underlined, and italicized

▶ Making text bigger or smaller

▶ Using different fonts

▶ Getting text back to normal

▶ Copying character formatting

▶ Changing capitalization

· ·

*T*he secret's out. We know this is really the chapter you've been looking forward to. The task of writing and improving text may be the heart and soul of creating a document and the job you spend the most time doing in Word-Perfect. But writing is also the hard part, with the ever-present challenge of trying to express your thoughts in a cohesive manner. If document writing is like class time in school, recess must certainly be when you add formatting to your characters. That's the fun part! Character formatting livens up a dull, monotonous document into a zesty manuscript that's ready to rumble.

When we talk about "characters," we're talking about the letters, numbers, punctuation, and other symbols from your keyboard that make up your text. WordPerfect enables you to control a lot about the way individual characters look. In addition to using underline, bold, and italic to add emphasis to your text, you can choose different typefaces and type sizes.

In this chapter, you explore how to add emphasis and apply all sorts of character formatting to your documents.

Adding Emphasis

Bold, *italic,* and <u>underline</u> are three methods for making a word or phrase stand out and make itself known. To add bold, italic, or underline to your text:

1. **Select the text that you want to emphasize.**

   See Chapter 3 for more on text selection.

2. **Click the Bold, Italic, or Underline button on the property bar.**

   As you probably can deduce, these buttons have the bold **B**, italic *I,* and underlined U on them. Alternatively, press Ctrl+B for bold, Ctrl+I for italic, or Ctrl+U for underline. WordPerfect displays the selected text in the font style that you chose.

The question of when to use each of these forms of emphasis is often a matter of style and preference, but here's a summary of common uses:

- **Bold:** Use bold for titles, headings, and other parts of your document that you want to leap off the page. Bold text may also be used occasionally for emphasizing a word in a sentence, though this is usually best left in the hands of italic or underline.

- *Italic:* Use italic to emphasize a particular word in a sentence, to define a term, or when typing the name of a book, film, or song.

- Underline: Use underline for headings or for strong emphasis of a word in a sentence. Underline is used also for formatting e-mail or Web addresses.

Typing and formatting at the same time

In the preceding section, we described a way to add bold, italic, and underline to text you've already typed. You can add text styles to your text also as you type it. Formatting while you type is slightly easier than walking and chewing gum at the same time. To emphasize text as you type it:

1. **Click the Bold, Italic, or Underline button on the property bar or press Ctrl+B, Ctrl+I, or Ctrl+U, respectively.**

   This step turns on the formatting.

2. **Type the text that you want to emphasize.**

3. **Turn off the formatting by clicking the same button or pressing the same key combination that you used in Step 1.**

Getting a clue from the property bar

Even if you can't tell by looking at the text, WordPerfect gives you a hint as to whether or not you're typing formatted text. The clue is to look at the Bold, Italic, and Underline buttons on the property bar. If any of them appears to be pressed in, the text you type or the text you have selected is formatted that way. If the buttons do not appear pressed, you know that the text doesn't have that property.

However, real life is not always so clear cut. Suppose you use the mouse to select a sentence. If a single word in the sentence is italicized, but the remaining words are not, the Italic button on the property bar doesn't look pressed in because the entire selection — the sentence — isn't italicized.

Because WordPerfect doesn't have a way to make the property bar's Italic button say "some text in your selection is italicized and some isn't," it does a natural thing when encountered with ambiguity: It punts! (Obviously, Word-Perfect missed the "when the going gets tough . . ." motivational speech.)

Changing the formatting of selected text

You can modify the formatting of the text you have selected, as follows:

1. **Select the text that you want to format or unformat.**

   Look at the property bar. If all the text that you selected is formatted, the relevant text-style button looks as though it's pressed in. For example, if all the text that you selected is bold, the Bold button looks as though it's pressed in.

2. **Undo the existing formatting by clicking the pressed button.**

   This step releases the button so that it isn't pressed in anymore, and the formatting should disappear. For example, to unitalicize an entire selected sentence, click the Italic button to make it look as though it isn't pressed in.

   If one click doesn't do the trick, some of the text probably *wasn't* formatted. It is now! Click the button again to undo the text formatting.

3. **To add formatting, click an unpressed button to format the text.**

   For example, to italicize an entire selected sentence, click the Italic button so that it looks pressed in.

   You can press the equivalent key combination (Ctrl+B, Ctrl+I, or Ctrl+U) to remove the formatting for the selected text. (Press it again if the formatting doesn't entirely go away.)

You can use more than one type of formatting at the same time. You can make text both ***bold and italic,*** for example. Just click both the Bold and Italic buttons on the property bar, or press Ctrl+B and then Ctrl+I; ditto to turn the formatting off.

When you make character formatting changes to your document, WordPerfect keeps track of your changes by adding secret formatting codes (called *reveal codes*). See Chapter 17 for information on how reveal codes work.

The Amazing Shrinking (or Expanding) Text

When you begin working with WordPerfect for the first time, the text you type is all 12-point size, a standard size for text in a document. (A *point* is the unit of measurement that typographers use to size text.) Although 12 point may serve a good purpose for paragraph text, it sure doesn't get your attention for the important stuff — such as the title of a document or a key heading. To make your text bigger, follow these steps:

1. **Select the text whose size you want to change.**

   You usually select an entire line when you change font size because a line with letters of different sizes usually looks strange. Try clicking in the left margin of the line you want to enlarge. (Check out Chapter 3 for the details about line selection.)

2. **Click the Font Size box in the property bar.**

   It's the box that has something like 12, for 12-point type, and a little down arrow beside it. When you click the arrow, a menu of font sizes drops down from the button, listing the standard sizes people usually use.

   As you move the mouse pointer up and down this list, you'll notice the window beside the list that has text that changes size based on your current selection. You'll also notice that the text you've selected in your document changes, based on the selected size, showing you what your text will look like. (See the "Getting a sneak peak with RealTime Preview" sidebar for more on this functionality.)

   If you decide at this point that this size business is a bad idea, just move the mouse pointer off the font size list without selecting a size and click the mouse button, or press Esc.

3. **Click one of the sizes on the list, or type a new size (such as 25 or 23.33), and then press Enter.**

   When you find the size you want, click it. Your text changes to the new size.

You can also set text back to its original size:

1. **Select the text again.**

2. **Click the Font Size button.**

3. **Select the same size that you used for the surrounding text.**

   If you've forgotten what size that was, select some text that looks the way you want this text to look. The leftmost items on the property bar show the selected text's font and font size. This is a handy way to find out what text size you're using.

Getting a sneak peek with RealTime Preview

WordPerfect 12 sports a handy capability called RealTime Preview, which allows you to preview the results of a formatting change on your document *before* you make it. For example, when you scroll through the font face or font size lists on the property bar, WordPerfect updates your document with the currently selected font face or size after a second or two. Previewing in this manner can save you a lot of time and steps in your decision-making process because the setting is not applied to your document unless you click the item. Most of WordPerfect's format commands support RealTime Preview.

Alternatively, don't forget about your good friend Mr. Undo, which we discuss in Chapter 3. You can always undo (choose Edit⇨Undo) a font size action if you want to return your text to its original size.

Keep in mind the following general tips on sizing your text:

- Headings in a document should generally be 16 or 18 points.
- Default paragraph text should be 10–12 points.
- If you plan to fax your document, make the text a minimum of 12 points. Faxes always look grainy, so they're much more readable if the type is larger.
- Text size is a funny thing. Depending on which font you're using, the same point size can look larger or smaller. For example, 12-point Arial looks larger than 12-point Times New Roman. Typographers have an explanation for this, but unless you have a keen and overwhelming interest in font metrics, we recommend that you just take our word for it.

Fontificating about Typefaces

We said at the outset of this chapter that character formatting was like recess, the fun part of word processing. If that's the case, fonts must be the shiny, new, curly-cue slide that all the kids line up to slide down during their 30-minute break.

Font is a popular term nowadays that commonly refers to what the text looks like. Fonts can be rather `dull and monotone`, somewhat everyday, kinda special, or *just plain radical*.

However, a typeface (or font face) is actually the term that describes a set of shapes for letters, numbers, and punctuation. For example, the common typefaces that you see on every Windows system are ones such as Times New Roman, Arial, and `Courier New`. In contrast, a font is a typeface plus a particular size and style (bold, italic, bold italic). So, whereas Times New Roman refers to a typeface, a font might be described as Times New Roman, 12 point, Bold.

More than any other formatting device, your selection of fonts radically affect the look and tone of your document and shows readers at a glance whether your document is considered formal or informal, for business or leisure, creative or technical. In addition, you can have hundreds of fonts at your disposal. (In fact, WordPerfect 12 Office comes with boatload of fonts that you can install and use.)

Here are some general tips when working with fonts:

- **Normal paragraphs:** Use a serif font for paragraph text. Serif fonts, such as Times New Roman, guide the reader's eyes in a straight line and are easier and faster to read than is sans serif, monospace, or fancy typefaces.

- **Titles:** Use a sans serif font, such as Arial or Tahoma, for titles and headings.

- **Variety in a document:** With the almost unlimited number of fonts at your disposal, it's easy to get carried away and use a bunch of different typefaces all over your document. If you're not careful, your document can begin to resemble an old ransom note, made of different letters cut from newspapers and magazines. In general, limit the number of typefaces in your document to two (or, at most, three): a sans serif font for your headings and a serif font for your text. Then you can add variety by using bold, italic, and underlining with these standard fonts.

Changing the font for a selection of text

If you want to change the font of a portion of a document, but not every part, all you have to do is select the text and go crazy (but not too crazy). The process is similar to changing the size of the text, which we discuss earlier in this chapter:

1. **Select the text whose font you want to change.**

   Take some care with what you select. Usually, all of a heading should be in the same font; sometimes the first word in a paragraph may be in a different font from the rest of the paragraph, but that's about it. Otherwise, select a whole sentence or paragraph.

2. **Click the little down arrow to the right of the current font name (usually** `Times New Roman`**) in the property bar.**

WordPerfect refers to this as the Font Face button because it shows the typeface of the font you're using. A list of available fonts appears to the left of the button. As you move the mouse pointer over this list of font names, the text you've selected appears in the highlighted font, and a sample of the font appears just to the right of the list. This feature is very cool — and helpful, because we can't remember what all these fonts look like. Also, RealTime Preview shows you what your document looks like with the selected font. (See also the "Getting a sneak peek with RealTime Preview" sidebar in the chapter.)

If you decide that the existing text looks better than anything you see in the font list, just move the mouse pointer off the font list and click the mouse button, or press Esc.

3. **Click a font that you like.**

   The selected text changes to the new font.

 If you use a number of font and size combinations over and over, check out the QuickFonts button on the property bar. That's the button that has a fancy-looking (almost unrecognizable) blue *F* with the yellow lightning bolt beside it (see the icon in the margin). It lists the last ten or so fonts you've picked from the Font Face list on the property bar. On the other hand, if you use the same font and size combinations a lot, you should also consider using styles, which we discuss in Chapter 9.

Choose a font for the rest of the document

If you want to change the font partway into a document, you can tell Word-Perfect that another font should appear from this point forward:

1. **Move your cursor to the location at which you want to use a new font.**

   If you want all the pages starting with page 2 to use a different font, for example, move your cursor to the top of page 2.

2. **Click the Font Face button in the property bar.**

   A list of available fonts drops down from the button.

3. **Choose a font from the list.**

   The font name in the property bar changes to the new font, and the text that comes after the cursor changes to the new font. You can do the same trick with the Font Size button. That's the one with the number, to the right of the Font Face button.

 Setting a font in this manner changes the font only for the unformatted text in the remaining part of the document. If you explicitly set font formatting for a chunk of text, WordPerfect won't override the formatting for that particular text piece.

You can use the same method to select a font at the beginning of the document by moving your cursor to the top of the document and then clicking the Font Face button. But a better way exists, as we describe in the "Character Formatting Central" section.

Embedding fonts in your document

Choosing the right fonts for your document can be tricky if you're sharing your document with other people. In general, for someone else to see the document in the font you chose, the desired font must first be installed on his or her computer. If that font is not available, WordPerfect makes a best guess and substitutes another similar style font. However, in spite of WordPerfect's good intentions, this could mess up your carefully formatted document.

The popularity of Windows has made it easier to choose fonts that most people will have on their machines. For example, you can count on everyone having Times New Roman and Arial. But you may have occasions where you want or need to choose something more unique or exotic.

Fortunately, WordPerfect enables you to embed fonts in the document itself so that whatever machine opens up the document can view it using the fonts you carefully selected. To do so, follow these steps:

1. **Display the Save File dialog box.**

   Choose File⇨Save for new documents or File⇨Save As for saved documents.

2. **Check the Embed fonts using TrueDoc(tm) check box.**

3. **Click Save to save the font-happy document.**

   The file is saved with the fonts embedded in it. You may notice that the size of the file is quite a bit larger, but what else could you expect from a document with a stomach full of fonts?

Character Formatting Central

In previous sections of this chapter, we just dip our toes into the vast ocean of character formatting, using text styles (**bold,** *italic,* and <u>underline</u>), font sizes, and fonts. In this section, we show you how to jump in with both feet. Rather than format your text piecemeal, wouldn't it be nice to see and change all the things you can control about your text in one unified display?

It can be done, and the Font Properties dialog box (shown in Figure 6-1) is the way to do it. To access, choose Format⇨Font, or press F9.

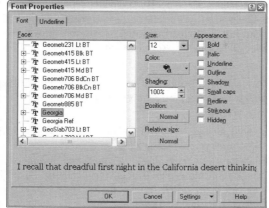

Figure 6-1:
Setting
more font
properties
than you
could ever
want.

Hot properties in the Font Properties dialog box

No, when we talk about "hot properties," we're not talking about real estate or movie stars. If you read Chapter 2, you know that *properties* is geek-speak for all-the-stuff-you-need-to-describe-something. So the font properties are all the things you can change about your characters, such as the typeface, size, style, and color.

Before accessing the Font Properties dialog box, you'll want to decide what text to apply the formatting to:

- ✔ To format a block of text, first select the text and then use the Font Properties dialog box to format the selected text.
- ✔ To format the rest of the text in the document, position your cursor at the point where you want the font to change and then use the Font Properties dialog box.

The lower part of the Font Properties dialog box contains some text, usually a snippet from your document. As you choose character formats in the dialog box, WordPerfect formats this text accordingly so that you can see how your text will look.

You can change all aspects of the font by applying changes as specified in the following list:

- ✔ **Typeface:** To change the typeface, choose a typeface from the Face list in the Font Properties dialog box. (You can get the same list of typefaces by clicking the Font Face button on the property bar.)

You may notice that some of the fonts have little plus signs in front of them. If you click the + sign, you'll see an expanded list of variations of the font, usually Bold, Italic, and Bold Italic. You can ignore those plus signs because you can apply these variations using the Appearance check boxes.

- **Size:** To set the font size (in points), choose a size from the Size list, which is the same list of sizes that you get when you click the Font Size button on the property bar.

- **Color:** If you want to add some pizzazz to your type, you can change its color and shading. Clicking the Color button displays a little box with 42 of WordPerfect's favorite colors for text, as well as the last few colors you may have chosen. Click a color. If you're picky, you can click the More button and select your color from a little color wheel showing all the colors your computer can display.

  You also can change the font color using the Font Color button on the property bar.

- **Shading:** Shading works with color, but it works best for black text. If you want gray text, try selecting smaller numbers in the Shading box. If you shade another color, you may well get either black or white, so try before you buy. Even more confusing, colors (particularly shaded ones) may appear differently on different computer screens and printers. You have been warned: Simple is often better.

- **Position:** Scientific types who want to create a subscript or superscript should click the Position box, which usually says Normal. WordPerfect displays a small pop-up list of your choices: Normal, Superscript, and Subscript. Click your choice.

- **Relative size:** We don't find the Relative Size setting to be useful very often. It does enable you to change the size of your text, but so does the Size box. It's true that if you use Relative Size and then change the Size setting, the small text stays small and the big text stays big, but we usually don't care.

- **Appearance:** On the right side of the Font Properties dialog box is a list of effects you can add to your text, including the ones we discuss earlier in this chapter: Bold, Italic, and Underline.

  If you want to use additional font styles that we haven't mentioned, check out the other options in the Appearance section of the dialog box. You can choose Outline, Shadow, Small caps, Redline, Strikeout, and Hidden. Not all effects work with all fonts (Outline is particularly temperamental), so check the preview at the bottom of the Font Properties dialog box.

Perhaps in a fit of overkill, WordPerfect devotes an entire box to describing how your underlines should look. That's what the Underline tab at the top of the Font Properties dialog box does. You can tell WordPerfect what to underline (Apply to), as well as the color and the line style to use.

After you select just the right formatting, click OK to exit the Font Properties dialog box. If you selected text before entering the Font Properties dialog box, the selected text is formatted; otherwise, the formatting starts at your current cursor position.

If you want to forget the whole thing, click Cancel or press Esc to escape from the Font Properties dialog box with your text unscathed. Or, if you click OK and decide your formatting decisions went horribly awry, never fear. Simply click the Undo button on the toolbar (or choose Edit➪Undo).

Formatting an entire document

What if you want to tell WordPerfect which font to use for the entire document, from soup to nuts? Every document has a *document default font,* which is the font that WordPerfect uses for all text except where you specifically tell it otherwise. WordPerfect uses this font not only for the regular text in the document, but also for page headers and footers (which we describe in Chapter 8) and for footnotes. To set the document default font:

1. **Press F9 or choose Format➪Font to display the Font Properties dialog box.**

   It doesn't matter where your cursor is when you perform this little operation; make sure, however, that no text is selected.

2. **Select the face, size, and other settings that you want to use as the default font.**

3. **Click the Settings button in the lower-right corner of the dialog box.**

   WordPerfect displays a list with some cryptic choices.

4. **Choose Set Face and Point Size as Default for This Document.**

   Presto! All the text in your document *that isn't otherwise formatted* takes on the new format.

Changing the default font for your documents

You can use the same technique we describe in the preceding section for formatting future documents. Whenever you use the File➪New command, or whenever you start WordPerfect, the program has to choose some font for your new blank document. When you find a font combination you like, open the Font Properties dialog box, select that font, click Settings, and select Set Face and Point Size as Default for All Documents. All future documents will use this font unless you format the text yourself.

Copying Character Formatting

After you format some text the way you want it, you can tell WordPerfect to format some other text the same way. (Very useful!) WordPerfect calls this feature *QuickFormat*. These steps show you how to use it:

1. **Move the cursor into the middle of some text that's formatted in a manner you want to copy.**

2. **Click the QuickFormat button on the toolbar (or choose Format⇨QuickFormat).**

   The QuickFormat dialog box is displayed, as shown in Figure 6-2.

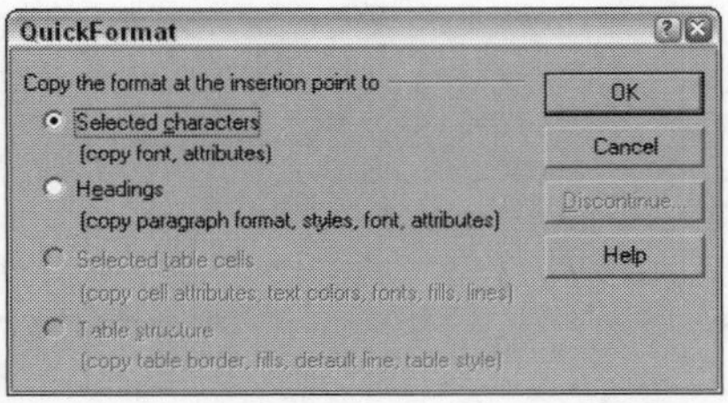

Figure 6-2:
In a hurry?
Use the
QuickFormat
dialog box.

> **QuickFormat**
>
> Copy the format at the insertion point to
>
> ⦿ Selected characters
>   (copy font, attributes)
> ○ Headings
>   (copy paragraph format, styles, font, attributes)
> ○ Selected table cells
>   (copy cell attributes, text colors, fonts, fills, lines)
> ○ Table structure
>   (copy table border, fills, default line, table style)
>
> [OK]
> [Cancel]
> [Discontinue]
> [Help]

3. **Choose between copying just the character formatting at the cursor selection (Selected Characters) or the character formatting *plus* the added formatting for the current paragraph (Headings).**

   For a description of paragraph formatting, see Chapter 7. For now, choose Selected Characters.

4. **Click OK.**

   The mouse pointer turns into the cutest-looking cursor we've ever seen: a little paintbrush (for character formatting) or paint roller (for paragraph formatting) with an I-beam insertion point next to it.

5. **Select the text to which you want to copy the formatting.**

   When the QuickFormat cursor is turned on, the text you select is instantly auto-formatted. QuickFormat remains on, so you can select other pieces of text in the document that you'd like to apply the same formatting to.

6. **To turn QuickFormat off, click the QuickFormat button again or begin typing (or right-click in the document).**

   When you do so, the cursor returns to its normal pointy self.

You can use QuickFormat to get rid of formatting, too. Select some unformatted text, click the QuickFormat button, and select some text that you wish you hadn't formatted. WordPerfect removes the formatting from the text.

Linking and Unlinking Formatting

If you choose the Headings option in the QuickFormat dialog box, WordPerfect remembers that you copied paragraph formatting from one heading to another, and it considers the two headings to be karmically *linked.* If you later change the formatting of the original heading, WordPerfect changes the formatting of the other heading, too — spooky!

You can unlink headings that have been linked by QuickFormatting so that you can format one without changing the format of the other. Check it out:

1. **Move your cursor to the heading that you don't want formatted.**
2. **Click the QuickFormat button on the toolbar.**

   The QuickFormat dialog box appears.
3. **Click the Discontinue button in the QuickFormat dialog box.**

   Now, do you just want to unhook this paragraph from the format or unhook this paragraph and all its friends (that is, all the paragraphs that use this formatting, no matter where they are in the document)?
4. **Click either Current Heading or All Associated Headings, depending on what you want to do.**
5. **Click OK.**

   Your headings' karmas are now all their own and no longer linked.

 Congratulations, you've just created and used your first styles. "Styles?" you ask. WordPerfect styles, which are just like QuickFormat, only better, are the subject of Chapter 9.

Changing Capitalization

dON'T yOU hATE iT wHEN yOU pRESS tHE cAPS lOCK kEY bY mISTAKE? In this situation, WordPerfect is your kind, thoughtful friend; it can correct the capitalization of text that you have already typed. To change some text into all CAPITAL LETTERS, all small letters, or even All Small Letters Except For The First Letter Of Each Word, follow these steps:

 1. **Select the text that you want to fool with.**

 2. **Choose Edit⇨Convert Case.**

    WordPerfect gives you three choices.

 3. **Choose lowercase, UPPERCASE, or Initial Capitals.**

    WordPerfect changes the text as requested. The text remains selected, in case you want to do anything else with it.

You can use these commands only if you've selected some text; otherwise, they're unavailable and appear dimmed on the menu. The Initial Capitals option isn't smart enough to know exactly which words to capitalize in a title or a name. After you use this option, you'll probably have to go back and make a few changes, to uncapitalize (smallize?) the first letters of prepositions, articles, and all those other types of little words.

Chapter 7

Sensational Sentences and Pretty Paragraphs

*W*hen you create documents in WordPerfect, you'll discover that margins and spacing are important because they can make your documents look much longer or shorter than they really are. Suppose that you're a student who has an assignment to write a ten-page paper. With schedules and priorities being what they are, however, not to mention movies and pizza bashes, you've had time to write only seven pages.

Not a problem. Widen those margins. Pad that line spacing. Add a little white space to your prose. You can inflate it like a hot-air balloon. (We're not suggesting any similarity to your prose, of course.) We can also address the opposite problem: packing it in. What if your boss reads only one-page memos, but you have a great deal of detail to include? WordPerfect to the rescue! Shave those margins, tighten that spacing, and maybe even shrink the font size a tad. You can squash everything in. If the whole thing still doesn't fit, just remove all the adjectives and adverbs.

Chapter 6 introduces document formatting in WordPerfect by focusing on the least common denominator in a document — the character. In this chapter, we move up the food chain a few notches to explore formatting for paragraphs and lines.

The Ruler (Kinda Sorta) Rules

You can control all sorts of things from the WordPerfect ruler, which we introduce to you in Chapter 2. But you can't do anything with it unless you can see it. If you don't see a horizontal strip just below the property bar, marked off in inches (or centimeters, for you jet-setters), choose the View menu from the menu bar and then choose Ruler. A check mark means that the ruler is visible; and no check mark means that it's not. If you see a check mark but don't see the ruler on your screen, get new glasses, squint harder at Figure 7-1, stop drinking so much coffee, clean the lint off of your screen, or go find your local WordPerfect wizard.

Tab settings button   Left margin marker   Margin strip   Right margin marker

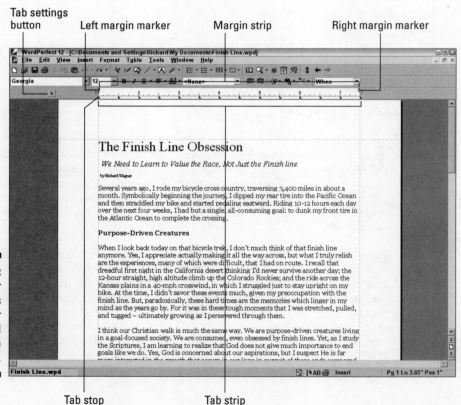

Figure 7-1:
The ruler
shows
all your
margins and
tabs as little
triangles.

Tab stop   Tab strip

The ruler shows you the margins and tabs that are in effect in your document at the point where your cursor is located. When you change settings on the ruler, WordPerfect updates your document. No information is really *stored* in, on, or around the ruler; it's just a nice graphical display of the state of your document. When you open another document, the stuff on the ruler changes to reflect the settings in the new document.

You can use the same View⇨Ruler command to get rid of the ruler later, when you finish with it.

Another way to display or remove the ruler is to press Alt+Shift+F3.

What are all those doodads on the ruler?

The ruler packs a great deal of information about margins and tabs into a small space. It's made up of two horizontal strips with accompanying little black doodads and, if you're lucky, a button off on the left side:

- **Margin strip:** A thin white strip at the top of the ruler shows you the margins for your document. Anything gray beyond the white ruler is considered outside the margins for the page. The two vertical lines at the left and right of the white bar can be used to set the margin.

- **Margin markers:** The gray markers at the top left and right side indicate the positions of the left and right margins. Truth be told, you probably won't use these paragraph margin gizmos too much because you can set paragraph margins in a different way (see "Indenting paragraphs," later in this chapter). But, hey, if nothing else, you can now amaze your friends with your newfound margin marker knowledge.

- **Tab strip:** A thin horizontal strip below the numbered part of the ruler contains little triangles. The triangles show the positions of your tab stops. A *tab stop* is the position across the line where the cursor moves when you press the Tab key.

- **Tab Settings button:** To the left of the ruler itself is a little triangle all by itself on a button. Clicking this button will display a menu for choosing tab settings. For more on all these tab types, see the sidebar "Types of tab stops and when to use which one," later in this chapter.

    The Tab Settings button appears only if you can view the left side of the page in your WordPerfect window. (For details on changing your view in WordPerfect, see Chapter 18.)

I always feel like somebody's watchin' me

Do all the doodads on the ruler intimidate you? Perhaps you feel like its little tab marks are little beady eyes staring at you, watching your every move? If this sounds like a 1980s song by Rockwell and you want your privacy back, feel free to hide the ruler by clicking View➪Ruler to uncheck the Ruler menu item. Fortunately, unless you're doing a lot of tab tweaking, you can get along just fine without the ruler because most margin and tab adjustments can be performed using alternative ways.

The ruler — why bother?

Margins and tabs can change as you go through your document; you can set them at the beginning of your document and change them wherever you want. That's why the ruler shows you the margin and tab settings that are in effect wherever your cursor is right now (not your mouse pointer, which moves whenever you move the mouse, but your cursor, which is the blinking vertical line in your text). If you want to include a long quotation in an article that you're writing, for example, you can choose to indent only the paragraphs that make up the quotation.

Besides seeing the current positions of your margins and tabs on the ruler, you can use the ruler to change them — that is, you can use the mouse to drag the little margin gizmos and tab triangles around on-screen. In the rest of this chapter, we usually tell you two ways (at least) to perform each formatting task: one by using a menu or pressing a key (and making choices in the resulting dialog box), and the other by using the ruler. You can decide which method you prefer; WordPerfect doesn't care which one you use.

Marginal Improvements

As you may recall from high-school typing class, the left, right, top, and bottom margins control how much blank space to leave along the edges of the paper. Usually, everything you type appears within these margins. The purpose of margins, of course, is to provide white space in which your reader can doodle while staring off into space. WordPerfect usually sets the left, right, top, and bottom margins to 1 inch, which is quite generous. You may want to make the margins smaller, to discourage excessive doodling.

Dragging the margin lines

By default, WordPerfect shows you where your left, right, top, and bottom margins are by using gray lines called *guidelines,* which you see on-screen in WordPerfect. If you're in Page view — the default view of WordPerfect 12 and accessed by View⇨Page — the lines are solid light gray and are on all four sides of the text on your page. If you're in Draft view — accessed by View⇨ Draft — the left and right margins are shown with dotted gray lines. (See Chapter 8 for more on different page views.) Note that the guidelines don't appear in the printed version of the document.

To turn the guidelines on or off, choose View⇨Guidelines. You see the Guidelines dialog box, shown in Figure 7-2.

Figure 7-2: WordPerfect is willing to provide all sorts of guidance.

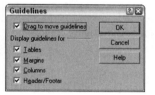

This dialog box enables you to choose which guidelines you want to see in the WordPerfect window. Not that we're gluttons for punishment or anything, but we find all the guidelines pretty useful and usually keep all the check boxes in this dialog box checked. If you don't want that much guidance, at least be sure that the Margins check box is checked so that you can change your margins by dragging them around.

There are a couple of squirrelly things about changing margins. The first is that no matter where *you* think you're changing the margins, WordPerfect changes them starting at the beginning of the paragraph that you're in. You can't change the margins partway through the paragraph.

Second, when you're changing margins, the position of the cursor and the mouse pointer are both important. The cursor (that's the blinking black line) controls *where* the change takes effect. The mouse pointer (the thing that moves on-screen when you move the mouse) controls *what* margin setting gets set. Follow these steps:

1. **Move your *cursor* to the tippy-top of the document.**

   If you want to change the margins for the entire document, it's important to start at the top.

Use the Ctrl+Home and Ctrl+End shortcuts to quickly maneuver from the top of the document to the bottom.

2. **Move your mouse pointer to the gray guideline that you want to adjust.**

   The gray guidelines surround the text on your page. When your pointer is on the gray guideline, it turns into a line with arrows pointing in the two directions in which you can drag the guideline.

3. **Drag the guideline where you want it.**

   A yellow hint window floats above your mouse cursor to display the precise margin size as you drag the mouse. When you release the mouse button, the guideline stays where you put it and the text in your document moves to stay within the margins. If you moved the left or right margin, the margin gizmos in the margin strip of the ruler move, too.

The preceding instructions worked because your text cursor was positioned at the very top of the document. However, if the text cursor was placed elsewhere on the page, your actions would set the margins from that point on through the rest of the document. Therefore, if you're in Page view and would like to change the margins for the entire document, we have an easier way for you to do this without fiddling with the text cursor:

1. **Position your cursor anywhere on the first page of your document.**

   It can be at the very top, but it doesn't have to be.

2. **Click and drag the guideline at the very top (or bottom) of the page in the margin white space — where the top (or bottom) and side margins meet in an X.**

   Any margin adjustment you make at that location affects the current page to the end of the document, regardless of where your cursor is on the page.

If you need to get precise with your measurements or you'd rather just use a nice, safe dialog box, read the section "Using the Margins dialog box." We prefer the guidelines, but feel free to suit yourself.

Using the Margins dialog box

If you don't like dragging things with the mouse, you can do all the same things in WordPerfect using dialog boxes. Here's how to change the margins:

1. **Move your cursor to the tippy-top of the document.**

   The quickest way to do this is to press Ctrl+Home.

2. **Choose Format⇨Margins or press Ctrl+F8.**

   This step displays the Page Setup dialog box, as shown in Figure 7-3. Here's another WordPerfect setting that looks like you just landed in the cockpit of a jet. You can safely ignore everything except the Document margins area in the lower right.

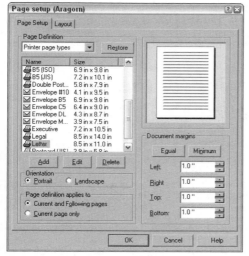

Figure 7-3:
Just set the margins and ignore the other stuff.

3. **Enter measurements in the Left, Right, Top, and Bottom boxes.**

   You can type numbers, or you can click the little up or down arrows to the right of each box to increase or decrease the numbers by $\frac{1}{10}$ inch per click. As you change the measurements, WordPerfect changes the margins on the little page diagram in the dialog box so that you can see the effect you'll achieve.

   If you want to know the minimum margins your printer is willing to print with, click the Minimum button. Or, if you want to make all four margins the same, click the Equal button. (*Hint:* The feature uses the margin measurement that's highlighted, usually the one you just changed.)

4. **To change the margins to the measurements you entered, press Enter or click OK.**

   If you'd rather forget the whole thing, press Esc or click Cancel.

You can also get to the Page Setup dialog box by

- Right-clicking the margin strip on the ruler and choose Margins
- Double-clicking the margin strip on the ruler
- Choosing Format⇔Page⇔Page Setup

When you set the margins and other paragraph formatting settings, WordPerfect inserts invisible, secret formatting codes that contain the new margin information. We'd tell you the names of these codes, but if we did, they wouldn't be exciting and secret anymore, would they? However, if you read Chapter 17, you'll discover these codes, how to look at them, and even how to delete them if necessary.

Changing margins for the rest of the document

Changes you make to the margins can affect the rest of your document. A lot of the time, this is what you want because your document can contain more than one distinct part (such as an executive summary followed by a detailed proposal). You can use different margins for the different parts of the document. (Okay, we're reaching for an example here, but it sounds plausible.)

To change the margins for the rest of the document, follow these steps:

1. **Move the cursor to the position where you want the margins to change.**

   This position is usually at the top of a page, but it doesn't have to be. Remember, your margin changes take effect at the beginning of the paragraph where the cursor is.

2. **Display the Page Setup dialog box with the Page Setup tab selected.**

   That is, choose Format⇔Margins or press Ctrl+F8 or double-click the margins strip of the ruler — you get the idea.

3. **Fill in the margin measurements you want to use.**

4. **Click OK or press Enter.**

   The dialog box goes away. The text following the cursor position moves to fit in the new margins. If you have guidelines displayed, they'll jog to indicate the new margins, too.

These steps show you how to do the same thing with the mouse and the guidelines:

1. **Move the mouse pointer to the point in the document where you want the margins to change.**

   To change the top or bottom margin, go to the first page on which you want to have the new margin, and use the top or bottom margin guideline on that page.

2. **Drag the guideline to the position where you want the new margin.**

   When you release the mouse button, WordPerfect sets the margin for the rest of the document from the position you chose, until you choose to change it again.

If you change the left or right margin again and again, the guideline starts to resemble an Etch-A-Sketch drawing, showing where it changes to the new position (see Figure 7-4).

Chapter 8 gets deeper and deeper into the details of page formatting, including the configuration of top and bottom margins.

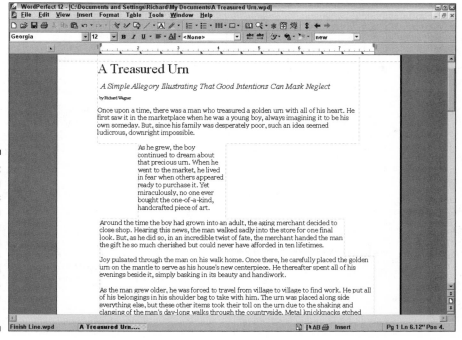

Figure 7-4:
Zig-zag guidelines result from changing margins in the middle of the document, but they're harmless.

Microsoft Word users: Go with the flow

If you have experience using Microsoft Word, one of the biggest hurdles to jump as you start to work with WordPerfect is a fundamental difference in the way WordPerfect handles document formatting. In Word, you typically format a specific text selection or the document as a whole.

In contrast, the position of your cursor is all-important in WordPerfect. In other words, *flow is everything.* Flow refers to the stream of text that goes through your document from the very top (Ctrl+Home) to the very bottom (Ctrl+End), something like water traveling down a river. When you make a formatting change in Word-Perfect, that change nearly always starts at the current position of the cursor and ripples through the rest of the document, unless

another command comes along downstream that changes the formatting again.

A good example of this difference is the Page Setup dialog box. In Word, no matter where your cursor is, whether it is on page 1 or 100, the settings you make in that dialog box, by default, affect the entire document. On the other hand, in WordPerfect's Page Setup dialog box, the settings made start at the page where the cursor is located and continue for the rest of the document.

Another way of looking at it is that Word enables you to swim upstream or downstream from the cursor's location, but WordPerfect really, really, really wants you to go with the flow and swim downstream.

Indenting paragraphs

When you use paragraph formatting, you can specify special margins for one or two paragraphs. If you include long quotations in your text to impress people with your intellect, you may want the quotations to be indented more than the rest of your prose. Although WordPerfect provides three separate features for accomplishing this task, we recommend changing the margins for one or more paragraphs by indenting them. The steps to indent follow:

1. **Move your cursor to the beginning of the paragraph you want to indent.**

2. **Right-click and choose Indent, or press F7.**

   (You can also choose Format⇨Paragraph⇨Indent.) The left margin of the paragraph moves to the right by one tab stop. (You can read more about tab stops later in this chapter.) Because you didn't actually change the margins, the guidelines do not change.

WordPerfect also provides the following useful variations:

- ✔ **Indent both left and right margins:** If you want to indent both the left and right margins for a paragraph, choose Format⇨Paragraph⇨Double Indent (or press Ctrl+Shift+F7).

- ✔ **Use a hanging indent:** A hanging indent may not sound politically correct, but you may jolly well want to include one in your document anyway. In a *hanging indent,* the first line of the paragraph is not indented, but the rest of the lines are. Choose Format⇨Paragraph⇨Hanging Indent (or press Ctrl+F7) at the beginning of the paragraph.

- ✔ **Indent multiple paragraphs:** If you want to indent several paragraphs, you can simply select the paragraphs and press F7 (or select the paragraphs, right-click, and choose Indent).

- ✔ **Modify indent sizes:** An indent code indents the paragraph one tab stop. To control how far your paragraph is indented, you can move your tab stops; see "Pulling Out the (Tab) Stops and Other Tab Tricks," later in this chapter.

How We Justify Things

Justification is a serious-sounding word — one that may make you think about moral imperatives, rationales for your actions, and other philosophical stuff. What a disappointment when you learn that it simply has to do with sticking spaces into lines of text. Such is life. In word processing and typesetting, justification deals with the moral problem of different lines of text being different lengths.

Our five favorite justifications

Most people think that there are four ways to justify text, but WordPerfect has the following five:

- ✔ **Left justification:** Text begins at the left margin and fills as much space as it takes up. Because different lines contain different text, the right edge of the text is uneven, or *ragged.* That's why this method is also called *ragged right.* Most of the text in this book uses left justification.

- ✔ **Right justification:** Works the same way as left justification, except that the lines are shoved over to the right margin. Now the left edge of the text is ragged, and the right edge is straight. (Wonder why nobody calls this *ragged left* or *straight right?*)

✔ **Center justification:** This method centers each line on the page. Both the left and right edges of the text are uneven. Titles look great centered; normal paragraphs look wacky.

 ✔ **Full justification:** The trickiest type; both the left and right edges of the text are nice and straight. How do you manage this type if different amounts of text are on each line? The extra space is broken into little pieces and stuck in among the words in the line, so that all the lines are padded out to fill the space between the left and right margins. Magazines, newspapers, and books usually use full justification, which is also called *justified text.*

 ✔ **All justification (as WordPerfect calls it):** Similar to full justification, only more so. In full justification, the lines at the end of paragraphs are exempt. If the last line of a paragraph contains two words, for example, the text begins at the left margin and stops where it stops. But with "all" justification, no line is safe from the Justifier — WordPerfect justifies *all* the lines. If the last line of a paragraph contains a word or two, no matter — WordPerfect sticks inches of white space between each letter, if that's what it takes to stretch the line out to the right margin. We don't imagine that you'll use this type of justification often; it looks downright weird. However, all justification can be useful if you decide to get deeply into tables and headings: Use it to S-T-R-E-T-C-H a heading across one or more columns.

Justifications for text: Left, center, right, and their friends

Justifying text is a lot like setting margins and indents. Check out the following steps:

1. **Decide how much of your document you're going to justify.**

   Depending on what you select, the same procedure can justify your whole document, a single paragraph, or a group of paragraphs.

2. **Move your cursor into position and make one of the following choices:**

   • To select the type of justification to use for the entire document, move your cursor to the beginning of the document.

   • To set justification for the rest of a document, move your cursor to the point at which you want the justification to change.

   • To justify only a paragraph or two, select the text that you want to justify.

3. **Click the Justification button on the property bar.**

   The property bar drops down a menu of the five types of justification. Alternatively, you can also choose Format⇨Justification from the menu.

4. **Click one of the justification types from the menu.**

   Alternatively, if you want to use shortcut keys, you can press one of these key combinations:

   - Ctrl+L for left justification

   - Ctrl+R for right justification

   - Ctrl+E for center justification

   - Ctrl+J for full justification

"All" justification has no key combination, which makes sense because we don't think people use it very often.

Justification for skipping Center and Flush Right

The particularly inquisitive reader may have noticed that, in the maze of WordPerfect menus, another location on the menu has Center and Flush Right commands. You can find these commands by choosing Format⇨Line. So what's the difference between centering your text with Format⇨Line and with Format⇨Justification? Format⇨Line applies only to the line you're in or the lines you've highlighted. Format⇨Justification applies to the *entire* paragraph you're in or the paragraphs you've highlighted.

For nearly all purposes, you're much better off using Justification because the option works as well on a single-line paragraph as well as on a multi-line one. The only two times we can think of to use Format⇨Line are if

✔ *You want to break a single line into several pieces.* Breaking a line into several pieces might be useful in a header or a footer; we talk about those in Chapter 8.

✔ *You know that you want to center (or flush right) just the one line you're currently typing.* Making a line flush right is useful for putting the date at the top of a letter. For an example, take a look at the sidebar "Inserting today's date on the right," later in this chapter.

Do *not* use Format⇨Line in the middle of a paragraph. If you have more text left in your paragraph than will fit on the current line, a minor train wreck will occur, and the letters in your paragraph will end up piled on top of one another. Don't panic, though. Just choose Edit⇨Undo (or press Ctrl+Z).

TIP

Using Hyphens to Hack Words in Half

In the days before word processors, hyphenation was a big deal for people. Heck, we even have a colleague who got a Ph.D. in Hyphenology. Back when you typed documents out on a typewriter, you had to make many decisions at the end of each and every line. The End-of-Line Soap Opera would go something like this:

> *Hmmm, do I have room to squeeze the word "contumelious" on the line before I run out of space? Nah, I don't think so . . . Then where do I hyphenate this crazy word? Perhaps after the m? Or maybe the l? Boy, I should have listened more during high school English class! Aw, heck, I'll just substitute the word "rude" instead. It means about the same thing and will definitely fit on the line without needing any stupid hyphen. Hyphens can be so contumelious!*

Hyphenation is far less of an issue today, particularly because word processors *wrap* the text for you. In fact, the only times we find it useful are on very narrow columns of text or when text is flowing around a picture (see Chapter 11 to find out more about that trick). If you decide you want words at the end of lines in your document to be hyphenated, you'll be glad to know that WordPerfect can do it automatically (sometimes correctly, occasionally incorrectly).

To tell WordPerfect to hyphenate words as necessary, follow these steps:

1. **Move your cursor to the beginning of the document.**

   Usually, you should use hyphenation on the entire document or not at all. Life is confusing enough as it is. You can't select a portion of your document and tell WordPerfect to hyphenate it, either. If you just want to hyphenate a portion of your document, go to the place where you want hyphenation to start and turn it on; then go to the place you want it to stop, and turn it off.

2. **Choose Tools⇨Language⇨Hyphenation.**

   WordPerfect displays the Line Hyphenation dialog box. Ignore the cute little diagram, the percentages, and everything. We've never met anyone who wanted to change the parameters that a word processor uses when it does hyphenation.

3. **Select the Turn Hyphenation On box.**

4. **Click OK or press Enter.**

   The dialog box closes.

At some point as you work on the document, WordPerfect decides that a word should be hyphenated because it doesn't fit at the end of one line. If that word is in the WordPerfect hyphenation dictionary, no problem! WordPerfect sticks in the hyphen and away it goes. If that word isn't in the WordPerfect dictionary, however, the Position Hyphen dialog box appears without warning, as shown in Figure 7-5.

Figure 7-5: Deciding where to split a word.

You have several options:

- ✔ Click the Insert Hyphen button to insert the hyphen where WordPerfect suggests.

- ✔ Press the left- and right-arrow keys on the keyboard to move the hyphen to a better place to split the word, and then click the Insert Hyphen button.

- ✔ Decide that this long word should really be two separate words. Choose this option if you left out a space accidentally (which is our top-rated typo). Click the Insert Space button.

✔ Decide that there's no good way to split the word in two and that the whole thing should be moved to the beginning of the next line. A classic example of this is the word *strength,* which has a bunch of letters but can't be hyphenated. (Isn't it amazing how much trivia we authors can dredge up?) In this case, click Ignore Word.

When WordPerfect hyphenates a word, it doesn't insert a plain old ordinary hyphen. No, it creates what it calls a *soft hyphen,* meaning that it will go away automatically if the word wrapping is changed. In contrast, a *hard hyphen* is one you put in yourself; it remains in the text even if the word wrap changes (which could leave it looking rather silly in the middle of a line rather than at its end). See Chapter 17 for more on the differences between hard and soft hyphens.

Pulling Out the (Tab) Stops and Other Tab Tricks

Tabs are mischievous creatures. What can be easier than pressing the Tab key to indent lines of your text? And yet, if you don't use tabs correctly, they can make a mockery out of your document formatting and can bite you in the back. You shouldn't be afraid of using them, but explore first how tabs work in your WordPerfect document.

Setting your tab stops where you want them

When you press the Tab key, WordPerfect indents the text at the next tab stop. A *tab stop* is a position across the line where tabs stop. By default, a line has a tab stop every half inch, though you can tweak the settings to your heart's content.

You can see the tab stops for your document using the ruler. (Choose View➪ Ruler or just press Alt+Shift+F3.)

On the tab strip (just below the inch markings) of the ruler, little black triangles mark the positions of your tab stops. The ones that WordPerfect provides are, by default, left tab stops (the most commonly used type) and are symbolized by triangles that point down and to the left.

You may not want a tab stop every half inch, and you may want to create tab stops of types other than left tab stops. If you're typing a list of names and phone numbers, for example, you may want just one tab stop at the position where you want the phone numbers to appear. Luckily, WordPerfect allows you to fool around with the tab stops at will.

Types of tab stops and when to use which one

WordPerfect has a bunch of different kinds of tab stops. This subject is kind of boring, but getting it right once will make your documents look much better. Don't worry about memorizing all these types of tabs; just remember that they're defined here the next time you wonder "How can I get this text to line up right?" Following is a description of the different types of tab stops, along with what happens when you press the Tab key to move to each type:

✔ **Left or L:** What you type appears to the right of the tab-stop position. On your ruler, left tab stops are indicated by little black triangles that point down and to the left.

✔ **Right or R:** What you type appears to the left of the tab-stop position. This tab stop doesn't sound too aptly named, does it? It's called a right tab stop because the text is flush right, or right aligned, at the stop. On the ruler, the triangles for right tab stops point down and to the right.

✔ **Center or C:** What you type appears centered on the tab-stop position. On the ruler, center tab stops are shown by little up-pointing triangles.

✔ **Decimal or D:** This type of tab stop is designed for numbers that have decimal points, such as columns of dollar amounts. WordPerfect positions the text with the decimal point at the tab-stop position; columns of numbers look so much tidier if their decimal points line up vertically. If you type something that has no decimal point, WordPerfect right aligns it. On the ruler, a decimal tab stop is indicated by an up-pointing triangle with a little dot in the middle.

✔ **Dotted versions of the preceding four types:** You can tell WordPerfect to display a line of dots (also called a dot leader) that leads up to the entry. You see this kind of thing in the table of contents of books such as this one. On the ruler, dotted tab stops are shown by triangles with dots above them.

Left	Center	Right	Decimal	Dotted Right
Tom	Jones	Blue	$150.00	.....Page 1
Jo	Bloggswirth	Greenish	.75 each	2
Sue	Fish-Frei	Purple	235	3
Mary	Green	Red	none	4

When you change or create tab stops, WordPerfect inserts a secret code into your document that contains the positions of *all* the tab stops that are in effect at that point. The tab stop changes that you make take effect at that point and continue for the rest of the document or until they encounter the next secret tab stop code. If you change your tab stops several times, with your cursor in different places, you can end up with a document that's littered with tab stop codes, and your tab stops may change when you don't expect them to.

Luckily, WordPerfect makes it easy to tell where you've changed your tab stop settings; a little *tab set icon* appears in the left margin of your document, with an arrow pointing to an indentation in a paragraph. (If you don't see the tab set icon, try changing the zoom on your document: Choose View⊅Zoom⊅Page Width. See Chapter 18 for all the details.) If you end up with unwanted tab stops in your document, you can right-click the tab set icon and choose Delete from its QuickMenu.

You have two ways to position your tab stops: Use commands or use the ruler. The command for setting tab stops, Format⊅Line⊅Tab Set, displays the Tab Set dialog box.

If you double-click a tab-stop triangle on the ruler, WordPerfect thinks that it's doing you a favor by displaying the dreaded Tab Set dialog box. Don't panic — just click the Cancel button or press Esc.

Slithering tab stops across the ruler

To move an existing tab stop, follow these steps:

1. **Move to the place in your document where you want the modified tab stops to take effect.**

   This spot is usually at the beginning of the document or a table. You can also click in the line where the tab stop that you want to change appears, or select the text that contains the desired tab stop.

2. **Click the little triangle for the tab stop that you want to move.**

3. **Hold down the mouse button and drag the triangle left or right along the ruler to its new position.**

   When you release the mouse button, WordPerfect moves the tab stop to the position where you left the triangle. A tab set icon appears in the left margin of your document (an arrow pointing to an indentation in a paragraph) showing that you've created a secret tab stop code here.

To move a bunch of tab stops at the same time, hold down the Shift key and drag the mouse across the tab stops that you want to move. When you release the mouse button, the selected tab stops appear against a gray background instead of a white one. You can then click the gray background to drag all these tabs to their new positions.

Removing unwanted tab stops

To get rid of a tab stop, follow these steps:

1. **Move to the place in your document where you want the change to take place.**

2. **Click the triangle for the tab stop and drag it down off the ruler.**

   You'll know you've dragged far enough when a cute little trash can appears as part of the mouse pointer. WordPerfect drops the tab stop in the trash can; you never see the tab stop again.

If you move or delete a tab stop by mistake, choose Edit⇨Undo or press Ctrl+Z to undo your change. You can also click the Undo button on the toolbar (the button with the U-turn arrow pointing to the left).

To get rid of all the existing tab stops, follow these steps:

1. **Right-click a tab strip on the ruler.**

   It doesn't matter whether you click a tab stop or between tab stops. A QuickMenu appears.

2. **Choose Clear All Tabs.**

   Blammo — no more tab stops.

Setting new tab stops

To create a new tab stop, follow these steps:

1. **Right-click a white area on the tab strip — that is, between two tab stops.**

   You see a QuickMenu that includes eight types of WordPerfect tab stops. For an explanation of the tab stop types, refer to the sidebar "Types of tab stops and when to use which one," earlier in this chapter. If you can see the tab indicator in the left margin, you can click there to see the same QuickMenu.

2. **Choose the type of tab stop that you want from the QuickMenu.**

   Now you're ready to create the tab stop. Get ready; this process is complex and painstaking. (Just kidding.)

3. **On the tab strip of the ruler (the part where the triangles appear), point to the position where you want the tab stop, and click.**

   WordPerfect creates the tab stop and the little triangle to go with it. A tab set icon appears in the left margin of your document to alert you to a change in tab stops.

After you have your tab stops where you want them, you're ready to use them.

To Tab or Not to Tab?

You must be thinking, "What's the big production about using tabs? Can't I just press the Tab key with the default settings and be done with it?" Yes, you can do that, but your documents work better (that is, they look better and are easier to edit) if you use tabs wisely. This section looks at the ways in which you're likely to want to use tabs.

Indenting the first line of every paragraph

To tab . . . Indenting the first line of each paragraph is one of the all-time-favorite uses of tabs. If you want to indent the first line of a paragraph, you can press the Tab key as you begin typing the paragraph. Or you can insert the tab later, after you type the paragraph. No big news here.

Or not to tab . . . If you want to indent the first lines of a *bunch* of paragraphs, however, you can tell WordPerfect to do it automatically, without your having to stick a tab at the beginning of each one. These steps show you how:

1. **Select all the paragraphs for which you want to indent just the first line.**

   The paragraphs must be together, with no other paragraphs, titles, or whatever mixed in. (You can always select one group of paragraphs at a time and repeat these steps for each one.)

   If you want to indent the first line of every single paragraph in the document, don't select any text; instead, move the cursor to the beginning of the document. If you want to indent all the paragraphs starting partway through the document, move your cursor to the point where you want this formatting to begin. Whew!

2. **Choose Format➪Paragraph➪Format.**

   WordPerfect displays the Paragraph Format dialog box, as shown in Figure 7-6.

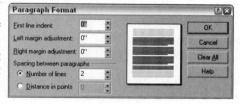

Figure 7-6:
Formatting a
bunch of
paragraphs
so that
their first
lines are
indented.

3. **In the First Line Indent box, enter the amount by which you want to indent each first line.**

   This amount is usually .25 or .50 inches.

4. **Click OK.**

   WordPerfect adds that little bit of white space at the beginning of each paragraph, just the way your typing teacher taught you. Look, Ma — no tabs!

Another way to display the Paragraph Format dialog box is to right-click the margin strip of the ruler and choose Paragraph Format from the QuickMenu that appears.

Words of wisdom on tabs

The Tab key can be a nifty little friend, but only when used smartly. With that in mind, consider the following pieces of advice on tabs:

- ✔ **Never use spaces to indent.** Whether you choose to use tabs or paragraph formatting, don't use spaces to indent paragraphs. In word-processing circles, this method is considered tacky. The problem with spaces is that they're different widths, depending on which font you use (see Chapter 6). Additionally, you can goof up your text justification by using spaces rather than tabs. In contrast, tab stops are always reliable, exactly the width that you see on the ruler.

- ✔ **Never indent all lines of a paragraph using tabs.** To indent *all* the lines in the paragraph, or all *except* the first line, refer to "Indenting paragraphs" earlier in this chapter. Never stick a tab at the beginning of each line of a paragraph. Yuck! Ptooey! If you do, when you edit the paragraph later, the tabs will be all over the place, and your paragraph will have unsightly gaps in all the wrong places. *Please* indent.

✔ **Use tabs only on the start of new paragraphs.** Whenever you use a tab to indent a line, make sure that you pressed Enter to end the preceding line. In other words, the line that you're indenting shouldn't begin as a result of WordPerfect's use of word wrap to fill the lines of a paragraph.

✔ **Use tabs to change the indent size later.** A major advantage of using tabs is that if you decide to indent your paragraphs by a different amount, all you have to do is slide that first tab stop over by a hair. Then all the tabs that depend on that tab stop move, too. When you perform this procedure, be sure that your cursor is in the right place: at the beginning of your document (assuming that you want to change the look of all the paragraphs in your document).

Tabbing yourself in the back

We know that tabbing backward sounds like a bizarre idea, but it's not the only one in the world of word processing. A *back tab* lets you tab backward to the preceding tab stop. WordPerfect sometimes uses back tabs without telling you. If you use the method for creating a hanging indent that we describe earlier in this chapter, WordPerfect indents the entire paragraph one tab stop and then enters a back-tab code to back up to the margin so that the first line isn't indented. Mercifully, WordPerfect performs this procedure automatically and spares you the gory details.

Tables: A 'real' alternative to tabs

Do you remember that 1970s diet soda called Tab? It's still around, but it sure is hard to find in your local grocery. When it was introduced, the drink was "all the rage" as the first popular sugar-free soda. Yet, for many, Tab's taste was an acquired taste. Given that people didn't like a "diet taste" to their soda, I suspect the makers of Tab went back to the drawing board and said "there has to be a better way." In doing so, they superseded Tab with the much better tasting, even more popular Diet Coke.

If you struggle with a bad aftertaste when using tabs in your documents, you'll be happy to know that for most purposes, you can use tables as an alternative to tabbed-up text formatting. For most people, tables are much easier to use and more intuitive to work with than are tabs. So, if you want to use the "real thing," see Chapter 10 to explore how to create and format tables in your documents.

You can use back tabs yourself, although why on earth you would want to escapes us. To insert a back tab, press Shift+Tab. If you want to type some text, such as *aaa,* on top of some other text, such as *bbb,* type **aaa**, press Shift+Tab to back up, and then type **bbb**. Looks just peachy, doesn't it?

We brought up the subject only to warn you in case you press Shift+Tab by mistake. If you see text stomping on other text, a back-tab secret code may be lurking in your document. See Chapter 17 to find out how to find and exterminate it.

Single Space, Double Space, Any Space

Double-spaced documents used to be the standard in the Typewriter Era, back when monospaced fonts made single-spaced text hard to read. But in this digital age filled with proportional fonts, most documents you create will be perfectly readable as single-spaced. However, in case you need to change the spacing between lines, WordPerfect can accommodate you:

1. **Move your cursor to the point at which you want the line spacing to change.**

   To change it for the entire document, move to the beginning of the docu-ment by pressing Ctrl+Home. To change the line spacing for a paragraph or two (for a long quotation, for example), select the text that you want to change.

2. **Choose Format⇨Line⇨Spacing.**

   WordPerfect displays the Line Spacing dialog box. See Figure 7-7.

Figure 7-7:
Double-spacing your document to make it look longer.

3. **Enter a number in the Spacing box.**

   Enter 2 to get double-spaced text, for example. You can enter fractions or decimals. To add just a little space between the lines, you can enter

1.1 or 1.2. Click the little arrows at the right end of the Spacing box to increase or decrease the number in the box a tad.

4. **Click OK or press Enter to dismiss the dialog box.**

WordPerfect does your bidding and adds the vertical space that you requested between each line of text.

Don't try to create a double-spaced paragraph by pressing Enter to add blank lines between your normal paragraph lines. You'll end up getting crazy formatting for your paragraphs when you try to edit them later.

Changing the Spacing between Paragraphs

You can tell WordPerfect to leave extra space between the paragraphs in your document and not add any between the lines of the paragraph. This capability results in text that looks sort of like this book does — an effect that we prefer over first-line indenting.

This procedure involves paragraph formatting and the use of the Paragraph Format dialog box, which we show you earlier in this chapter (refer to Figure 7-6). Follow these steps:

1. **Move your cursor to the beginning of the document by pressing Ctrl+Home.**

Assuming that you want to use this kind of thing for the entire document, that is.

2. **Choose Format⇨Paragraph⇨Format.**

WordPerfect displays the Paragraph Format dialog box (refer to Figure 7-6).

3. **In the Number of Lines box, enter the number of lines that you want between paragraphs.**

Entering 1 means that you want no extra space. We recommend entering 1.5, which adds a blank half-line between each paragraph — enough to separate the paragraphs visually. (Don't we sound like we know what we're talking about?)

4. **Click OK or press Enter to leave the dialog box.**

Beyond the List Horizon

People tend to think in lists — to-do lists, grocery lists, America's Most Wanted lists, seven steps to successful tango dancing, David Letterman's Top Ten lists, The Part of Tens in *For Dummies* books, and so on. It comes as no surprise then that creating lists is one of the most commonly performed tasks you can perform with a word processor.

Adding bullets to existing paragraphs

A *bulleted list* is used to set apart a bunch of related lines or paragraphs in your document. To add a bullet to an existing paragraph, follow these steps:

1. **Position your cursor anywhere in the paragraph to which you'd like to add a bullet.**

   Because a bullet applies to the entire paragraph, you can position at the start of the paragraph, the middle, or the end.

2. **Click the Bullets button on the toolbar.**

   A bullet is added to the start of the paragraph and then text is indented to the first tab stop. For more on tab stops, see the "Pulling Out the (Tab) Stops and Other Tab Tricks" section earlier in the chapter.

If you'd like to add bullets to several paragraphs, select the paragraphs with your mouse and click the Bullets button on the toolbar. A bullet is added to each paragraph.

Creating a new bulleted list

If you would like to create a list from scratch, follow these steps:

1. **Move your cursor to the start of an empty line to which you want to add a bullet.**

2. **Click the Bullets button on the toolbar.**

3. **Type the text for the bulleted item and press Enter.**

   When you press the Enter key, WordPerfect moves the cursor to the next line and assumes that you want this line to have a bullet, too.

4. **If you need to add a new bulleted item, type the text here. Repeat as necessary for each item in your list.**

5. **When you're finished with the last item in your list, press Enter again to create a new, blank bulleted line.**

6. **Click the Bullets button on the toolbar to turn off Bullet formatting.**

   You can also press Backspace on a new line to turn off bullets.

Using an arrow, a block, or a smiley for a bullet

If variety is the spice of life, sooner or later you're going to get bored with the same small black dots that you use for bullets. It's a good thing, then, that WordPerfect has a vending machine's supply of bullets that you can use for almost every conceivable need.

To use a different type of symbol for the bullet:

1. **Position your cursor on a new line or in a paragraph whose bullet you want to change.**

   If you position the cursor in a paragraph that already has a bullet, Word-Perfect will just swap out the old bullet and replace it with the new one you select.

2. **Click the down arrow next to the Bullets button on the toolbar.**

   A menu of bullet types appears. Your options include small dots, large dots, diamonds, blocks, triangles, and check boxes.

3. **Click the bullet type that you'd like to use.**

   Or, if none of these standard types of bullets suit your fancy, click the More button to display the Bullets and Numbering dialog box (see Figure 7-8). You can choose from an even greater number of bullets here or click the More Bullets button for an even greater selection. Ignore the other settings in this dialog box for now. If you're industrious, you can click the Create button in the Bullets and Numbering dialog box to create your own bullet.

4. **Click OK when you're finished.**

   WordPerfect updates the document.

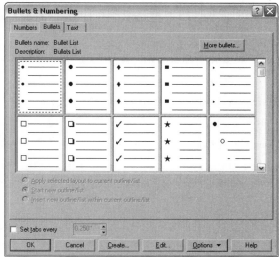

Figure 7-8:
Create
bulleted
lists faster
than a
speeding
bullet.

Creating multiple levels of bullets

You can create multiple levels of bulleted lists — something like a list within a list. To *demote* a list item (or move a list item to the next tab stop to the right):

1. **Position the cursor on the bulleted item that you want to demote.**

2. **Click the Demote button on the property bar.**

   The bulleted item will move to the right one tab stop.

If you create multiple levels of bulleted lists, we recommend using a different bullet type for each level. Different bullets make for easier reading and are quicker for the human eye.

Alternatively, if you have multiple levels of lists and would like to promote a list item (or move its indention one tab stop leftward), do the following:

1. **Position the cursor on the bulleted item that you want to promote.**

2. **Click the Promote button on the property bar.**

   The bulleted item will move to the left one tab stop.

Numbering an existing set of paragraphs

You can have WordPerfect automatically number a list. If you have a group of paragraphs that you'd like to transform into a numbered list, follow these instructions:

1. **Select the paragraphs that you'd like to number.**

   If you need a primer on text selection, go to Chapter 2.

2. **Click the Numbering button on the toolbar.**

   Numbers are added to the start of each paragraph, and text is indented to the first tab stop. (For more on tab stops, see the "Pulling Out the (Tab) Stops and Other Tab Tricks" section earlier in the chapter.)

Creating a new numbered list

To create a new numbered list from scratch, follow these steps:

1. **Move your cursor to the start of an empty line that you'd like to have numbered.**

2. **Click the Numbering button on the toolbar.**

3. **Type the text for the paragraph and press Enter.**

   WordPerfect moves the cursor to the next line and increments the number in your list by one.

4. **When you're finished with the last item in your list, press Enter again to create a new, blank numbered line.**

5. **Click the Numbering button on the toolbar to turn off Numbering formatting.**

Chapter 8

Perfect Pages and Dashing Documents

. . . .

In This Chapter

▶ Sizing up the page

▶ Tweaking margins

▶ Beginning pages where you want

▶ Making sure text stays together

▶ Centering a page from top to bottom

▶ Viewing your document in multiple ways

▶ Putting numbers on your page

▶ Adding headers, footers, and watermarks

▶ Force fitting your document into a page length

. . . .

Chapter 6 explores formatting of characters, the plankton in the vast sea of documents. Chapter 7 talks about formatting in the salt-water schools of margins, indents, and tabs. In this chapter, you discover how to format the Great Tuna, the document as a whole. You'll cast your nets sizing, centering, and numbering the page and then look at adding things such as headers and footers.

Any tuna will tell you that a key to creating great-looking documents comes from knowing how to format at the page and document levels. So read on, or you'll have a whale of a time the next time you need to format a document.

Setting the Page Size

WordPerfect can be a busybody. It wants to know the type of paper you want to print on (letterhead? envelopes? labels?) and the paper's size. Unless you tell it something different, WordPerfect assumes that you're going to use the usual letter-size paper that you stick in the printer in the usual way. If you plan to print on the paper sideways (known as *landscape orientation*), however, or if you plan to use legal-size paper, envelopes, or paper with letterhead across the top or down the sides, you'd better tell WordPerfect about it; otherwise, you may run into trouble with your margins.

To tell WordPerfect about the size of the paper on which you plan to print your document, open your document and follow these steps:

1. **Move your cursor to the beginning of the document by pressing Ctrl+Home.**

   Because paper size is something that usually applies to the entire document, set the cursor at the beginning.

2. **Choose Format⇨Page⇨Page Setup.**

   WordPerfect displays the Page Setup dialog box, as shown in Figure 8-1. The Page Setup tab displays paper sizes WordPerfect thinks you might be interested in. If the Page Setup tab is not selected, click it.

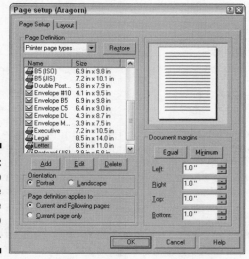

Figure 8-1:
Setting up
your page
in the Page
Setup
dialog box.

The Page Definition area contains a combo box (that displays by default the Printer page types) along with a list of page definitions. The Letter page definition is probably highlighted in the list, but the items in the list you see depend on the type of printer you use (different printers accept different paper sizes) and the item you selected in the combo box. Our list includes the following:

- A4 (European paper, a tad bigger than American letter size)

- Envelope #10 (a regular business envelope)

- Envelope DL (yet another envelope size)

- Legal (legal-size paper, which is longer than letter size)

- Letter (our favorite)

3. **To use a different paper size, click the page definition that you want to use.**

    The page size that appears highlighted in the Page Definition list is the one that you're currently using for this document.

4. **Click OK.**

Use landscape printing for documents that are too wide to fit on the paper the regular way, especially for tables that have many columns. Also, people occasionally "ooh" and "ahh" when they see a document printed sideways on the page. We have no idea why that happens, but the ooh-and-ahh effect is another good reason to use it.

Adjusting the Top and Bottom Margins

After WordPerfect knows the size of your paper, it has opinions about your margins. Unless you tell it otherwise, WordPerfect assumes that you want 1-inch margins all the way around the page, measuring from the edge of the paper. We generally find this measurement to be a little too airy and spacious for our tastes, so we usually reduce the margins — unless we're getting paid to write by the page, of course.

To change the left or right margin, refer to Chapter 7, which explains how to use the ruler, guidelines, and the Page Setup dialog box for this task.

To change the top or bottom margin, open your document and follow these steps:

1. **Make sure you're in Page view by choosing View⇨Page (or pressing Alt+F5).**

    Page view shows you the top and bottom margin guidelines and allows you to see these margin changes right on your screen.

2. **Move your cursor to the page at which you want the new margins to take effect.**

    To change the top or bottom margin for the entire document, move to the first page by pressing Ctrl+Home. To change the margin beginning at another page, position your cursor somewhere on that page.

3. **Click the top or bottom margin guideline on your page and drag it to a new position.**

As you drag the guideline, a pop-up window appears to tell you the current measurement of the margin (in inches by default).

4. **When you have the margin at the desired place, release your mouse.**

Alternatively, if you have shaky hands and don't like to adjust the margin with your mouse, use a dialog box approach. To do so, open the document and follow these steps:

1. **Position the cursor on the page where you'd like to begin the margin change.**

2. **Choose Format⇨Margins or press Ctrl+F8 to display the Page Setup dialog box.**

   If you get the urge, you even can display the dialog box by double-clicking the part of the ruler that shows the margins. If the Page Setup tab isn't selected, click it (refer to Figure 8-1).

3. **Fill in the measurements for the top and bottom margins.**

   The little page diagram changes to show you how the page will look, more or less.

4. **Click OK.**

   In Page view, you'll see the changed margins immediately. If you're using Draft view (described later in this chapter in the section "Looking at Different Views of Your Document"), the only difference in the look of the page is that the page breaks move.

Starting a New Page

When you're typing text, WordPerfect's job is to keep track of how much text will go on a page. When you get to the bottom of a page, WordPerfect puts a couple more quarters into the coin slot for you and dishes out a brand new page for you to continue your work.

WordPerfect keeps track of where on the page each line appears as you're typing your text. You can always see your position on the page by looking at the application bar, which appears on the bottom right of the WordPerfect window and displays your current page, line position, and column position.

But what if you don't want to fill a page before starting the next one? You can insert a secret code that tells WordPerfect to skip to the top of the next page, regardless of whether this one is full. This feature is called a *page break*. The page break that WordPerfect sticks in when a page is full is called a *soft page break*. A break you add yourself is called a *hard page break*. (See Chapter 17 to find out about the difference between hard and soft codes.)

To insert a hard page break, just press Ctrl+Enter. Poof! Your cursor dashes down to the top of a new page. If you were in the middle of the line, the part of the line after your cursor moves down to the new page with you.

To get rid of a hard page break, move your cursor to the very beginning of the page *after* the page break and press the Backspace key. This step backs you up, and with luck, it deletes the page break in the process. Alternatively, you can move your cursor behind the last character *before* the page break and press the Delete key — same idea. If this step doesn't work, see Chapter 17 to find out the secret code that WordPerfect uses for the page break and delete the crazy thing.

You may be tempted to begin a new page by pressing Enter over and over until your page is full of carriage returns and you arrive at the top of the next page. It may seem logical and easy to break a page this way, but don't. Trust us. Here's why: If you edit the earlier part of your document so that it gets just a teeny bit shorter, everything shifts up a tad. Now you have too few returns to fill the page, and the text begins at the bottom of the preceding page rather than on a new page — not the effect that you want. Take our advice: Insert a hard page break instead. It's so much less work!

Keeping Text Together

You have complete control over where hard page breaks occur because you put them in yourself. But WordPerfect sticks in soft page breaks whenever it decides that no more lines can fit on a page. Sometimes, it chooses singularly bad spots to begin a new page. A technical term was created for lousy positioning of page breaks: *bad breaks*. (We always thought it was a skiing term.)

Avoiding broken homes (widows and orphans)

Your document looks lousy when a paragraph begins on the last line of a page so that only one line of the paragraph appears before the page break. This traditional typesetting no-no is called an *orphan*. A *widow* occurs when the last line of a paragraph appears at the top of a page all by itself.

Luckily, you don't have to know about this stuff or even think about it because WordPerfect does your worrying for you. Follow these steps to avoid the dreaded social disease of bad breaks:

1. **Move your cursor to the beginning of the document by pressing Ctrl+Home.**

The following command and the resulting secret code apply to the entire document.

2. Choose Format⇨Keep Text Together.

WordPerfect displays the Keep Text Together dialog box, as shown in Figure 8-2. The dialog box contains three settings that have to do with positioning page breaks, and we discuss all three in this chapter. Our immediate concerns, however, are those widows and orphans.

Figure 8-2:
Widows and orphans, unite with Keep Text Together.

3. Click the box called Prevent the First and Last Lines of Paragraphs from Being Separated across Pages.

4. Click OK or press Enter to leave the dialog box.

Now WordPerfect avoids leaving widows and orphans on pages. Instead, it moves page breaks up or down a line as necessary. The pages won't be completely full, but that's the price you pay for family cohesion.

Keeping your text together

Your document may contain information that should not be split over a page break. A columnar table looks crummy if it's split up, for example, unless it's longer than one page. You can select part of your document and tell Word-Perfect, "Let no page break enter here!" Follow these steps:

1. Select the text that you want to keep together.

Refer to Chapter 4 to find out how to select text, if you don't already know. For tables, be sure to include any headings or titles.

2. Choose Format⇨Keep Text Together.

WordPerfect displays the Keep Text Together dialog box (refer to Figure 8-2).

3. Click to add a check in the Keep Selected Text Together on Same Page box.

4. Click OK or press Enter.

Block Protect sounds like the maneuver that a 2-year-old uses when another kid comes to visit, but WordPerfect isn't talking about that kind of block. In earlier versions of WordPerfect, selecting text was always called "marking blocks," and doing anything with a bunch of text was called a "block operation." Although WordPerfect has adopted Windows-speak, which requires that you refer to a bunch of text as a "selection," references to blocks still exist.

Keeping your head together

Leaving a heading stranded all alone at the bottom of the page while the text that follows the heading begins on the following page is considered tacky and gauche.

Unlike the method for preventing widows and orphans, which requires you to issue one command at the beginning of your document, the method for keeping your heads together with your content requires you to issue a separate command for *each* heading.

If you're working on a long document, the prospect of manually entering this command for every possible heading may not seem very attractive. One alternative to this time-consuming problem is to use styles to format your headings; jump to Chapter 9 if this subject interests you.

To prevent WordPerfect from separating a heading from its body, open the document in question and follow these steps:

1. **Move your cursor to the beginning of the line that contains the heading.**

2. **Choose Format⇨Keep Text Together.**

   WordPerfect displays the Keep Text Together dialog box (refer to Figure 8-2 again). Look at the Conditional End of Page section of the dialog box.

3. **Click the box called Number of Lines to Keep Together, so that it contains a check mark.**

4. **Type a number in the text box.**

   To keep the heading line and the first two lines of the text that follow it together, enter 3. If you use a blank line to separate the heading from the text, you may want to enter 4.

5. **Click OK or press Enter to leave the dialog box.**

Now if the heading and the first few lines that follow can't fit at the bottom of the page, WordPerfect moves the whole kit and caboodle to the top of the next page.

Don't use too many Block Protect and Conditional End of Page settings in your document, or WordPerfect will have a heck of a time finding anywhere to put page breaks. The best solution is to avoid using lots of headings with large fonts. Instead, if you have a long document with many headings, decrease the font size of the headings to eliminate many of the conditions that cause widows and orphans.

Centering a Page, Top to Bottom

When you create a title page for a document, it's nice if the titles appear in the middle of the page, both up and down and left to right. Chapter 7 talks about how to center text between the left and right margins (oh, all right — move to the beginning of the line and press Shift+F7). The following steps show you how to center the titles top to bottom. Of course, you can press Enter a bunch of times above the titles, but this is a baaaad idea. Let WordPerfect put your titles in exactly the right place by following these steps in an open document:

1. **Move your cursor to the top of the page that contains the text to be centered top to bottom.**

   In most cases, this page is the first page of your document.

2. **Choose Format⇨Page⇨Center.**

   WordPerfect displays the Center Page(s) dialog box, as shown in Figure 8-3.

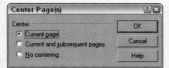

3. **To center this page, choose Current Page.**

4. **Click OK or press Enter.**

   WordPerfect moves the text on the page up or down as necessary.

To revoke centering on a page, move your cursor to the top of the page, choose Format⇨Page⇨Center to display the Center Page(s) dialog box, and choose No Centering.

You may have centered all your pages without knowing it. Suppose that you're working on page 12 of an existing document, and you decide that this would be a good place to start a new page. Press Ctrl+Enter, and suddenly, to your chagrin, you notice that all this white space appears at the top and bottom of *page 12*. What's going on here? Somewhere in your document you probably have a Center Page(s) code that is secretly telling WordPerfect to perform this dastardly deed. All your pages so far have been centered top to bottom, but because they're full of text, you didn't notice. Now that page 12 has only a little text on it, you do notice. Check out Chapter 17 to find out how to hunt down and eliminate the little varmint (er, we mean reveal code).

Looking at Different Views of Your Document

WordPerfect can show your document from several angles, depending on how closely you want the view to resemble the printed page. This list shows the different views that you can choose:

- ✔ **Page view:** WordPerfect shows how your page will look when you print it. You see the full page, including all margins, headers, and footers. This is the default viewing option. For details, see Chapter 18.

- ✔ **Draft view:** The focus with this view is on the text. Page breaks appear as horizontal lines across your document, and you can't see top or bottom margins, extra space on a partially full page, headers, footers, or page numbers.

- ✔ **Two Pages view:** You can see two pages side by side, which can be helpful when you're checking out a document's formatting. However, unless you have Superman-like vision or a life-size monitor, the teeny-weensy text will be illegible.

Table 8-1 summarizes when to use each of these views. To switch between them, choose View from the menu bar and then choose Draft, Page, or Two Page.

Table 8-1	Recommended Uses for Document Views
View	*When to Use It*
Page view	Best all-around, general-purpose view. When you want to see both page formatting and text as you write.
Draft view	When your focus is completely on the text, and you don't want to be distracted with the document's formatting.
Two Page view	When you want a bird's-eye view of your document layout.

A quick way to jump to Page view is to swat Alt+F5. A fast way to switch to Draft view is to press Ctrl+F5. There's no keyboard shortcut to Two Page view, but that's okay because you probably won't use it that much anyway.

Numbering Pages

Few things are more annoying than a sheaf of unnumbered pages that are out of order. Don't look like a schnook; number your pages.

For some strange reason — probably some quirk of software history — WordPerfect has not one but two ways to number pages:

✔ Choose Format➪Page➪Numbering to tell WordPerfect to begin numbering the pages. You can tell WordPerfect where the numbers should appear and also enter other text (such as today's date or the document title) to include with the page number.

✔ Choose Insert➪Header/Footer to define a header or footer, and include page numbers in the header or footer.

There's little difference between these two approaches. These steps show how to use the first method to number your pages:

1. **Move your cursor to the top of the page on which you want page numbers to begin.**

   If your classy-looking document has a cover page, for example, you can begin numbering on the next page.

2. **Choose Format➪Page➪Numbering.**

   WordPerfect displays the Select Page Numbering Format dialog box, as shown in Figure 8-4.

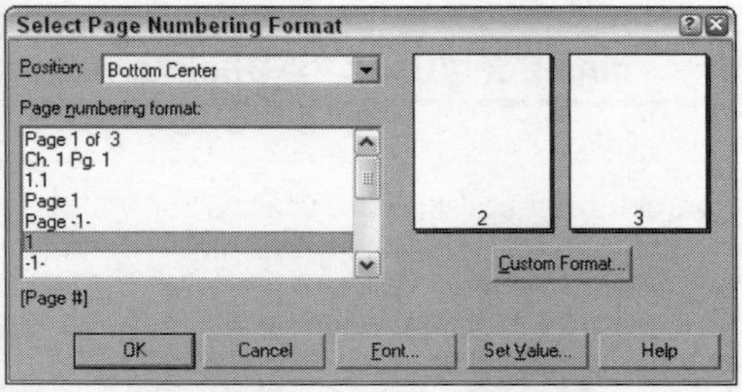

Figure 8-4:
Tired of boring page numbering? Here's your chance to spice things up.

Select Page Numbering Format	
Position: Bottom Center	
Page numbering format:	
Page 1 of 3	
Ch. 1 Pg. 1	
1.1	
Page 1	2
Page -1-	3
1	
-1-	
	Custom Format...
[Page #]	
OK Cancel Font... Set Value... Help	

3. **Tell WordPerfect where to print the page numbers.**

   Click the Position box to see a drop-down list of 11 choices for placing the number (No Page Numbering, Top Left, Top Center, Top Right, Top Outside Alternating, Top Inside Alternating, Bottom Left, Bottom Center, Bottom Right, Bottom Outside Alternating, Bottom Inside Alternating). Select the option of your choice.

   Outside Alternating is just right for documents printed on both sides of the paper (this book, for example) because the page numbers appear on the outside edge of each page. In other words, the page numbers appear on the right side of odd-numbered pages and on the left side of even-numbered pages. Inside Alternating indicates that the page numbers appear on the left side of odd-numbered pages and on the right side of even-numbered pages.

   Fortunately, you don't have to remember which numbering format is which. After you select a format, just check out the example of the page numbering format on the right side of the dialog box.

4. **In the Page Numbering Format box, choose what text you want to appear beside your page number.**

   The simplest choice is 1, for plain, unadorned page numbers. But we think that looks a little naked on reports (as opposed to books, where people kind of expect it). If you click the Page -1- format, that's exactly what your page numbers will look like.

5. **Choose the font for your page numbers.**

   If you want the page number to appear in a different font than the rest of the document, click the Font button and choose the font and font size in the Font dialog box (we describe this dialog box in Chapter 7). Then click OK to return to the Select Page Numbering Format dialog box.

6. **Click OK to bug out of this dialog box.**

Now WordPerfect prints page numbers on this page and on all the following pages in the document, even pages that you add later.

For all you roman numeral fans

You don't have to use boring, pedestrian arabic numbers for your page numbers. You can use small roman numerals to number the pages in the introduction of a report, for example. To tell WordPerfect which type of numbers to use (roman or arabic), follow these steps:

1. **Move your cursor to the top of the page on which you want the numbering to begin.**

2. **Choose Format⇨Page⇨Numbering.**

3. **Scroll down through the Page Numbering Format list until you find the lowercase roman numeral *i*.**

   The settings in this list start with regular old arabic numbers, but there are zillions of choices; you decide how you want your page number to look by selecting one.

4. **If you can't find a format you like, do the following:**

   a. **Click the Custom Format button.**

      The Custom Page Numbering dialog box appears.

   b. **In the text box labeled Custom Page Numbering Format, enter text until the sample looks the way you want your page numbers to look.**

      When you get to the place in your page number text where you'd like the page number to appear, select the number you're interested in from the five lists above the box where you're typing, and click Insert in Format. For example, you might type **Goofy Report, Page**, select *I,II,III* from the Page list, click the Insert in Format button, and then type **Preliminary**. Your page numbers would read *Goofy Report, Page I Preliminary*.

   c. **Click OK when you're finished with the Custom Page Numbering dialog box.**

5. **Click OK to leave the Select Page Numbering Format dialog box and save your selection.**

You even can switch page number styles partway through the document: Just move your cursor to the top of the page on which you want the style to change and then follow the preceding set of steps.

Starting over again at 1

If you want to change your page numbering partway through a document, you can. If your report titled "Ten Thousand Uses for Chocolate" begins with an Introduction, for example, you can restart the page numbering at 1 on the first page that follows the introduction. Follow these steps:

1. **Move your cursor to the top of the page on which you want to restart page numbering at 1.**

2. **Choose Format➪Page➪Numbering.**

   WordPerfect displays our friend the Select Page Numbering Format dialog box.

3. **Click the Set Value button.**

   The Values dialog box appears with the Page tab selected.

4. **In the Set Page Number box, type the number you want this page to be.**

   In this case, you want this to be page 1, no matter how many pages of Introduction you write.

5. **If the Make Sure That Always Keep Number the Same option is not selected, click it.**

   This option ensures that the page that the cursor was on when you changed this setting will always be numbered 1.

   The Let Number Change as Pages Are Added or Deleted option does just that. If you add a page to the Introduction, the page that you originally insisted should have the number 1 now has the number 2. This option is useful if you are inserting unnumbered pages into a document from another source (graphs or figures, for example).

6. **Click OK to leave the Values dialog box.**

Adding Heads and Feets

Now that we've gone through all the gory details of page numbering, we admit that we usually don't use the Select Page Numbering Format dialog box to number our pages. We usually have lots of other things that we want to include at the top or bottom of each page, such as the title of the document, today's date, and notes that say *Draft* or *Confidential!* or *This Document Will Self-Destruct In Five Seconds!*

Two neat things about headers and footers are that they can contain almost anything — one line of text or even a picture — and they're shown on each page of your document. Also, your document can contain two different headers (Header A and Header B) and two different footers (Footer A and Footer B, believe it or not), so you can print different headers and footers on the facing pages of documents that are printed on both sides of the page.

Making a header or footer

These steps show how to make a header or footer:

1. **Choose View⇨Page or press Alt+F5 to switch to Page view so that you can see the headers and footers that you create.**

   Headers and footers are invisible in Draft view. You're probably already in Page view, but we want to make sure.

2. Move to the beginning of your document by pressing Ctrl+Home.

If you want headers and footers to begin partway through your document, move to the top of the first page on which you want the header or footer to appear.

3. Choose Insert➪Header/Footer.

The Headers/Footers dialog box appears, as shown in Figure 8-5.

Figure 8-5:
If your mission is to define headers and footers, start here.

4. Choose the header or footer that you want to create.

If you plan to use one header or footer for the entire document, we recommend sticking with Header A or Footer A to avoid confusion. Or, if you plan to use two headers or two footers (to number facing pages, for example), choose Header A and Footer A or Header B and Footer B.

You can have several Header As, Header Bs, Footer As, or Footer Bs in your document. If you think that this arrangement would be confusing, you're right; don't use it.

5. Click Create.

This step tells WordPerfect to create a header or footer for your document. WordPerfect adds a blank line at the top (for headers) or bottom (for footers) of the page; you can begin typing your header or footer in this line.

Headers and footers get their own guidelines. You can drag all margins but the top margin of a header (you have to change the page's top margin) or the bottom margin of a footer (you have to change the page's bottom margin).

If you use multiple headers or footers, make sure you define one header or footer for odd pages and the other for even, as we explain later in this chapter. If not, you could have headers or footers printing on top of each other, a confusing situation.

Typing the text in a header or footer

Now your job is to type the text that you want to appear in this header or footer. The new line that WordPerfect adds to your document (see Step 5 in the preceding section) is no ordinary new line — this line is in a special zone that will contain the text for your header or footer. You can't use the cursor-control keys to move between the header or footer zone and the rest of the document. You can use the mouse to click where you want to edit; this action enables you to switch between editing the regular document and your header or footer.

While you're editing a header or footer, WordPerfect really would prefer that you stay focused on what you're doing. So, some of the buttons on the toolbar and some menu commands get fuzzy and unusable when you're editing a header or footer. For instance, you can't use the New, Open, Save, and Print buttons on the toolbar or their equivalent menu commands while you're editing a header or footer. C'est la vie.

To enter the text in your header or footer, follow these steps:

1. **Move your cursor to the header or footer zone, if it's not already there.**

   You can tell when you're editing a header or footer because the property bar acquires the header/footer buttons on its right side, as shown in Figure 8-6. You can tell also by looking at the window's title bar, which displays not only the name of the document that you're editing but also the name of the header or footer that you're working on, such as zukesoup. wpd - (Header A).

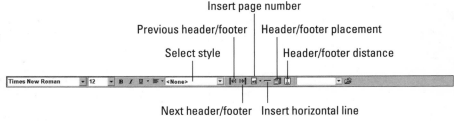

Figure 8-6:
The property bar for headers and footers.

2. **Type the text.**

   You can control the font, font size, and text style in the usual ways (refer to Chapter 6). Fonts for headers and footers should generally be smaller (such as 8 point) than the normal document text.

3. **To include the current page number in the header or footer, move your cursor to the place where you want the page number to appear.**

4. **Click the Page Numbering button on the property bar.**

   This button has a little *#1* on it. When you click the button, a little menu appears.

5. **Choose Page Number.**

6. **Click the Close button (the rightmost button) on the property bar to get back to the real world.**

When you type the text of your document, you don't have to leave room for the headers or footers. WordPerfect sticks them in at the top and bottom margins of the page and shoves the other text out of the way.

If you want to print the current date in the header or footer, press Ctrl+Shift+D. If you want your header or footer to contain lines, boxes, or even pictures, see Chapter 14.

You can format the text in your headers and footers by using the same commands that you can use for text in the rest of your document. Commands that you can't use appear dimmed in the WordPerfect menus.

If you can't see your headers or footers, you're probably using Draft view. Choose View⇨Page (or press Alt+F5) to switch to Page view.

Controlling where headers and footers print

After you create a header or footer and type its text, you can tell WordPerfect which pages to print it on. Click the Header/Footer placement button on the property bar (labeled in Figure 8-6).

You need to be typing in the header or footer to see that button on the property bar. See the preceding section, "Typing the text in a header or footer," for hints on how to display the header/footer property bar.

WordPerfect displays the Placement dialog box for whichever header or footer you're looking at, as shown in Figure 8-7. Choose Odd Pages, Even Pages, or Every Page, and then click OK.

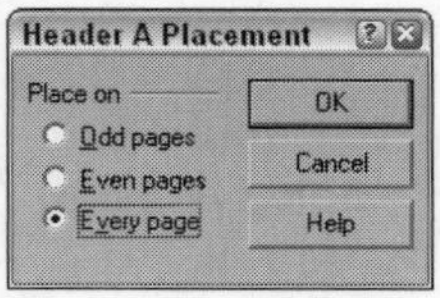

Figure 8-7:
Choose
where to
place the
header.

Header A Placement	
Place on	OK
○ Odd pages	
○ Even pages	Cancel
⦿ Every page	Help

Don't print it here!

You can tell WordPerfect not to print the header or footer that you just went to so much trouble to create. Why would you want to? We can think of these two good reasons:

> ✔ You don't want the header to print on the first page of your document. When you write a letter, for example, you may want all the pages except the first one to have a header that says *Authored by Thurston Howell III, Sept. 8, 2004, Page 2* (with the correct page number, naturally). Therefore, you want to suppress the header or footer for one page.

> ✔ Your document may have two or more sections, and you may want to use a header or footer for only the first section. You can discontinue the header or footer for the rest of the pages in the document.

To suppress a header or footer for one page, follow these steps:

1. **Move your cursor to the page on which you don't want to print the header or footer.**

   Make sure that your cursor is not in the header/footer area.

2. **Choose Format⇨Page⇨Suppress.**

   WordPerfect displays the Suppress dialog box, as shown in Figure 8-8.

3. **Choose the header or footer that you *don't* want to print.**

   If you don't want any headers, footers, or watermarks, click to put a check mark in the All check box.

4. **Click OK.**

   The headers or footers disappear from the page, only to reappear on the next page.

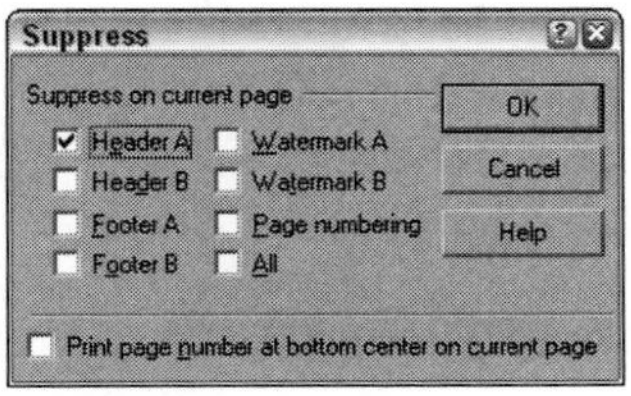

Figure 8-8:
Don't suppress your page formatting needs. Use the Suppress dialog box.

Discontinuing headers and footers

When you want a header or a footer to stop appearing after a certain page, you *discontinue* that header or footer. Follow these steps:

1. **Move to the first page on which you don't want the header or footer to print.**

2. **Choose Insert⇨Header/Footer.**

3. **Choose the header or footer that you want to discontinue.**

   If you want to discontinue all the headers and footers, you have to repeat these steps for each one. (Sigh.)

4. **Click the Discontinue button.**

   The dialog box disappears in a puff of bytes, and so does your header or footer from this page and all subsequent pages in the document.

Getting rid of a header or footer

If you change your mind about a header or footer, and you want to get rid of it for good throughout your document, you can delete it. However, no menu, toolbar button, or mouse click action does this task for you. Instead, you have to do it the techno-geeky way — by working with WordPerfect's secret formatting codes known as reveal codes. See Chapter 17 for the details.

Splish, Splash . . . Adding a Watermark to Your Document

A watermark sounds like something you get on your document when you drop it in a mud puddle or bump into someone at the water cooler. But a *watermark* is actually a lightly shaded image or text appearing in the background on your page. A watermark can be useful for a variety of purposes:

✔ Using *Draft* as a text watermark helps ensure that no one mistakes a preliminary document for a final one.

✔ Using *Confidential* reinforces that special care should be taken when handling or disposing of the document.

✔ A watermarked logo of your company can be a subtle and impressive addition to a proposal.

✔ If you're daring, adding something like *Charles needs a raise!* as a water-mark on your weekly memo to your boss can be a subliminal way to ask for a salary increase.

Adding and editing a watermark

To add a watermark to your document, follow these steps:

1. **Position the cursor on the page on which you'd like the watermark to start.**

   If you want a watermark to appear on each page, make sure your cursor is on page 1.

2. **Choose Insert➪Watermark.**

   The Watermark dialog box appears, as shown in Figure 8-9.

Figure 8-9:
Defining a
background
watermark.

3. **Click the Create button.**

   A new blank document window appears. This is isn't a normal docu-ment; it's the watermark editing window. Notice that the end of the docu-ment name on the WordPerfect title bar says (Watermark A).

4. **Add the text or graphic that you'd like to use as a watermark.**

   Everything you add to this document window will appear behind your normal document text. Therefore, we recommend that you add a single graphic or a large text message (such as *Draft* or *Confidential*), so that the watermark doesn't distract the reader from the document itself.

   Note that the property bar has special properties for watermarks, as shown in Figure 8-10. (See "Tweaking your watermark settings" in the next section for more on these property bar buttons.)

5. **Click the Close button on the property bar.**

   WordPerfect returns you to the normal view of the document. If you're in Page view, the watermark is displayed as the background of your page.

Figure 8-10:
The
property bar
for editing
watermarks.

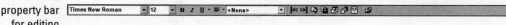

If you'd like to edit the watermark you've just created, choose Insert⇨ Watermark, make sure Watermark A is selected, and click Edit. WordPerfect will take you back to the watermark editing window.

Tweaking your watermark settings

When you're in the watermark editing document window, you can use several buttons on the toolbar:

- The Watermark Previous button is used only if you've defined two watermarks. It takes you to Watermark A if you're in Watermark B.

- The Watermark Next button is also used only if you've defined two watermarks. When clicked, it takes you to Watermark B if you're in Watermark A.

- The Clipart button displays the Scrapbook dialog box to add clipart to your watermark. See Chapter 11 for more on working with clipart.

- The Image button displays the Insert File dialog box, which allows you to select a graphic for use in your watermark. See Chapter 11 for more on working with images.

- The Insert File button displays a dialog box that allows you to select an existing document to be used as a watermark.

- The Watermark Placement button enables you to specify whether you want the watermark to go on even pages, odd pages, or all pages.

- The Watermark Shading button allows you to control how dark or light the watermark shows through on your document. In most cases, the lighter, the better.

When you're finished making adjustments, click the Close button on the property bar to return to your document.

Restricting or removing your watermark

You don't have to use a watermark on every page. In addition to the Watermark Placement button, which enables you to place the watermark on even pages, odd pages, or all pages, you can further restrict the usage of a watermark. You can also get rid of it altogether. Consider the following:

- ✔ **Discontinue your watermark:** You can stop a watermark from appearing after a certain point in your document. To do so, choose Insert➪ Watermark to display the Watermark dialog box. Select the watermark you want to discontinue (usually Watermark A if you only have one watermark defined), and click Discontinue.

- ✔ **Suppress a watermark for a specific page:** If you'd like to avoid placing a watermark on a specific page in your document, choose Format➪Page➪ Suppress. Check the Watermark A or Watermark B check box (or both) and click OK.

- ✔ **Delete a watermark:** Perhaps you're having second thoughts on adding that *Charles needs a raise!* watermark to your memo and would like to delete it. If so, position your cursor at the top of the first page in which the watermark appears. (Press Ctrl+Home if you defined the watermark on the first page.) Then, choose Insert➪Watermark. In the dialog box, select the appropriate watermark (usually A) and click Discontinue.

The Big Squeeze: Using Make It Fit to Tweak Your Document's Length

In the introduction of Chapter 7, we hit on a practical and pragmatic truth concerning document creation — sometimes the page length of a document is as important as the document's content. If you have a 12-page term paper requirement, you'd better have a dozen pages to turn in, even if WordPerfect is telling you that you have only nine pages so far. Or, if you have only a single page for telling your boss why you need that raise after all, you better figure out a way to cram 101 reasons into that 8½ x 11-inch sheet of paper.

If you read Chapters 6, 7, and 8, you discovered that font size, margins, and line spacing all have an effect on the length of your document. However, suppose you've tried your best but can get only 11 of those 12 pages for your term paper. Or, perhaps you have one minute to stuff a three-page treatise on salary increases into a single-page memo for your boss to take to a budget planning meeting. For these occasions, you don't need a hammer to pound your document into submission — you need a sledge hammer!

WordPerfect gives you a sledge hammer to squeeze or expand your document into the exact page length you need. To do so:

1. **Choose Format⇨Make It Fit.**

   The Make It Fit dialog box is displayed, as shown in Figure 8-11.

Figure 8-11:
Word-
Perfect's
Machiavelli-
an feature,
Make It
Fit, makes
the end
(of the
document)
justify the
means.

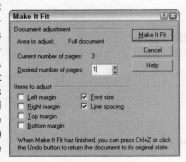

2. **In the Desired Number of Pages box, enter the number of pages your document needs to be.**

   WordPerfect isn't a miracle worker and won't do ridiculous adjustments, such as a 40-point font size, to accomplish the task. Therefore, the number of pages that you can enter must be within 50 percent of the current page count.

3. **Select the items that you give WordPerfect permission to adjust, including the margins, font size, and line spacing.**

4. **Click the Make It Fit button and let WordPerfect do its magic.**

If you have second thoughts, you can always undo your operation by clicking the Undo button on the toolbar.

Chapter 9

Documents with Style

● ●

● ●

*B*efore the Industrial Revolution, everything — be it a sword, house, or horse cart — was built in a custom, one-of-a-kind fashion. A craftsman, such as a blacksmith, would specialize in creating something by hand. The major strengths of this approach were quality products and attention to detail, but it was also highly inefficient in time and cost.

Over the past couple of centuries, technology and innovation gave us the "assembly line" mindset. Instead of custom building a car, for example, you define what a car is, make identical parts, and then assemble those parts in a highly structured, efficient process.

In WordPerfect, you have a similar choice when formatting your documents: custom (direct formatting) or assembly line (styles). You *custom format* your document by directly formatting each block of text as you get to it. This is the method we've been talking about in the earlier part of this book. Using *styles* allows you to format similar parts of your document in an identical manner.

We think *styles* are the most useful but least used feature of WordPerfect. In this chapter, you discover how to work with styles to format your document. We also discuss why you should use styles instead of relying solely on the direct formatting approach.

Perhaps best of all, while the assembly line method has some major drawbacks in the real world (homogenization, dehumanization, and so on), styles have no harmful side effects, other than the brief time it takes to understand how to use them and set them up in your document.

Direct Formatting: Natural but Highly Inefficient

Nearly every document you create has a built-in structure to it. For example:

- ✔ All good business letters have a date, address, salutation, body text, and signature.
- ✔ Memos have a title, headings, and body text.
- ✔ A lengthy research paper or book utilizes a title, subtitle, a heading structure, body text, headers, and footers.
- ✔ Newsletters have titles, article titles, picture captions, and more complex formatting.

One of the natural ways in which you express the structure and organizational cues to the readers of your work is to format documents consistently from beginning to end. If all top-level headings look alike, all picture captions are the same format, and so on, you keep readers, figuratively, on the same page. Other practical reasons exist for following this reasoning when formatting your document. For one thing, you may have no other choice. Perhaps your boss wants all headings in your document to be a 16-point bold Arial font and indented ¼ inch from the left margin. (Likewise, you probably want to take this as a hint that all the numbered steps and bulleted lists are consistent in appearance, as well.)

Formatting a document is a repetitive process. To get consistency, you need to format each heading in your document the same way. If you use a custom direct formatting approach, you manually format each of the headings yourself using the various font and paragraph formatting options. But the problem is that you have to first remember the various options and then apply all of them every time you encounter a new heading or add one. If there are just a couple of headings, it's not a big deal. But what if you have 20, 30, or even more? That's a lot of work you're doing over and over and over again!

Now suppose you took the time to format each of the 30 headings in your document to your boss's specifications. However, just before lunch, you find a memo on your desk stating that the new corporate standard for all headings this week is 18-point italic Tahoma font, indented ½ inch from the left margin. Using the direct approach to formatting, this news is "groan city" because you now get to spend your lunch hour reformatting your headings one at a time.

This direct approach to formatting is the way many people work in Word-Perfect. Unfortunately, as you can see, it is also highly inefficient because formatting is *always* a repetitive process.

Using Styles to Get Consistent Document Appearance

A WordPerfect *style* is a combination of various types of formatting, such as fonts and indentation — the kind of stuff that you typically do with the Format commands — that you name (such as `Heading 1`). By using specific styles, you can apply formatting with a simple click of the mouse.

For example, suppose you'd like your headings to all be 18-point italic Tahoma font and indented ½ inch from the left margin. You can define this formatting once and assign it a name (for some reason, `Heading 1` seems like a good name). Then, when you want to format a heading, you select the text and assign it the `Heading 1` style.

Notice the two advantages that styles have over the direct formatting approach:

- **Define once, apply anywhere:** Regardless of the number of headings you have in your document, you define the formatting for that type of heading only once. Each heading gets the formatting properties the instant you assign a style to it.

- **Update styles automatically:** You'll never lose your lunch hour again when you need to change formatting for a particular style. If you change the formatting defined for a style, those changes ripple throughout your document, changing appearances wherever you applied that style.

Direct versus style: Who wins?

When you format text using styles, a bit of a conflict occurs in places where you formatted the text directly using the Format command or the function keys. WordPerfect resolves this conflict in favor of the directly formatted text. For example, if you indent a paragraph by using Format⇨Paragraph⇨Indent or pressing F7, and then you apply a paragraph style that is not indented, the indentation remains. Directly applied formatting can be tricky to remove, too, and often requires you to delete the reveal codes discussed in Chapter 17. If you use styles, be somewhat diligent about using them. As much as possible, do not revert to your old, unprincipled ways of formatting your text directly using the Format menu's commands.

Understanding the Types of Styles

Before you get started working with styles, it's helpful to understand the different kinds of styles in WordPerfect. Specifically, you can work with three types of styles:

- **Character styles:** Affect the format of characters, such as their font, whether they're bold or italic or underlined, and their color. In fact, pretty much anything you can find under the Format⇨Font command can be part of a character style. (Character formatting is the focus of Chapter 6.)

- **Paragraph styles:** Includes all the things in character styles (so that's all the Format⇨Font stuff) along with paragraphy things such as center or right justification (you can read about them in Chapter 7), tab settings, and borders around paragraphs (which we talk about in Chapter 10).

- **Document styles:** Includes just about all the formatting you can think of, at all levels of the document — character, paragraph, and page (see Chapter 9). However, document styles are used far less than character or paragraph styles.

Creating Styles with QuickStyle

The real key to knowing everything about styles lurks at the bottom of the Format menu, under Format⇨Styles. We'll get to that soon in the "Understanding Built-In Styles" section. However, there's a shortcut to creating character and paragraph styles. You can begin by formatting a bunch of text the way you want it. When you've finalized the appearance, you record the various formatting as styles. Because it's straightforward, WordPerfect calls this formatting QuickStyle. The following sections explain how to do it.

WordPerfect doesn't allow you to create actual *document styles* using Quick-Style. To create a document style, see the "Creating and applying a document style" section later in this chapter.

Creating a character style using QuickStyle

Think of creating QuickStyles as creating *styles by example* — you format a chunk of text the way you like and then name it as a style.

Suppose you want all the foreign words in your document to be in bold and italic. Just create a style called Foreign and apply it. These steps guide you through this process:

1. **Format some text in your document as an example for WordPerfect.**

   Preferably, format some text that you want to apply the style to anyway. For example, to start creating a style that will format text as bold and italic, select the text and then press Ctrl+B and Ctrl+I.

2. **Click the Select Style list on the property bar and select QuickStyle at the very bottom of the list.**

   The Select Style list on the property bar is the drop-down list just to the left of the abc button; it usually says <None> until you start creating styles. When you select QuickStyle, the QuickStyle dialog box appears. Another way to display the QuickStyle dialog box is to choose Format⇨ Style (or press Alt+F8) and then click the QuickStyle button.

3. **Make up a name for your style and type it in the Style Name box, where your cursor awaits you.**

   A good style name might be something like *Foreign*. Don't exceed 20 characters; WordPerfect doesn't allow more than that limit.

4. **You can type something in the Description box that describes the style's purpose.**

   Adding a description can be useful if someone else will be using the styles you create. You could type something such as *character formatting for foreign text.*

5. **In the Style Type area at the bottom of the dialog box, click Character with Automatic Update.**

   This step tells WordPerfect to create a character style (see Figure 9-1).

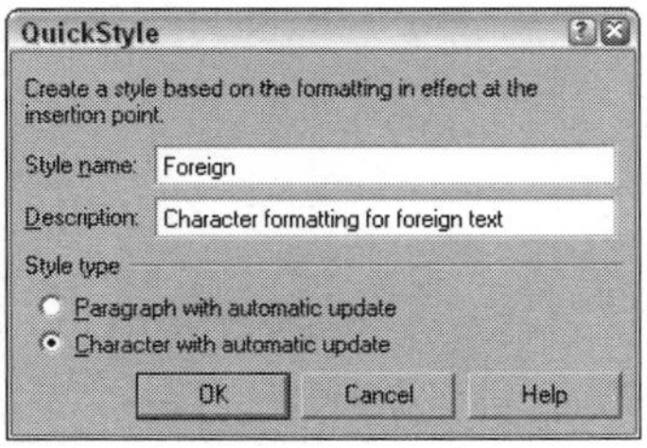

Figure 9-1:
In a rush? Speed through style creation using the QuickStyle dialog box.

QuickStyle

Create a style based on the formatting in effect at the insertion point.

Style name: Foreign

Description: Character formatting for foreign text

Style type
○ Paragraph with automatic update
● Character with automatic update

OK   Cancel   Help

6. **Click the OK button.**

The QuickStyle dialog box goes away, and WordPerfect creates the style. It also applies the style to the selected text, but it may not tell you about that in the Select Style list. No matter — click in the middle of the styled text, and you'll see the Select Style list change.

7. **If you see the Styles dialog box, click Insert.**

If you used the QuickStyle button to display the QuickStyle dialog box (in Step 2), you see that dialog box again when you close the QuickStyle dialog box. You also see your new style highlighted in the Available Styles list.

That's it — you did it. You've created a style called *Foreign,* which you now can apply by name to any selected text in your document.

Although styles can be updated automatically or manually, styles you create using QuickStyle are automatically updated (the typical option).

Creating a paragraph style using QuickStyle

Certain types of formatting do not belong in a character formatting style. For example, indentation and other things you usually do with the Format⇨ Paragraph command belong in a paragraph formatting style. Paragraph styles, however, are inclusive and can include *both* paragraph-type things and character-type formatting, such as bold and font styles.

To create a paragraph style, you perform the same steps as you do to create a character style, but when you get to the QuickStyle dialog box, make sure to select the Paragraph with Automatic Update Style type.

Applying Styles

Whether you want to use built-in styles (see the "Understanding Built-In Styles" section later) or ones you've created, you apply styles in the same manner:

Quick, Henry, the QuickStyles!
No, the QuickFormat!

Personally, we think that the WordPerfect folks have gone a little overboard with all this Quick-this and Quick-that stuff. Just exactly what is the difference between QuickStyles and Quick-Format? If you're as confused as we are by all this quick-stuff, here's the low-down:

	QuickStyle	**QuickFormat**
What it does	Picks up formatting from whatever text is selected and creates a style with a name you choose.	Picks up formatting from whatever text is selected — and lets you paint that format onto other text. Everything painted in the same format is linked and automatically updated if one is updated.
What kind of style it creates	Character style or paragraph style	Character style or paragraph style (although paragraph formatting is called "headings" in the QuickFormat dialog box).
Automatically updated?	Yes	Yes
How you create one	1. Select some text. 2. Select QuickStyle from the Select Style list on the property bar or choose Format⇨Style and click QuickStyle.	1. Select some text. 2. Click the QuickFormat toolbar button (the button with the paint roller on it) or choose Format⇨QuickFormat command.
How do you apply one to your text?	1. Select some text. 2. Select the style name from the Select Style list on the property bar; or choose the Format⇨Style, click the style name, and click Apply.	As soon as you create the QuickFormat style, your cursor turns into a cursor-with-a-paint-roller. As you highlight text, the text acquires the style you just created. Everything that gets formatted in that way becomes linked. In the process of doing its job, QuickFormat also creates styles, giving them names such as QuickFormat1. As a result, you can also apply QuickFormats as you would regular styles! Click the QuickFormat button again to stop QuickFormatting.

Oh, and don't forget the QuickMenu! That's the menu you get when you right-click some text. You can do QuickFormat from the QuickMenu, but you can't do QuickStyles. Go figure. Quickly.

- **Applying character styles:** To apply your character style, select some text and click the Select Style button on the property bar. This time, the Style list contains your style. Click it to apply it to your text. The text you selected now has the formatting of this style.

- **Applying paragraph styles:** Applying paragraph styles is much like applying character styles. Put your cursor in the paragraph that you want to style (you don't have to select text when you want to format just one paragraph). If you want to format multiple paragraphs, select them. Then click the Select Style button on the property bar. When the Style list appears, click the style name you want to apply.

WordPerfect tells you what style is applied to the paragraph in which the cursor is located. Just look in the Select Style box on the property bar, or in the general status section of the application bar at the bottom of the screen (just to the left of the current line and page number). If you've used paragraph styles in your document, both those places display the name of the style applied to the current paragraph. Clicking the Select Style box enables you to select another style for the paragraph. If you select a style and nothing happens, you've selected a character style. Generally, this is a bad idea; see the sidebar "The Enter key is broken."

The Enter key is broken

If you're typing along and decide that you want your text to be formatted as you type, you probably want to be using a paragraph style. If you have a little text inside a paragraph that you want formatted specially (such as foreign words), you probably want to be using a character style. "What's the difference?" you ask. You won't notice one until you get to the end of a paragraph. Then you press the Enter key and expect a new paragraph to begin. Instead, *nothing happens!* You're typing and applying a character style at the same time.

If you select a character style (either from the Select Style button on the property bar or from the Style dialog box) and continue to type merrily along, the behavior of the Enter key changes. Instead of starting a new paragraph, it inserts a code to turn the character style off and then on again. It does *not* start a new paragraph. We have to admit that this is one of the more mysterious behaviors in WordPerfect. You have been warned.

To solve this problem, press the right-arrow cursor key to move your typing cursor *beyond* the closing character style code. This code is invisible unless you open the Reveal Codes window (which you don't have to do to use this trick). If you *do* open the Reveal Codes window (discussed in Chapter 17), what's going on should become pretty clear.

Understanding Built-In Styles

Before you go on to modifying styles, we should introduce the *built-in styles,* called Heading 1 through Heading 5 and DocumentStyle. Unsurprisingly, Headings are styles for your headings and subheadings. Their definitions are preset, for convenience, because headings are what most people use styles for most of the time. To see them, click the Select Style button on the property bar.

Heading styles

Heading styles (Heading 1 through Heading 5) do nice things, such as make your headings all bold and enter them in the table of contents (if you ask WordPerfect to create a table of contents). They're nicely specified styles, which is fortunate because changing them often requires you to understand (ugh!) secret reveal codes (see Chapter 17).

You apply heading styles in the same way you apply any other paragraph style: With your cursor in the paragraph to be formatted, click the Select Style button on the property bar and select a heading style. After you apply these styles, you may want to use them to create a table of contents. If you do, take a look at Chapter 12.

DocumentStyle

The other built-in style, DocumentStyle, specifies the way that your text looks when you create a document, before you do anything to change its appearance. You don't have to apply DocumentStyle; it happens automatically at the beginning of your document. Unless you apply other styles, all the text in your document is formatted according to DocumentStyle.

DocumentStyle is the central place where your choices are recorded when you use either Format⇨Font⇨Default Font (described in Chapters 7 and 19) or File⇨Document⇨Default Font (mentioned in Chapters 10 and 19).

If you want to add or change something in DocumentStyle or a heading style, check out the Styles Editor, described in "Creating and Modifying Styles," later in this chapter.

If you want to remove something, you have to deal with secret codes, which are discussed fully in Chapter 17.

DocumentStyle is the default document style for a WordPerfect document.

More built-in styles

WordPerfect comes with a grab bag of predefined styles. They're not usually listed in the Style list, but you can bring them in by following these steps:

1. **Choose Format⇨Styles.**

   The Styles dialog box appears.

2. **Click the Options button, and choose Settings from the list that drops down.**

   The Style Settings dialog box appears. WordPerfect System Styles is a check box with two additional selections: WordPerfect heading styles (which is selected now, and causes you to see the Heading 1 through Heading 5 styles) and WordPerfect heading styles and all other system styles.

3. **Click the WordPerfect Heading Styles and All Other System Styles setting.**

4. **Click OK.**

   You can then choose among all built-in styles in the Available Styles box.

If you open a Microsoft Word document in WordPerfect, WordPerfect imports all styles with the document. As a result, these Word styles are added to your styles list automatically.

Exploring the Styles Dialog Box

So far, we've managed to do everything we need to do with styles without opening the Styles dialog box, the control panel for styles. Figure 9-2 shows you what the Styles dialog box looks like.

Figure 9-2:
Your style management control panel.

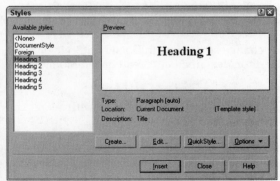

To display the Styles dialog box, choose Format⇨Styles. You can also access this dialog box also by clicking the box on the application bar that tells you the name of the style while the cursor is on styled text. (When the cursor is on unstyled text, the box tells you whether you're in insert mode or typeover mode, and clicking it does not display the Styles dialog box.)

To select a style, double-click the style name in the Available Styles list to apply it to the currently selected text (for character styles) or to the place where the cursor is (for paragraph or document styles). Table 9-1 gives you the lowdown on what else you can do with the Styles dialog box. We talk in detail about modifying styles in the next section.

Table 9-1	Stylish Options
Option	*What It Does*
Available Styles	Displays the name of every style defined in the current document
Create	Displays a blank Styles Editor dialog box so you can create a style
Edit	Displays the Styles Editor dialog box for the style highlighted in the Available Styles box
QuickStyle	Displays the QuickStyle dialog box and creates a style with the same format as the text at the cursor location
Options	Provides further options for styles: Settings, Copy, Delete, Reset, Retrieve, and Save As
Insert	Applies the highlighted style to (a) the highlighted text if the style is a character style, (b) the highlighted paragraphs or the paragraph that the cursor is in if the style is a paragraph style, (c) the rest of the document if the style is a document style, or (d) nothing if there isn't any text highlighted and the style isn't a document style
Close	Closes the dialog box
Help	Displays a WordPerfect Help screen for styles

Creating and Modifying Styles

The Styles dialog box is also your gateway to creating styles from scratch and modifying styles that came with WordPerfect or that you created with QuickStyle or QuickFormat. That's right: You can apply or change those QuickFormat styles just like any other style. Modifying styles requires that you know something about reveal codes (see Chapter 17). Fortunately, the task is worthwhile. Nothing is as satisfying as having every paragraph in your document hooked up to a style, so that you can change the formatting of whole swathes of documents at will through the Styles Editor.

When you click the Create or Edit button in the Styles dialog box, you get to the heart of styles: the Styles Editor. (If you're a frequent flier in the Reveal Codes window, you can double-click a style code there as well to see the Styles Editor.) Check out Figure 9-3 and the descriptions in Table 9-2.

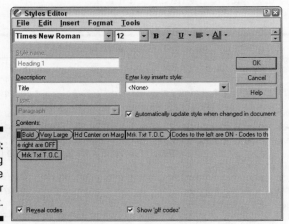

Figure 9-3:
Tweaking
styles in the
Styles Editor
dialog box.

Table 9-2	Options in the Styles Editor
Option	*What It Does*
Styles Editor menu bar and Formatting property bar	Insert codes to format your text. The most often used formatting commands are in the Format menu. Choose Format⇨Font to display the Font dialog box, or choose a font name from the list on the property bar.
Style Name	Identifies the style you're using.
Description	Lets you wax eloquent about your style.
Enter Key Inserts Style	Tells WordPerfect what the style of the next paragraph should be.
Type	Lets you control whether you're using a character or paragraph style.

Option	*What It Does*
Automatically Update Style When Changed in Document	When checked, enables you to change the style automatically when you change the format of some styled text in the document.
Contents	Shows you all the secret codes WordPerfect uses to make the style happen. (See Chapter 17.)
Reveal Codes	Displays formatting codes in the Contents box.
Show 'Off Codes'	Enables you to insert codes that will take effect when the style ends.

Creating a style from scratch

Armed with the Styles Editor (which you access by choosing Format⇨Styles and then clicking the Create button) and the descriptions in Table 9-2, here's how you go about creating a style from scratch:

1. **In the Style Name box, type a name for your style.**

   You can make the name up to 20 characters long. Because the Style List on the property bar shows you only the beginning of the style name unless you click it, you might want to make sure that you can tell one style name from another using only the first few letters of the name.

2. **Select a type for your style.**

   Create a character style if you don't want your style to apply to the entire paragraph. Create a paragraph style if you want to control margins and indenting or you want the entire paragraph to have a single "look."

3. **Tell WordPerfect that your style should automatically update.**

   We recommend automatic updating; you can always turn it off later if you don't like it.

4. **Format!**

   Go wild. At the top of the Styles Editor, you see the property bar. You also see a miniature version of the WordPerfect menu. The menu commands are there for two reasons:

   - To format your text
   - To help you correct your text

   For example, if you include any regular text in the Contents box, you can spell check it. Forget about such frivolity; you're here to format text, so just stick to that.

Unfortunately, you don't get a sample of what your text is going to look like, so you just have to envision it from looking at the codes. Don't forget — you can always format first and then create the style using QuickStyle.

5. **Click Enter Key Inserts Style, if you care.**

This feature really asks, "What do you want to happen when you're typing along in this style and you spawn a new paragraph by pressing Enter? Do you want the new text to continue in this style, or what?" When you click the down arrow to the right of the associated box, you see that you have three possible answers to this nitpicking question:

- **<None>** means "Turn off the styles altogether when I press Enter."

- **<Same Style>** means "Begin a new paragraph in this same style even if I press Enter."

- **Named styles in the Style List** (Heading 1, Heading 2, and so on) means "Begin a new paragraph with this *other* style I specified." These *chaining styles* are useful when styles normally follow each other. For example, you may want to have a Subtitle style follow your Title style or Normal Paragraph style follow a Heading style.

Character styles should *never* insert <Same Style>. Why? Because, for reasons known only to the WordPerfect folks, the Enter key, when used in a character style, doesn't start a new paragraph. Instead, it just goes on to the next style. See the sidebar "The Enter key is broken" previously in this chapter.

6. **After you've completed all your formatting, click the OK button.**

You're back at the Styles dialog box.

7. **Click Insert to apply the style you just made to the selected characters or paragraph.**

Alternatively, you can click the Close button to get rid of the Styles dialog box. Your style is defined, but it's not in use yet. Or you can keep defining styles and choose one to apply when you're finally ready to leave Style land.

To change something about a style (say you want to change bold to underline), you probably have to use the Reveal Codes box by pressing Alt+F3 (or choosing View⇨Reveal Codes). Look in the Contents window at the bottom of the Styles Editor dialog box for a suggestive word, such as Bold. Double-click it, and the Font dialog box appears. Now you can make your change. Close this dialog box, and you change the code.

To delete something in the Contents window, such as a font size code, click it and then drag it out of the Contents window and into the real world (anywhere outside the Contents window), where scummy reveal codes can't survive.

If you make a mistake while you're modifying styles in the Styles Editor dialog box, the Undo command on the Styles Editor menu bar can help you. Just choose Edit⇨Undo.

Modifying styles

The Styles Editor (remember, you get there by choosing Format⇨Styles and clicking Edit) is the place to change existing styles as well. In fact, the only difference between changing a style and creating one is that you don't get to type a name for the style. Look at the preceding section on creating styles from scratch for the blow-by-blow description.

Creating and applying a document style

You may want to create a style that goes into effect at a certain point in a document. This type of style is called a *document style,* and it's a little weird. Unlike character and paragraph styles, a document style has no predetermined point at which it ends. As a result, it generally continues until another document style begins.

Document styles can include not only the formatting that you can add to a document with the Format⇨Page command, but also anything else that you do from the Format menu, including Font, Line, Paragraph, and Column commands. For that matter, document styles can do darn near anything from the Insert, Tools, Graphics, and Table menus, including inserting page breaks, changing headers and footers, inserting dates, inserting graphics, or making quacking noises.

Using a document style is a good way to set up the overall layout of a document, including the margins, the paragraph formatting for most paragraphs, and the font for most text.

As we mentioned before, you can't create a document style by using the QuickStyle method; you must use the Create method (see "Creating a style from scratch," earlier in this chapter). When you're prompted to select a style type, select the Document option. Aside from that, it behaves pretty much like a regular style.

To apply a document style, first position your cursor where you want the style to begin (typically before a paragraph). Next, select the document style from the Styles list in the property bar. The document style is then applied at this location in your document.

Turning Off Styles

Suppose that you applied a style, and you're merrily typing along, updating your resume to include the phrase *Mastery of WordPerfect styles.* You finish a delightfully styled paragraph, press Enter, and bingo! — you start another similarly styled paragraph. This automatic spawning of a similarly styled paragraph is lovely, but what if you don't want another similarly styled paragraph?

Or suppose that you're typing a letter to Aunt May in a character style that uses the lovely ShelleyVolante font, and you want to turn it off to write a more legible note to your nearsighted Uncle George. Do one of these two things:

✔ To turn off a paragraph style in the paragraph in which your cursor is located, click the Select Style button on the property bar and then click <None> in the list.

✔ If you've been typing along in a character style and now want to turn it off for the following text, press the right-arrow key on your keyboard. This step moves your cursor past the `Style-end` reveal code. When you type again, the style is no longer in effect.

TIP

Revealing your secret style codes

If you understand reveal codes in WordPerfect (see Chapter 17), you probably understand the bottom window of the Styles Editor dialog box. It shows which codes are being included in the style, just as a Reveal Codes window does.

Moreover, you probably understand why character and paragraph styles are denoted as (Closed) and document styles are denoted as (Open). *Closed* is another word for paired style codes; *open* means single style codes.

When WordPerfect applies a closed style (character or paragraph style) to your document, it uses pairs of codes to bracket the affected text. These codes use only the style name, which gives you complete freedom to edit the style definition without putting a bunch of screwy codes in your text. When WordPerfect applies an open style (document style), it uses single codes, again, using only the style name. Magically, these (unpaired) style codes can apply character formats such as bold text, even though bold text requires a paired code. Works anyway — go figure.

Reusing Styles

Reusing work is always a smart idea, and styles help you reuse your formatting efforts. You can reuse styles in any of three ways:

- ✔ Retrieve the styles from an existing document into a new document.
- ✔ Add the styles to the default WordPerfect template.
- ✔ Save the styles in another file.

Copying styles from an existing document

Retrieving styles from another document is the lazy way to do it and, therefore, our favorite. Follow these steps:

1. **Choose Format➪Styles.**

   You see the Styles dialog box.

2. **Click the Options button.**

   Now you see the Options drop-down menu.

3. **Choose Retrieve.**

   The Retrieve Styles From dialog box appears, as shown in Figure 9-4.

Figure 9-4:
Don't redo, retrieve instead. That way, you don't have to re-enter your styles from one document to the next.

4. **Type the name of the document from which you want to retrieve styles.**

   Or you can click the file folder icon to select the file from a list (this works the same way as opening files, described in Chapter 1).

5. **If you want just the user styles or just the system styles, click the appropriate option.**

   Normally, you get both. WordPerfect asks whether you want to override the current styles.

6. **Click OK.**

   In all likelihood, you want to override the current styles.

7. **Click Yes.**

Adding styles to the default WordPerfect template

Suppose you'd like to copy your styles to a central location so that whenever you use WordPerfect, you can get to them. One way to do this is to copy your styles to a document template that automatically brings in styles when you create a new document using that template. (Chapter 12 describes templates and all the wonderful things you can do with them.)

If most of the documents you create will use the same styles, copy your styles to WordPerfect's default template, on which all documents are based. (This approach is also great for pack rats, who don't mind if every style that they ever create is stored in one place.)

To copy styles to the default template, follow these steps:

1. **Choose Format⇨Styles.**

   You see the Styles dialog box.

2. **Click a style that you want to copy.**

3. **Click the Options button.**

   The little Options menu pops up (or down).

4. **Click Copy.**

   The Styles Copy dialog box appears, as shown in Figure 9-5.

Figure 9-5:
Copying
styles using
the Styles
Copy dialog
box.

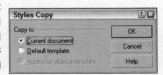

5. **Click Default template in the Copy To area.**

6. **Repeat Steps 1–5 for each style that you want to copy.**

From now on, whenever you create a new document, these styles are available.

Saving styles in a separate file

You may want to save your styles to a separate centralized location and bring them in only when you need them. This method has the advantage of enabling you to save all your styles — styles for memos, for example — under a name such as memos.sty.

To save your styles to a file, follow the instructions below:

1. **Choose Format⇨Styles.**

   You see the Styles dialog box (refer to Figure 9-2).

2. **Click a style that you want to copy.**

3. **Click the Options button.**

   The little Options menu pops up (or down).

4. **Click Save As.**

   The Save Styles To dialog box appears (see Figure 9-6).

Figure 9-6: Think global. Save styles in a location beyond your document.

5. **Type a directory and filename.**

   Or you can click the file folder icon to use a dialog box for this procedure. For some reason, WordPerfect doesn't add a file extension for you. So, give the file an extension that will remind you of styles, such as .sty.

6. **Click OK.**

To use these styles, just open your new document, choose Format⇨Styles, click the Options button, and then choose Retrieve.

Getting Rid of Styles

After a while, particularly if you're of the pack-rat persuasion and keep all your styles in the same place, you'll want to delete a few of them. However, you can delete only your own styles, not the built-in styles.

Follow these steps to delete some styles:

1. **Choose Format⇨Styles.**

2. **Click a style that you want to delete.**

3. **Click the Options button in the Styles dialog box.**

   If the Delete option appears dimmed, you're trying to delete a built-in style. Stop that.

4. **Click Delete in the menu that drops down.**

   A dialog box appears, showing a list of all the styles you can delete, as shown in Figure 9-7. The style you selected is highlighted. Select as many additional styles from this list as you want (hold down the Ctrl key as you click the style names).

   The options at the bottom of this dialog box allow you to either delete the style definition and take out all the codes for that style in your document (that's the Including Formatting Codes option), or remove the definition but leave the formatting in place (that's the Leave Formatting Codes in Document option).

Figure 9-7:
Hasta la
vista, bad
style!

5. **Choose either Including Formatting Codes or Leave Formatting Codes in Document.**

6. **Click the OK button.**

   All traces of the styles disappear from the Available Styles list and from your document.

Part III

Making Your Documents Come Alive

The 5th Wave   By Rich Tennant

"I appreciate that your computer has 256 colors.
I just don't think that they all had to be used
in one book report."

In this part . . .

Text is the "meat and potatoes" of any word processing document. But if you held a fancy banquet and served your guests just meat and potatoes, they'd probably be falling over each other to leave early and finish their meal elsewhere. No, your guests would be expecting soup, salad, vegetables, and dessert. In the same way, if your WordPerfect documents are well-written but are filled top to bottom with just text, the readers of your documents — we hate to say it — may end up getting b-o-r-e-d and surf the Web instead.

To prevent this from happening, Part III shows you how to add many features to your documents, including tables, borders, lines, and pictures. You also discover how to create documents using professional looking templates. Who knows, perhaps by the time you finish with this part, your documents will be so nice-looking that they'll be devoured like a tasty five-course meal. Bon appétit!

Chapter 10

Formatting Beyond the Text

● ●

In This Chapter

▶ Adding borders

▶ Dividing text into columns

▶ Arranging text in tables

▶ Presenting text in boxes

▶ Drawing lines and arrows

● ●

The terrific thing about today's word processors is that you can dress up a document in ways that only a designer, typesetter, or printer could do a few years ago. The trouble is that people (your boss, for example) know that the technology is available, so they expect people (you, for example) to do this kind of thing.

But wait, there's more. WordPerfect performs not only word processing but also drawing, charting, spreadsheet-like calculating, and elements of type setting.

The problem for regular people like you is getting around all the fancy stuff so you can do the basic stuff. That's what this chapter is all about. We don't give you a course in spreadsheets or computer graphics; we just help you get started creating borders, backgrounds, basic columns, tables, and boxes for your documents.

Specifically, here's what we talk about in this chapter and why you want to know this info:

- ✔ **Borders and backgrounds:** You'll want to know about these because everything you put into your document (including paragraphs of text) can have its own border and background.

- ✔ **Columns:** Columns come in handy when you want to create newsletters, compile lists, or cram a whole bunch of text onto a page.

- ✔ **Tables:** Many types of information that you work with can be structured in a table format, whether you're displaying a list of information or presenting a budget report.

- ✔ **Boxes:** In WordPerfect — as in real life — boxes are where stuff goes. Stuff, in this case, is pretty much everything except the main text of your document. Stuff like lines and blocks of text, which we talk about in this chapter, either are in boxes or act pretty much like they are. Pictures, graphs, and drawings, which we talk about in Chapter 11, are also all in boxes.

Adding Borders and Backgrounds

For some reason, nothing looks as neat as having a nice fancy border around your text. At least, that's what the folks at WordPerfect must believe, because their border features allow you to choose among a dizzying array of tasteful (and not so tasteful) borders. You can fill the background of your document with subtle, interesting, or downright bizarre patterns.

Some of these features can be useful if you want to create a fancy document — a certificate, for example. (See Chapter 12 for the particulars on creating certificates.) But unless you use these features carefully, it's easy to end up with a document that simply looks amateurish. Use borders wisely.

Basic borders

To put a snazzy border around part of your document, first decide where you want to put it. Your choices are pages, paragraphs, or columns, which give you borders down the side of the page, the paragraph (and that includes each paragraph in multiple columns), or the whole area in columns, respectively.

For the basic once-over, we'll choose paragraphs because all border controls work basically the same way. Follow these steps to add a border to a paragraph:

1. **Put the cursor anywhere in the paragraph you want to box.**

2. **Choose Format⇨Paragraph⇨Border/Fill.**

   The Paragraph Border/Fill dialog box appears, as shown in Figure 10-1. You see the same dialog box if you click Border/Fill in the Columns dialog box.

   The Page Border/Fill dialog box (which appears when you choose Format⇨Page⇨Border/Fill) displays some fancy borders that aren't available in the Paragraph (or Columns) Border Fill dialog box. We talk about the fancy option in "Some miscellaneous thoughts about borders," later in this chapter.

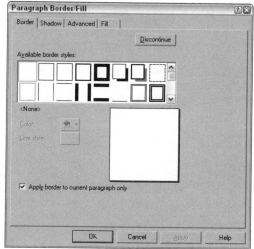

Figure 10-1:
Add borders
to your
document.

3. Scroll through the box labeled Available Border Styles and click the style you want to use.

Zillions of borders are available — okay, maybe not zillions, but a lot. If you don't find one that you like, you can set the color, line style, and shadow direction yourself, if you don't have anything better to do. Or choose "none" — the blank square in the top-left corner of the Available Border Styles box.

4. Decide whether you want to apply the formatting to the paragraph or the entire document.

You're not quite finished yet. In the bottom-left corner of the dialog box you see the Apply Border to Current Paragraph (or Page or Column Group) Only check box. If you leave this box checked, that's exactly what WordPerfect does. But if you want the fancy formatting to apply to the entire document, *un*check this box. All the following pages (or paragraphs or column groups) will have this border.

5. Click OK or Apply.

When you click OK in the Paragraph Border/Fill dialog box, the border is added to the paragraph and the dialog box closes. To keep the dialog box open to add more formatting (say, to add a border *and* a shadow to the paragraph), don't click OK after you choose a border style — click Apply. When you click Apply, the dialog box stays open, and you can add more formatting to the paragraph.

Phil . . . for all that white space behind your text

Phil (or, rather, Fill) shows up when you click the Fill tab of the Border/Fill dialog box (see Figure 10-2). However, depending on the choice you make, this option can make your text illegible by putting a pattern behind it.

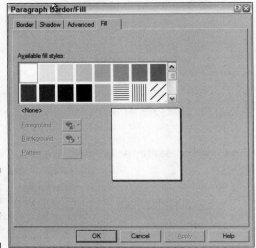

Figure 10-2:
Adding fill
to your
document.

If you want to put a light-gray pattern behind something to make it stand out, make sure that your printer and your copier are up to the job of printing or copying this stuff. Otherwise, you'll end up with a smudge instead of readable text.

When you've configured the fill settings, click OK to close the dialog box.

If you decide at a later time to remove the borders and fills, just click the Discontinue button in the Border/Fill dialog box. Poof!

Some miscellaneous thoughts about borders

"But I'm not an artist!" you cry nervously. "What am I going to do with all these borders and backgrounds, other than make my documents illegible?" This section lists some things that you may want to do:

✔ **Put a fancy border around the entire document.** In the Page Border/Fill dialog box (refer to Figure 10-1), click the down arrow next to the Border Type box and select Fancy to see some pretty neat borders that you can use for certificates and the like.

✔ **Put a line below a heading.** Another common technique is to add a line below a heading as a way to offset sections in a document. To do so, select the Thin Bottom border style from the list of available border styles. We find this one of the most useful aspects of the Borders feature.

✔ **Limit your borders to the paragraph, page, or column that your cursor is in.** In the Border/Fill dialog box, click the box in the lower-left corner that says Apply Border to Current *whatever* Only. Checking this box is an alternative to selecting an area of text before you issue the Border/Fill command.

✔ **Put lines between columns.** If you're dealing with a document in columns (such as a newsletter), place the cursor anywhere in the columns and choose Format➪Columns➪Border/Fill. Three borders near the end of the Available Border Styles list apply specifically to columns. Click the vertical line (it's the fifth choice from the end of the list). Under the border style samples, the name Column Between appears. If you don't see it, keep clicking around until it appears; it puts a line between your columns. The border to the left of the vertical line adds space for lines around your columns but doesn't put in the lines (an obscure but useful function if you have some columns with lines and some without). And the border to the left of that is a box with a line down the middle. This border is the Column All border; it puts borders around the set of columns, including lines between your columns. For more about columns, see the next section "Dividing Text into Columns."

✔ **Change the way borders and lines between the columns look.** After you select Column Between or Column All, you can click the Color and Line Style buttons. You can choose any color and any thickness for your lines.

✔ **Turn off borders.** Place your cursor where you want the borders to stop, and then click the Discontinue button in whichever border dialog box you're using (Paragraph, Page, or Columns).

✔ **Don't use borders at all.** Use a horizontal or vertical line. We talk about these in detail in the section "Drawing Lines and Arrows in Your Document," later in this chapter.

Dividing Text into Columns

Columns are great for newsletters, newspapers, magazines, scripts, lists, and certain charts or tables. With newspaper and magazine documents, even if you don't print the document yourself, you can use columns and the correct character and paragraph formatting to determine approximately how long your article will be when it is printed.

WordPerfect can lay out columns in the following four styles (when was the last time we said that there was only *one* way to do something in WordPerfect?):

- **Newspaper:** Fills one column to the end of the page before beginning another column. Use this option for a typical newsletter.

- **Balanced newspaper:** Continuously shuffles your text to make sure that all columns are of more or less equal length. Use this style (which has nothing to do with a balanced editorial policy) when a document alternately uses a single column and multiple columns, such as when you have a long, multicolumn list in the middle of a regular document. You can use it also for ending the last page of a multicolumn newsletter before the end of the physical page.

- **Parallel:** Creates rows across your columns and creates cells of text in a manner similar to a table. When you use this style, you create a row one cell at a time by inserting a hard column break when you want to begin writing the next cell to the right. This style is useful for documents such as scripts and contracts.

- **Parallel with block protect:** Similar to Parallel, but makes sure that automatic page breaks don't mess things up if your rows must continue on the next page.

If all these styles sound confusing, take heart. The WordPerfect Columns dialog box (explained in the "Adding columns with precision" section) shows you neat pictures of what type of columns is used for each option.

Adding columns with just two mouse clicks

To add standard newspaper columns to your document, follow these steps:

1. **Place your cursor where you want columns to begin.**

   If you want your entire document except for the title at the top to appear in two newspaper columns, for example, move your cursor to the first line after the title.

2. **Click the Columns button on the toolbar.**

   The Columns button has three little columns of parallel blue lines.

3. **Select the number of columns that you want (usually 2 or 3) from the menu list.**

   You're finished.

Adding columns with precision

If you'd like to have greater control over the size or style of columns in your document, add them by following these steps:

1. **Place your cursor where you want columns to begin.**

   If you want your entire document except for the title at the top to appear in two newspaper columns, for example, move your cursor to the first line after the title.

2. **Choose Format⇨Columns.**

   The Columns dialog box appears, as shown in Figure 10-3.

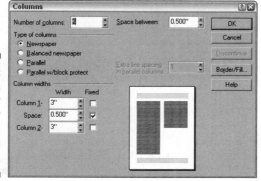

Figure 10-3: Getting, like, totally columnar with the Columns dialog box.

3. **Choose the number of columns that you want.**

   In the upper-left corner, in the Number of Columns box, WordPerfect suggests two columns (unless you are working with text that's already in columns, in which case you see the current setting). Change this number by typing a number or by clicking the up or down arrow next to the Number of Columns box.

4. **Choose the type of columns that you want.**

   In the Type of Columns section, choose one of the options (Newspaper, for example), which we described previously.

5. **Adjust the column widths or spacing, if you want.**

   In the Column Widths section, WordPerfect suggests nice, even column widths with a ½-inch space between them. It allows column widths to vary if you change the page margins, but it prevents the spacing between columns from changing — that is, it keeps the spacing fixed.

To fix (or unfix) any column or space-between-columns dimension so that it doesn't vary, click the box in the Fixed column to the right of the Width setting.

To change widths, click the Width box and edit the value by typing and deleting, or click the adjoining up- and down-arrow (increment and decrement) buttons. Use the " symbol for inches or *mm* or *cm* for metric values.

If you want all the spaces between the columns to be the same size, you can adjust the intercolumn spacing using the Space Between setting next to the number of columns. But be careful — if you change the value in this box, *all* the spaces between the columns (even ones that you changed by hand) will be set to the new column-spacing size.

If you make your columns look sort of like a table by using Parallel or Parallel with Block Protect, you can also specify the number of blank lines that WordPerfect leaves between rows. Click the up- or down-arrow button in the small box with the long name (Extra Line Spacing in Parallel Columns).

If you click the Border/Fill button in the Columns dialog box, you'll be in the Border/Fill dialog box, which we talk about in the first section of this chapter.

6. **Click OK.**

The hyperobservant will have noticed that the word Insert on the application bar (between the picture of the printer and the position on the page) has changed to indicate what column you're in, usually Col 1 at this point.

Turning off the Columns function

To turn off columns at some point in your document, place your cursor where you want things to go back to normal. Then choose Format⇨Columns, or click the Col 1 button on the application bar (the button appears where you usually see the Insert/Typeover indicator). The WordPerfect Columns dialog box appears; click Discontinue. Alternately, click the Columns button on the toolbar and select Discontinue from the menu that drops down.

If you're going to turn off columns in your document, you probably want to be using Balanced Newspaper columns instead of plain Newspaper columns. Plain Newspaper columns will most likely leave you with an entire blank column at the place where you turn columns off.

Bad breaks and what to do about them

There are good breaks, and there are bad breaks — column breaks, that is. WordPerfect decides where to break your columns depending on many factors, including the type of column. But when your columns don't break where you want them to (or break where you don't want them to), you can regain some control by inserting hard column breaks.

To insert a hard column break, follow these steps:

1. **Place your cursor before the line (or word or character) where you want a column to begin.**

2. **Press Ctrl+Enter to insert a hard column break.**

Column breaks don't always behave as expected. The resulting behavior depends on which type of columns you have: Newspaper, Balanced Newspaper, or one of the Parallel styles. The following list shows the types of columns in the column-break story:

- **Newspaper:** Column breaks begin a new column in the way that you think they should.

- **Balanced Newspaper:** A column break begins a new block of balanced columns; it's almost like turning columns off and then on again. This style probably isn't what you have in mind if you're trying to correct the way that WordPerfect balanced your columns. Rather than use a column break to change the balance, try regular Newspaper columns.

- **Parallel or Parallel with Block Protect:** A column break moves you across your current row to the next column. It doesn't put you at the top of a new column, as you might expect. When you insert a column break at the end of the row, you're back in the left column, in a new row.

Putting selected text in columns

Sometimes you want to put a block of text in columns. You might put a long list of words, such as a packing list, into several columns to save space, for example.

Begin by highlighting the block of text that you want to columnate. (Columnarize? Columnify?) Next, choose Format⇨Columns. In the Columns dialog box, choose the style that you want. The Balanced Newspaper style probably works best, unless you want to control where the columns break, in which case you should use the Newspaper style. Then click OK. If you want Newspaper columns, you can use the Columns button on the toolbar. Choose the number of columns you want, and you're all set.

Using highlighted text in this way is equivalent to turning columns on, typing all the text in the block, and then turning columns off.

Column breaks are invisible no matter what you do, unless you use the Reveal Codes window (see Chapter 17). If you want to delete hard column breaks, have faith that they are located just before the first character in a column (or just before the current "cell" in a Parallel-type column). To delete hard column breaks, place your cursor before the first character in the column and then press the Backspace key. (Don't try to delete soft column breaks — the ones WordPerfect puts in.)

Presenting Text in Tables

WordPerfect does tables. And then some. In fact, you can think of WordPerfect as a word processor that has swallowed a spreadsheet program. It can compute sums of columns and rows. It can even compute the standard deviation of the arc tangent of the logarithm of the net present value of your mortgage, over multiple random variations of the interest rate. Blech!

Fortunately, for those of us who would just as soon leave spreadsheets to the accounting department, WordPerfect also makes it easy for you to create more ordinary tables.

Making tables with Table QuickCreate

The fastest way to create a table is to use the Table QuickCreate button on the toolbar. Follow these steps:

1. **Click the toolbar button that looks like a little grid and hold down the mouse button.**

   As you hold down the mouse button, a grid appears. You can use this little grid to tell WordPerfect how big to make your table.

2. **Drag the mouse pointer down and to the right on the grid to highlight the number of rows and columns that you want.**

   For example, 5 x 2 represents a table with five columns and two rows. The number of columns and rows appears above the grid.

3. **Release the mouse button.**

   Your table is ready.

4. **To fill your table with goodies, simply click in a cell and type.**

   You can use text, numbers, and even graphics, and you can format your text in the usual way by using the Format commands.

When to use columns and when to use a table

It's not always obvious when to use tables and when to use columns. In many cases, either one will do. In general, use columns when you have a lot of text and you're willing to have the text move from one column to another depending on how your page layout goes. Use tables when you have shorter text but the placement of text beside each other is important. You can do that with parallel columns with the Block Protect function enabled, but using a table is usually easier. Moreover, if you need more than four columns, you need a table.

If you want to do special table-ish things, you'll be pleased to know that the property bar now contains a bunch of table-ish buttons, as shown in Figure 10-4. Just as a Graphics drop-down menu appears on the property bar when you're working with boxes, a Select Table menu appears on the property bar now. It's quite useful, as you can see.

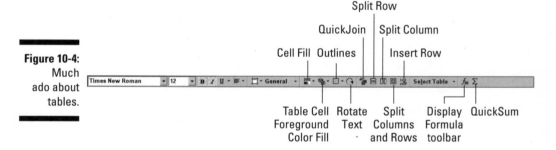

Figure 10-4: Much ado about tables.

Adding rows and columns

To make tables larger or smaller (that is, to increase or decrease the number of rows or columns), you use the Table menu.

These steps show you how to add one or more rows or columns:

1. **Click any row or column that will adjoin your new row or column.**

   Click anywhere in the bottom row, for example, to add a new row to the bottom of your table.

2. **Choose Table⇨Insert.**

   The Insert Columns/Rows dialog box appears. You can access the same Insert command also by using the right-click QuickMenu.

3. **In the Insert section of the dialog box, click Columns or Rows.**

   If you want more than one new row or column, type the number in the box next to Columns or Rows, or increment the number by clicking the adjoining up or down arrow.

4. **In the Placement section of the dialog box, click Before if you want the row to go above (or the column to go to the left) of the cell that you selected in Step 1; otherwise, click After.**

   To add a row to the bottom of your table, for example, click After.

5. **Click OK.**

To quickly insert a row, click the Insert Row button on the property bar (labeled in Figure 10-4).

To delete a row or column from your table, follow these steps:

1. **Click anywhere in the row or column that you want to delete.**

   For multiple rows or columns, click and drag to highlight them.

2. **Choose Table⇨Delete.**

   The Delete Structure/Contents dialog box appears.

3. **In the Delete section, click Columns or Rows.**

4. **Click OK.**

Deleting tables, rows, and columns

To delete the entire table, begin by highlighting all the cells. The quickest way to do that is with the Select Table button on the property bar. Then, if you press the Delete key on your keyboard, the Delete Table dialog box appears. You can delete the entire table by clicking Entire Table. Or, if you prefer (and this is kind of a nice feature), you can delete only the table contents and leave the table framework behind by clicking Table Contents Only. Then click OK.

To delete the contents of a bunch of cells, highlight them and press the Delete key. You don't get any warning, but the contents are gone. (Never fear, you can always get them back by choosing Edit⇨Undo.)

TIP

Microsoft Word users: Be selective

If you previously created tables using Microsoft Word, we want to point out that Word and WordPerfect differ in how you select rows, columns, and the entire table. Microsoft Word enables you to select a row or column by positioning the mouse cursor outside the margin of the row or column you want to select and then clicking. In contrast, to select a row or column in WordPerfect, you position your mouse inside a cell and hover over the left side (for rows) or top side (for columns) until the cursor changes to an arrow. Next, double-click to select a row or column.

Additionally, Microsoft Word allows you to select a table by hovering your mouse over a table and clicking its handle. With WordPerfect, you can triple-click on the left or top side of a cell to select the entire table. (Alternatively, you can use the Select Table drop-down menu on the property bar.)

Changing column width

Changing individual column widths is simple. Click the vertical line that divides the columns and drag it. The mouse pointer turns into a little horizontal-arrow gizmo to tell you that you're moving a column divider. When you release the mouse button, the column divider moves over so that the column on one side of the line gets wider and the other one gets narrower.

If you hold down the Ctrl key while you move the column divider, only the column to the left of the divider gets wider or narrower as you move the divider. The column to the *right* of the divider line stays the same size. The entire table gets wider or narrower to provide the space you need. The columns to the right of the divider line just *move* instead of being resized. This feature can be handy.

Another convenient feature is WordPerfect's capability to set column width automatically to match the widest entry in the column. Follow these steps:

1. **Click a cell somewhere in the column you want to resize.**

2. **Choose Table⇨Size Column to Fit.**

TIP

Changing the width of more than one column or the entire table is not hard, but it requires that you use a slightly intimidating dialog box. You can change other aspects of your table's appearance in this dialog box — such as left or right justification, the alignment of numbers, column margins, table left or right justification on a page, and even making slanted table headings (you find this option on the Skew tab). But because SpeedFormat, which we discuss in the next section, does such a good job with all this formatting, we won't go into detailed instructions here.

Take a deep breath and follow these steps:

1. **To change the width of several columns, highlight the columns by clicking and dragging across them. To change the column widths of the entire table, click anywhere in the table.**

2. **Choose Table➪Format or press Ctrl+F12.**

   The Properties for Table Format dialog box appears. The options across the top enable you to specify whether you want to format an individual cell, a column, a row, or the entire table.

3. **Decide whether you want to change the column width for the entire table or only one column.**

   To change the column width for the entire table, click Table. To change the column width for an individual column, click Column.

4. **Change the value in the Column Width box (the box marked Width).**

   Click in the box and type a new number, or click the up arrow and down arrow buttons. If your table is set to take up the full width of the page, click the up arrow button until WordPerfect won't increase it any more. Your columns will get as wide as they can.

5. **Click OK or press Enter.**

   If you don't notice any difference in your table, go back to the Properties for Table Format dialog box and look on the Table tab again. See whether the Table Position on Page combo box is set to *full.* If it is, your table is set to take up the entire page width, so it doesn't much matter what width you set for the columns; WordPerfect is still going to make your table take up the entire page width. Change it, if you like.

The Properties for Table Format dialog box has a nifty feature on the Cell tab. If you want to put a diagonal line in a cell, this is the place.

Formatting with SpeedFormat

Tables often look best when certain rows or columns are specially formatted with bold, italic, or colored shading. The fastest and hippest way to format your table is to use SpeedFormat. Follow these steps:

1. **Click anywhere in your table.**

2. **Choose Table⇨SpeedFormat.**

   The Table SpeedFormat dialog box appears (see Figure 10-5), displaying a list of named table styles on the left.

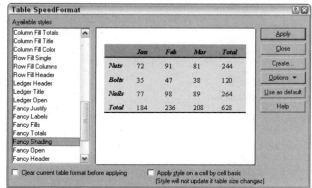

3. **In the Available Styles list, select a style.**

   SpeedFormat shows you an example of how that style looks. The example in the dialog box is just that — an example. SpeedFormat doesn't actually enter things into your table for you, such as typing titles or creating totals. Instead, it formats the table with various fonts, row and column widths, alignments, and borders. You take care of typing stuff.

   To quickly look at the available SpeedFormats, click <None> in the Available Styles list. When you press the down-arrow key on your keyboard, the next style is highlighted, and its sample appears.

4. **Click the Apply button.**

   SpeedFormat applies your chosen table style to your table.

If you later insert rows or columns into the table, WordPerfect automatically formats them in the same style. If you insert a column after a totals column, for example, WordPerfect formats the original totals column as an ordinary data column, and the new column takes the appearance of the original totals column. If you prefer that SpeedFormat leave its cotton-pickin' hands off your new rows or columns, click the check box marked Apply Style on a Cell by Cell Basis when you choose your style in the Table SpeedFormat dialog box.

Formatting with speed?

Okay, okay, we know you must be wondering what's up with the name *SpeedFormat*. After all, for nine chapters in this book, we've been talking about QuickThis and QuickThat. Now, out of the blue, here comes SpeedFormat. What gives? We're guessing WordPerfect used *Quick* with every possible and conceivable word and was forced to move on to the prefix *Speed*. Besides, QuickFormat was already taken. (As discussed in Chapter 9, QuickFormat is a feature that allows you to quickly format text based on other text.)

After WordPerfect exhausts the *Speed* prefix, we'd like to humbly suggest new feature names for future versions of WordPerfect: ZippyFormat, TurboPoweredMenus, HyperVelocityBullets, AlacrityStyles, and ElFastoCorrectoMundo.

Dealing with incredibly complex spreadsheet-like tables

Spreadsheet-like tables don't have to be incredibly complex, but they certainly can get that way. Tables become like spreadsheet programs when they begin to calculate values automatically. To show you how this process occurs in WordPerfect, we focus on a simple example of summing rows and columns. For more complicated stuff, use Quattro Pro, which is included with your WordPerfect Office 12 CD.

First, however, you need to keep a couple of things in mind when creating a spreadsheet-like table:

- **Every cell in a table has a reference name that describes its row and column position.** Rows use single letters, beginning with *A* in the top row. Columns use numbers, beginning with *1* in the left column. The top-left cell, therefore, is A1, and so on. Users of Excel, Quattro Pro, and other spreadsheet programs should feel right at home.

- **Calculations are based on formulas that you enter (in a special, invisible way) in the cell in which you want the answer to appear.** To add cells A1 and B1 and put the answer in C1, for example, the formula A1+B1 must be specially stuffed into cell C1. We talk more about this subject in a minute.

Look at the simple budget shown in Figure 10-6, which has sums of columns.

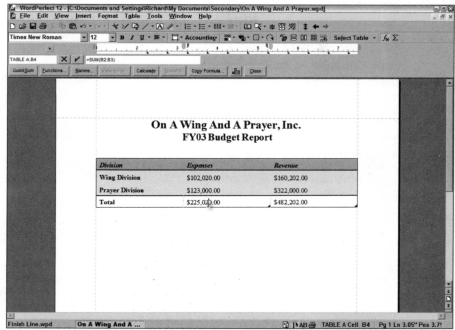

Figure 10-6:
A report
with a
complicated
table.

It's pretty hard to tell that formulas, not numbers, are entered in the total rows and in the far-right column. The only way to tell, in fact, is to turn on the Formula toolbar. To turn on the Formula toolbar, which enables you to enter or see formulas, click the Display Formula Toolbar button on the property bar (labeled in Figure 10-4), or choose Table➪Formula Toolbar. (Click the Formula toolbar's Close button to make the bar go away.)

The white box on the left side of the bar shows you which table WordPerfect thinks you're in (such as A, B, or C) and in which cell your cursor is located. In Figure 10-6, that location is Table A, cell C4 — the sum of the FY03 revenue.

The other white box shows you the formula in this cell: +SUM(C2:C3). The colon (:) means "through," so this formula means "Sum cells C2 through C3." (Does this look like a spreadsheet formula, or what?)

To create this formula, click the formula box and type the formula, or click the QuickSum button. If you type the formula, click the adjoining check-mark button to test the formula and insert it into the cell.

The QuickSum button is kind of magical. It inserts a formula for the sum of cells either above or to the left of the cell in which you're putting the formula. It also adds a little blue triangle to the bottom-right corner of the table cell, letting you know that the contents are a calculated value. QuickSum is pretty intelligent about doing this correctly, but sometimes it guesses incorrectly about what you want.

Try it. If the QuickSum button makes a wrong guess, you can always edit the formula in the formula box. Don't forget to click to add a check mark to the left of the formula box (refer to Figure 10-6) when you finish.

Values must already be in the cells for the QuickSum button to work. Put the values in first and then use the QuickSum button.

To get your numbers to look as pretty as ours do in Figure 10-6, with dollar signs and stuff, click in a cell that you want to format and then choose Table⇨ Numeric Format or press Alt+F12. The Properties for Table Numeric Format dialog box appears (catchy name, huh?). This dialog box enables you to format an individual cell, a column, or the entire table. Rather than fool with the details of how to format your numbers, WordPerfect has defined some number types, such as fixed (decimal-point numbers), scientific, currency, and accounting. Choose the number type you want and trust that WordPerfect will make your numbers look right.

If your numbers *don't* look right, you can always specify a different number type. In the Properties for Table Numeric Format dialog box, specify whether you want to format the cell that your cursor is in, the column, or the entire table. Click a selection in the Format for Numbers section (check out the example in the Preview section) and then click OK.

To perform multiplication and other simple calculations, such as computing the percentage change year to year, you can use these symbols in your formulas:

- ✔ * (Multiply)
- ✔ / (Divide)
- ✔ + (Add)
- ✔ – (Subtract)

You can access other formulas by clicking the Functions button in the Formula toolbar, but, hey — use QuattroPro if you're really serious about using formulas. This is all pretty heady stuff for a mere word-processing program.

Corralling Text in Text Boxes

Suppose that you're reading a serious article — in *People* magazine, for example — about a celebrity ("Tom Hanks: Movie Star or Alien from Outer Space?"). In the corner of the page, bordered in fuchsia, are two columns of text about some frivolous, annoying peripheral subject, such as "Tom Hanks and Cher: Separated at Birth?" Guess what? You, too, can make annoying sidebars such as this one in your document by using text boxes.

Actually, you should read this section if you're going to create *any* type of box in your WordPerfect documents. Plain old text boxes like the one we just described, some tables, pictures, even equations use this box stuff. So it's handy to know. All the boxes in WordPerfect work pretty much the same way. We'll use text boxes to introduce them.

To create a text box, choose Insert⇨Text Box or click the Text Box button on the toolbar (it's the one with the letter *A* inside a rectangle). Poof! A box appears in your document. (In the unlikely event that no box appeared, see the sidebar "It's not a drag to create boxes where you want them.") WordPerfect decides where to put the box and what it should look like. Your cursor is inside the box, so type away to your heart's content.

It's not a drag to create boxes where you want them

If you put a lot of boxes in your documents, you probably have opinions about where they should be. Rather than have WordPerfect just stuff them into your documents willy-nilly and then force you to move them around, WordPerfect is willing to take some direction as to where and how boxes should be created. You tell WordPerfect what to do by using WordPerfect settings.

We talk all about WordPerfect settings in Chapter 18. The quick preview goes like this: Choose Tools⇨Settings to display the Settings dialog box. This rather peculiar box just displays a bunch of tasteful icons with captions. Click the Environment icon. The Environment Settings dialog box appears.

Click the Graphics tab. In the upper-left corner of this dialog box is a check box labeled Drag to Create New Graphic Boxes. Make sure that this box is checked, click OK, and then click Close to get back to what you were doing. Now, instead of creating boxes for you where *it* pleases, WordPerfect will let you create the boxes pretty much wherever *you* please. When you choose Insert⇨Text Box (or click the *A* button on the toolbar), your mouse pointer changes to a hand holding a rectangle. When you click and drag this cursor diagonally, a dashed-line rectangle appears. This rectangle defines the location and size of your text box.

So is it better to work with Drag-to-Create or have WordPerfect create your graphics boxes for you? Your choice. We prefer the Drag-to-Create method (call us control freaks).

You can format this text using the Format commands, just as you would format any other text. You even can put text in columns. Don't try to use the Format commands to change the border of the text box, though; all you get are boxes within boxes. If the text box is the wrong length or width, don't worry about it now; just type the text. You can change the box dimensions when you're finished.

You may decide that the box has a few of problems. Perhaps it's not exactly where you want it. Or maybe you don't like its border. Never fear. You can change all that, too. Just read on.

Selecting your box

If you click *in* a box, WordPerfect obliges by thinking about the contents of your box. If you click *outside* the box, WordPerfect obliges by thinking about the text outside your box. You can select your box in three ways. Not all of these ways work all the time, so it's good to know all three of them:

- **Right-click the contents of your box:** *This is the most reliable way to select a box.* WordPerfect responds with a QuickMenu that contains a Select Box command. Click that command, and the box is yours.

- **Click the border of your box:** This tactic works if you can see the border of your box but WordPerfect's attention is elsewhere.

- **Click the contents of your box:** This works if the attention of WordPerfect is elsewhere and your box is not showing its eight handles. However, it doesn't work for text boxes. For text boxes, and for boxes WordPerfect is already thinking about, clicking the contents of the box makes Word-Perfect select the contents rather than the box itself.

Moving a box to more or less where you want it

Okay, you've typed a bunch of text in your box, and it's grown to suit. It's just not quite where you'd like it to be. No problem. Because this is the box you're typing in, it should have eight little square blocks around it, called *handles*. Click and hold the mouse button anywhere along the outside of the box *between* the handles. You'll know you're in the right place if your mouse cursor turns to a four-headed arrow. When you click and start to drag, that box moves anywhere you want it to.

Making a box more or less the right size

Resizing a box is just about as challenging as moving the box is. Find those eight handles around the outside of the box and drag one of them to resize the box. Once again, your cursor changes to tell you that you're in the right place. In this case, you get a two-headed arrow pointing either up and down (you can make the box taller or shorter), left and right (you can make the box wider or narrower), or diagonally (you can drag the corner of the box and change both its width and height at the same time). Go wild.

Changing everything else about a box

Usually, when you're working with the text inside the box, the property bar gives you information about type fonts and sizes and the like. But click the outline of the box (with its eight handles), and the property bar starts with the word *Graphics*. And it's a good thing it does, too, because there are about a million things you might want to do to your box.

Getting the property bar to display the *box* properties, as opposed to the properties of the text inside or outside the box, can be a little tricky. You must click the edge of the box itself. A telltale sign that you've done what you need to do is that the two- or four-headed arrow and the handles appear, and the box property bar (see Figure 10-7) appears as well.

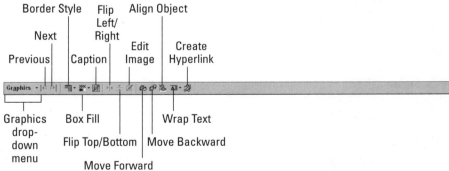

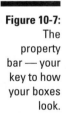

Figure 10-7: The property bar — your key to how your boxes look.

A few of these buttons are pretty simple:

✓ **Previous Box and Next Box:** Rather than having to find them and click them, these handy buttons, which appear on the far left side of the property bar, take you to all the other boxes in your document while your mind is on boxes. If either one of these buttons appears dimmed, it's because your document has no previous or next box.

✔ **Border Style:** Located just to the right of the Next Box button, this button gets you into the border formatting land we talk about in "Basic borders" at the beginning of this chapter.

✔ **Box Fill:** Right next to the Border Style button is Phil, the fill guy we talk about at the beginning of this chapter in "Phil . . . for all that white space behind your text."

The rest deserve a look in a little more detail.

The Graphics drop-down menu

What is this drop-down menu doing on the property bar? Normally, menus are on the menu bar. However, because a whole bunch of commands are meaningful only when you've selected a box (technically, a graphics box), WordPerfect displays this drop-down menu only when a graphics box is around to edit.

You can do only two things of major importance with this menu that you *can't* do anywhere else: set the exact position of your box and set the exact size of your box.

Moving a box exactly where you want it

Earlier in this chapter, we talk about dragging the border of the box (between the handles) to move it around. That may be fine if you don't care *exactly* where your box goes. But if you want to specify the gory details, the Box Position dialog box, (see Figure 10-8) is for you. To display this dialog box, choose Graphics⇨Position.

Figure 10-8:
The massively overcompli-cated Box Position dialog box comes in three flavors.

Because boxes aren't part of your text, WordPerfect needs to decide where they should go on the page and what should happen to them if the text on the page changes. This last point, what happens when the text changes, is why the Box Position dialog box has an Attach Box To setting. You can attach your boxes to a page, paragraph, or character.

Relative to a page

Boxes that are set relative to a page are fixed not to a specific page, but to a specific physical location on a page. Text can come and text can go, but the box always appears in the same place on the page. Ahh, but *which* page, you ask. It all depends on the amount of text you have in your document. Your box may appear on page 2 or on page 5, say, but regardless of the page number, the box appears at the same place on the page.

If you always want a box to appear on page 2 and only page 2 of your document (regardless of what other text is on that page), create the box on page 2. Choose Graphics➪Position to open the Box Position dialog box. After you select Page in the Attach Box To field, click Box Stays on Page option, in the lower-left corner of the dialog box. Now your box stays on page 2, regardless of how much text you insert before it or how much text you delete. In fact, if you delete all the text from page 2, you may end up with a page containing *only* the box you created. That's what you said you wanted, so that's what WordPerfect does.

You might think that specifying *where* your box is going to appear on the page would be straightforward, but this is WordPerfect. You have *many* options. To start with, you specify the horizontal and vertical position of the box. But relative to what? For the horizontal position, you can specify that you want your box placed relative to the edged of the paper, relative to the margins of your text, or relative to columns (if you have any on that page).

After you figure out what you're going to attach your box to, you figure out relative to where: the left or right margin or the center of the page? Or the left edge of the paper (in case the margins change)? The left column, the right column, or the center of the columns? Usually, you'll want to choose relative to the left or right margin. Choose relative to the left edge of the paper if your box is big enough that it might not fit between the margins. You may need to experiment until you find what you like.

Relative to a paragraph

Boxes attached to paragraphs move with the paragraph they're attached to. If you add text before the paragraph, your box moves down the page with the paragraph; if you remove text, your box moves up the page. Telling WordPerfect where your box should appear relative to a paragraph is simpler than telling it where a box should appear relative to a page. The horizontal options are pretty much the same. But for the vertical options, you can specify only where the box should appear relative to the paragraph. In most cases, you'll want your boxes to be relative to the paragraphs they're near.

Relative to characters

You can also attach boxes to characters. You can think of a box like this as being a special character that you can draw by yourself. If you actually want to draw it, look at Chapter 11. But if you just want some text to move around in your document as if it were a character, you're in the right place. Of course, you have a dizzying array of options for locating your box. Luckily, the Box Position dialog box does a nice job of illustrating the options. Our guess is that you'll want to use the Content Baseline option, even though that's the scariest sounding. It just means that the bottom of what's in the box should line up with the bottom of the text on the line.

Making a box exactly the right size

As you might imagine, if dragging isn't good enough for determining exactly where your box should go, it's probably not good enough for determining how big your box should be either. So, to complement the Box Position dialog box, WordPerfect has the not-quite-so-massively-overcomplicated Box Size dialog box, as shown in Figure 10-9. To get to the Box Size dialog box, choose Graphics⇨Size. In this dialog box, you can enter an exact height and width for your box. This feature is useful because it gives you the option of maintaining the proportions of your box. When you drag the corners of your box around, you can stretch the box like Silly Putty, an approach that works better for some boxes than for others.

Figure 10-9:
Size your box just the way you want it.

If you want to keep the original height-to-width proportions of your box, resize it by using the Box Size dialog box and then click the Maintain Proportions option. If you click Maintain Proportions in the Height area, you can change the width, and WordPerfect adjusts the height automagically. If you click Maintain Proportions in the Width area, you can probably guess what happens.

If you want your box to run the full width of the page, click Full in the Width area. If you want your box to run the full height of the page (perhaps you want a tasteful stripe up the page), click Full in the Height area.

Don't click Full for both height and width.

Adding captions to your boxes

It's virtually impossible to use regular document text to put a caption where you want it, such as below a box. You have to use the special Caption feature. When you click the Caption button on the graphics property bar (labeled in Figure 10-7), WordPerfect creates a little typing space below your box and suggests a caption. If you don't like WordPerfect's suggestion, press the Backspace key to delete WordPerfect's suggested caption (*Figure 1,* or whatever). Alternatively, you can add your caption to the beginning and end of WordPerfect's suggestion.

As you type your caption, you can use any of the usual Format commands and buttons, adding bold or changing type size at will. When a caption already exists, the Caption button takes you to the caption text so you can edit it. You also can click the caption text to edit it, too.

You can delete a caption, but you wouldn't know it by looking around Word-Perfect. To do so you need to have the box selected and the Graphics menu displayed (refer to Figure 10-6). Choose Graphics⇨Caption to display a dialog box that has more options about captions (and captions about options) than a reasonable person wants. Ignore them all and click Reset. WordPerfect warns you that you are (gasp!) about to delete your caption. If you click OK, Word-Perfect provides absolutely no indication that you have deleted your caption, but rest assured that your caption is gone, gone, gone!

When all is said and done, we think captions are great, although it may take you a little time to get them set up exactly the way you want them. Captions help people find their way around your document, and they look pretty classy.

Text wrapping

Text wrapping is kind of like gift wrapping, with a twist (or is that a bow?). When you have a box on a page, you have to decide what WordPerfect should do with the text of your document when it gets to the box. Figure 10-10 shows you the Wrap Text drop-down list that you get when you click the Wrap button on the property bar (labeled in Figure 10-7).

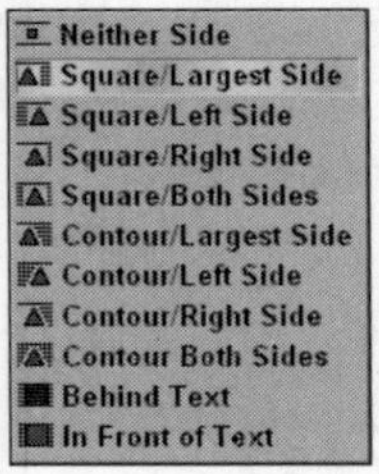

Figure 10-10:
Text
wrapping
your box in
time for the
holidays.

Neither Side
Square/Largest Side
Square/Left Side
Square/Right Side
Square/Both Sides
Contour/Largest Side
Contour/Left Side
Contour/Right Side
Contour Both Sides
Behind Text
In Front of Text

Although several text-wrapping options are available, they can be broken into three basic categories:

✓ **Neither Side:** Jump over the entire box, leaving white space to the right and left of the box. That's what we've done with the figures in this book.

✓ **Square:** If your box isn't exactly in the middle of the page, the space on one side will be smaller than the space on the other side (at last, a use for high-school geometry!). WordPerfect will be perfectly happy to figure out which side is smaller, leave the smaller side blank, and run the text down the wider side of the page. In fact, that's what WordPerfect does unless you tell it otherwise, and it's not a bad choice.

✓ **Contour:** Run the text around the box, assuming that the reader's eye will just skip over the box. This is usually not a good idea unless your box is rather small. Otherwise people get confused and don't know whether to read down one side of your box and then down the other, or across the page, skipping the box.

The Text Wrap button on the property bar makes it easy to select what kind of wrapping you want. In case you've forgotten, the only way to see the property bar for the box itself, instead of for the contents of the box, is to click the outline of the box; you should see those eight square handles around the edge of your box (see "Changing everything else about a box," earlier in this chapter).

When you click the Text Wrap button, you get a list with the options we just described, and a few additions. Don't worry about contours just yet; we talk about them in Chapter 11 when we talk about pictures. You can also have your box block out the text that it's sitting on top of (that's the In Front of Text option), or have the text march right over your box (Behind Text).

You also can tell WordPerfect how you want it to do text wrapping by right-clicking your box. Click the Wrap command, and you'll see the Wrap Text dialog box, which illustrates the text-wrapping options.

Drawing Lines and Arrows in Your Document

In the ceaseless quest to make documents on computer screens look more and more like documents on paper, word processors feel compelled to let you scribble on your document, just like you might with a pen or pencil. Actually, this capability can be useful if you want to emphasize something or draw a visual connection between elements of your document. WordPerfect is uncommonly accomplished in this area. You can easily draw horizontal and vertical lines in your document, and, with a little more effort, draw lines and shapes anywhere you want to.

To draw a horizontal line, press Enter to make a new paragraph, place your cursor there, and choose Insert⇨Lines⇨Horizontal Line or press Ctrl+F11. For a vertical line through most of your page, choose Insert⇨Lines⇨Vertical Line or press Ctrl+Shift+F11.

You can change the length of the horizontal or vertical line and change its location by editing it. *Very slowly* pass your mouse cursor over the line you just inserted. At some point the cursor should turn into a right arrow. That's your cue to right-click. On the QuickMenu, you see the choice Edit Horizontal Line (or Edit Vertical Line). If you're tired of your line, you can also delete it from this menu.

WordPerfect has a more useful kind of line it calls a draw line. You can decide not only where a draw line should begin and end but also a lot more about what it should look like than boring old horizontal and vertical lines.

Add draw lines to your document by choosing Insert⇨Shapes⇨Lines. Your cursor turns into a set of crosshairs. Click *and hold down* the mouse button where you want one end of the line to be and then drag the line to where you want the other end to be.

Your line is actually in a box, so all the things we mention earlier about text boxes apply. The reason you can see the text behind your line is that the text wrapping for the box is set to In Front of Text.

Again, the property bar has mutated to include some new buttons that you haven't seen before (see Figure 10-11). A couple of these are worth pointing out; we encourage you to explore the rest.

Figure 10-11:
The
property
bar and
the secret
of arrows.

To transform your plain old line into a pointed arrow, click one of the property bar's Arrowhead buttons (the fourth and fifth buttons from the right). From the Arrowhead lists, choose a point for the front of the arrow and a tail for the end of the arrow. Or use two pointy ends. Sometimes it takes a little doing to figure out which end gets which arrow, but you can change them as often as you want.

Chapter 11

Saying It with Pictures

*U*ndoubtedly, Michelangelo had fewer tools for painting the Sistine Chapel than WordPerfect provides for creating and working with graphics. We have yet to rise to Michelangelo's level and create artistic masterpieces inside our documents, but our falling short isn't WordPerfect's fault. No, we have to admit that we're, shall we say, artistically challenged (in other words, we stink!). Even though we're much better writers than artists, WordPerfect does give us enough artsy tools for spicing up our bland documents with graphics.

In this chapter, you explore how to insert a picture, a diagram, or a chart that you got from the Web, WordPerfect, or somewhere else. You also discover how to create a simple picture or chart right inside WordPerfect. Who knows, maybe in the process, you'll discover you have a knack for this art stuff. Carry on, Michelangelo!

Working with Graphics

A few basics before we jump in here:

- ✔ **All pictures live in boxes.** We talk a lot about boxes in Chapter 10.

- ✔ **All boxes have borders and backgrounds.** That's why we talk about them in Chapter 10, in the first section.

✔ **You can select boxes and the pictures that are in them in two ways.** If you're typing along in your text and you click a box, you get black handles and no border around your box (unless your box itself has one). This means that the box itself is selected. Pull on one of the handles, and the box changes size and shape. The contents are stretched like Silly Putty to fit the new shape of the box. See Figure 11-1 to see a stretched picture. (If you stretch an image by accident, click some text in your document. Then you can use Edit⇨Undo to restore the picture to its previous state.)

If you're typing along in your text and you *double-click* a box, you get the same black handles, but you also get a dotted-line border (whether or not your box itself has a border). Drag the handles to change the size of the box without affecting the contents of your box. Figure 11-2 shows the dotted-line border and what appears when you drag one of the handles. In this case, we've made the box narrower and chopped off part of its contents, but we could just as easily have made the box bigger to make room for more contents.

Figure 11-1:
S-t-r-e-t-c-h-i-n-g a picture.

Figure 11-2:
By dragging
the left
handle, we
cropped the
image.

Inserting some of Corel's clipart into your document

Here's the simplest way to insert a graphic into your document. We'll insert into the document one of the clipart images that Corel includes with Word-Perfect. Proceed as follows:

1. **Choose Insert⇨Graphics⇨Clipart.**

   Or click the Clipart button on the toolbar.

2. **Scroll down through the Scrapbook until you see an image you like.**

   The image we've chosen is the bear face a few clicks down the list.

3. **Select the image and click the Insert button.**

   Alternatively, you can drag the image from the Scrapbook window into your document. You might want to move the Scrapbook off to the side of the document by clicking and dragging the Scrapbook window's title bar (that bar, the one that says Scrapbook, appears just above all the images) until you can see the place where you want your image inserted.

4. **Get rid of the Scrapbook by clicking the Close or Minimize button.**

Your cursor now merrily blinks at just the point where you left it, and your graphic should appear in your document. Overall, not too difficult. Figure 11-3 illustrates our copy of a cowboy and an accountant shaking hands. (We're wondering how many people find this particular piece of clipart useful.)

This graphic is in a box. To move the graphic, click the edge of the box and drag it around. To change the graphic's size, select it and then click the corners and drag them around. To add a border to the graphic, select it and then click the Border Style button on the property bar. These mysteries and more are described in loving detail in Chapter 10.

If dragging and dropping images from the Scrapbook into your document doesn't work for you, click the image you want in the Scrapbook and then click the Insert button. This method has the added advantage of removing the Scrapbook from your screen when you click the Insert button.

Keep in mind that the proportions you see on-screen may not match the ones you'll see when you print. Print a test of your document to check it before you print 20 copies for the next company meeting.

You can also size the image to exact dimensions by right-clicking the image and choosing Size from the Image QuickMenu that pops up.

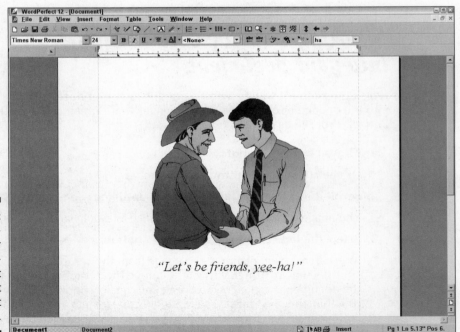

Figure 11-3:
The ever-popular Cowboy-Accountant Summit clipart picture.

"Let's be friends, yee-ha!"

How to see where you're going

To make it easier to see where you're positioning an image, zoom out to Full Page view before you begin positioning or sizing your image. Click the Zoom button on the toolbar — the button with the magnifying glass icon — and select Full Page from the drop-down list.

When you finish positioning and sizing the image, click the magnifying glass button again. Make your Zoom selection from the choices in the list to return to editing your document.

Selecting clipart from the Internet

If you don't see a picture you like under the Clipart tab in the Scrapbook dialog box, click the Internet button in that same dialog box. If you're online, you'll be connected to the WordPerfect Office Web site at www.corel.com, where you can choose from a boatload of additional photos, clipart, and more.

This Web page has some handy instructions that tell you how to proceed. Basically, you save the Scrapbook file that's on the Internet to a folder on your local hard drive. Then, when you're back in WordPerfect, you click the Import Clips button in the Scrapbook dialog box and select that file in the Insert File dialog box.

Inserting a picture from somewhere else into your document

Whew! Well, if the clipart that comes with WordPerfect and the graphics available on the WordPerfect Office Web site don't work for you, you can always use one taken with a digital camera, scan one with a scanner, download one from the Web, or even borrow a picture from a friend or co-worker. WordPerfect is happy to insert just about any ol' image file into your document. Here's how — we skip the steps where you beg and grovel to get the other person to share the picture:

1. **Make sure that the graphics file is on a disk in your PC (or on your network).**

   You'll need to remember where you saved the file, such as your My Pictures folder; otherwise, you'll have to search for the file on your disk.

2. **Choose Insert➪Graphics➪From File.**

   The Insert Image dialog box appears.

3. **Double-click the filename, or click the filename and click Insert to insert the picture into your document.**

You may have to dig down through some folders to get to the graphics files.

If you need to get a preview of the picture, click the View button on the toolbar and then choose the Thumbnails option. (Yes, the Insert Image dialog box has a Preview feature, but it's pretty useless because it doesn't support most graphic types, such as JPG or BMP. Use the Thumbnails preview instead.)

The rules for clipart apply also for a graphics file you insert: It's a box, it can have borders, and you can move it and resize it just like any other box. To resize a box, double-click the image until you get the dotted-line border (refer to Figure 11-2); otherwise, WordPerfect will be happy to stretch your picture for you when you drag the handles, and that usually looks odd.

Creating Your Own Graphics

If you couldn't find any art that suits your document, or if you found some but decided that it needs a little touch-up, WordPerfect is all set for you. It contains a set of drawing tools that will let you do the basics and then waste days refining every single dot on your screen or on your paper. So what if you're not Norman Rockwell — with WordPerfect, you can still create your own home-style graphics and have them look . . . well, okay. Hey, at least it's easy to stay inside the lines.

When you create a WordPerfect document, you type text into WordPerfect. Simple enough. When you create a text box, you add something that is non-text to your document: a box. What's inside the box is more text. In Chapter 10, we talk about things you can do to these boxes. Because the boxes contain text, you can do all sorts of text-ish things to the text in them — the kinds of things we're talking about all through this book.

But the box may contain a picture, and just as a document is made of text, a picture is made of *objects*. Here's a quick run-down of what a picture can contain:

✔ **Dots:** A dot of color in your picture. Usually, dots come in groups, and together they're trying to be a picture of something. Pictures made entirely of dots are called *bitmaps*. You can insert a bitmap into your drawing from a file or from a scanner, but you don't draw one.

✔ **Lines:** A line or curve from one point to another. Nothing too special here. You can draw as many lines as you want in your picture. Straight lines are the simplest, but WordPerfect also knows about curved lines.

✔ **Enclosed shapes:** Three or more lines (or a curve) that enclose some space. These shapes automatically close themselves, so if you're drawing a box, for example, you don't have to manage to click precisely back on the starting point when you finish the fourth side. The space inside the enclosed shapes can be filled with a solid color or two-color pattern called a *fill*.

✔ **Text:** You know all about text by now; we've been talking about it for more than a hundred pages. Each individual letter or other character inside a WordPerfect graphic, however, has two parts: the thin line around the outside and the space inside it.

Fine, you say, but you don't want dots and lines and shapes in your document. You want, for example, a map with some notes on it. Never fear! Out of these four ingredients you can create anything! Sort of like geometry meets physics. Let's get familiar with the building blocks.

Drawing a line in a document

Drawing in WordPerfect documents is kind of like playing with those famous Russian lacquered dolls that nest inside one another. Inside your document you put a box, and inside the box, you put a line. To start simply, open a document, blank or otherwise, and put a box and a line in it:

1. **Choose Insert⇨Graphics⇨Draw Picture to insert a drawing box into your document.**

   You see a drawing box appear on the screen, with the WordPerfect drawing tools listed on the left side of the window. That's your cue that you've entered the world of drawing.

2. **Select the Line Drawing tool.**

   To do so, click the down arrow beside the Line Shapes button on the Drawing toolbar and then click the first button in the list.

3. **Click and drag across your drawing box.**

   You end up with a line inside your drawing box.

Being careful where you click

Now that you have a line inside a box along with some text in your document, you must be careful where and when you click something. You can click in four, count 'em, four *kinds* of places in your document: the text, the box, the *inside* of the box, or some *object* inside the box. The main things that change are the property bar and the kind of handles (see Chapter 10) that appear on your screen. Figures 11-4 through 11-7 illustrate all four different kinds of places.

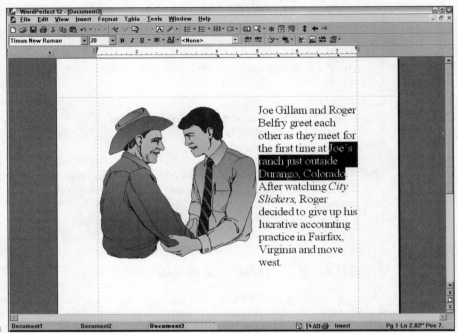

Figure 11-4:
Selecting
text in
Word-
Perfect.

Figure 11-5:
Drag the
handles to
stretch the
drawing.

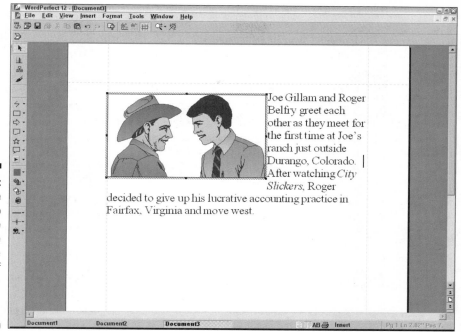

Figure 11-6:
Drag the handles to change the size of the box and the amount of the picture displayed in the box.

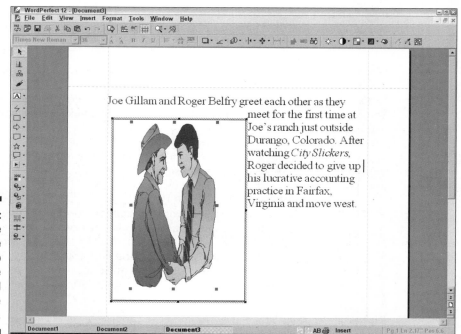

Figure 11-7:
Move the inside handles to change the size and shape of the object.

Because clicking is now somewhat confusing, here's how to select each one:

- **To select text in your document:** Click anywhere in the text. If something inside the box is selected, you may have to click twice.

- **To select a box:** If text outside the box is currently selected, click anywhere on the box. If something inside the box is currently selected, click outside the object.

- **To select the drawing:** Double-click inside the box, but not on any object inside the box. If an object is selected, you can click any place where the cursor changes to a black left arrow.

- **To select an object in the drawing:** Click the object.

So now you know how to get into and out of drawings in WordPerfect. In the following sections, we assume that you've selected the drawing you're interested in and that you may or may not have selected an object within the drawing.

Whipping shapes into your drawings

WordPerfect has far too many built-in shapes for us to describe each one in detail. We do, however, list the categories of shapes and offer some notes on how to draw each one. At the end of this section, we talk about things that are common to all the shapes. After you've selected your drawing, you can insert shapes in your drawing by choosing Insert➪Shapes and then selecting the category and the shape you want. (Alternatively, you can use the Drawing toolbar to select the category and shape of your choice.)

WordPerfect has so many shapes to choose from that the shapes are grouped into categories. The categories also have selections on the toolbar. The pictures in the margin show you which shape in the category is currently active. You can select the other shapes in the category by clicking the little down arrow to the right of the button.

We're assuming from here on that you've already selected the drawing by double-clicking it. With the drawing selected, choose from any of the following categories of shapes:

- **Line shapes:** Click and drag in your drawing to create the type of line you see on the button. Depending on the shape you choose, you may have to double-click to stop drawing. Those who can draw with a mouse might find the Freehand shape (the button with the pencil on it) particularly useful. Those of us who couldn't draw if our lives depended on it should probably stick to straight lines and preformed shapes, such as squares and rectangles.

- **Basic shapes:** This category includes squares, cubes, and ovals. Choose the shape you want, and drag the crosshairs until the shape is the size you want. If you didn't get it right the first time, click the shape and drag the handles.

✔ **Arrow shapes:** You have more arrows than Robin Hood ever knew existed. Select one, then click-and-drag in your drawing. Watch your arrow grow as you move the cursor in your drawing.

✔ **Flowchart shapes:** For those who can't resist diagramming data flow, this category gives you a selection of the most frequently used flow-charting symbols. Map your input, output, databases, and files to your heart's content. Click the symbol you want, and drag across the space you want it to cover.

✔ **Star shapes:** Click the down arrow on the button, select the shape you want, and drag it to size in the drawing. Some of these stars look like banners you can use to dress up your document.

✔ **Callout shapes:** You know those billowy circles that appear above char-acters' heads in cartoons? This is how you make them! Click one of the callout shapes and drag it around until you get the size and shape you want in your drawing. The direction you drag determines which direc-tion the pointer on the callout goes.

✔ **Action shapes:** These are actually buttons you can put in your docu-ment to highlight paragraphs or add pizzazz to boring pages of text. For example, the question mark button is a dandy way to spotlight Help paragraphs in your text.

After you finish drawing any one of these shapes, it's surrounded by handles. By pulling on the handles, you can reshape the object. More importantly, you can *right-click* the object and see a QuickMenu directly related to the object. Our two favorite QuickMenu choices are Edit Points (it enables you to change any start or end point you used to draw the shape) and Object Properties (it displays a dialog box full of things about your shape). Figure 11-8 shows you the Object Properties dialog box. Its Fill, Line, and Shadow tabs are very much like the border and fill settings we look at in Chapter 10.

Figure 11-8:
Setting the
fill, line, and
shadow for
something
you drew
in your
drawing.
You can
even fill with
dinosaurs!

All graphics aren't the same

You can work with two major types of graphics in WordPerfect: bitmaps and vector graphics. It's helpful to understand their differences when you try and resize or edit them.

✔ **Bitmap graphics:** A bitmap graphic is a pattern of colored dots (called *pixels*) that combine to form a picture. A photograph you've scanned into your computer and that scenic wallpaper on your Windows desktop are examples of bitmaps. If you zoomed in on a bitmap graphic with the right software, you'd see that the image is composed of countless, individually colored dots that form a mosaic.

Bitmap graphics are used for photos and other images that need sharp definition or rich colors. The disadvantage to bitmap graphics is that you lose quality the moment you resize them. When you shrink a picture, the quality loss is usually not too noticeable. But when you enlarge a bitmap out of proportion, the picture quality can be conspicuously degraded.

Bitmaps are the most popular type of graphic used on Web pages and in Windows and will often be the graphic type you'll get from the Web or another person. However, when printing a bitmapped image in your

WordPerfect document to a printer, the edges of the images can be ragged, so make sure you test the image before using it.

Popular bitmap file types are GIF, JPG, and BMP.

✔ **Vector graphics:** Vector graphics are made up of a bunch of lines and curves (called, appropriately enough, *vectors*) that together form the shape of the picture. Unlike bitmaps, these lines and curves can be shrunk or stretched as much as you want without losing any quality because the graphic is generated by mathematical calculations rather than using pixels. However, vector graphics never look as realistic or have the detail that bitmaps do.

Popular vector file types are WPG and WMF.

In WordPerfect, clipart, TextArt, and the shapes you create while drawing are vector graphics. Photos you insert from the Scrapbook are bitmaps.

If you are having trouble understanding the differences between the two, think of bitmaps as being photorealistic images and think of vector graphics as more like sketches or drawings.

Putting text in your drawings

WordPerfect is, after all, all about words. So it shouldn't be too surprising that you can type right in your drawing. WordPerfect helps you put four kinds of text objects into your drawing: a line of text, a box full of text, a bulleted list, or some TextArt. (There's so much to TextArt that it gets its own section, right after this one.)

Text in a drawing behaves a little differently than text in a text box. The main difference is that you can change the size of text in a drawing by dragging on the handles that surround it (after you've put it in your drawing). Instead of being defined by point sizes (see Chapter 6), the text can grow and shrink with infinite variability. You can add two types of text to your drawings:

- **Text line:** A line of text is just that. With your drawing selected, choose Insert➪Text Line and click someplace in your drawing. Whatever you type stays on one line. If the line is too wide for the drawing, it gets chopped off instead of wrapping to a second line.

- **Text boxes:** Text boxes in pictures act very much like text boxes in text. With your drawing selected, choose Insert➪Text Box to create one. When you do, you see that the cursor turns into a little hand holding a box. As you click and drag, you are determining how wide your text box will be (don't worry, you can change the box's width later). When you release the mouse button, you can type in your box. Many of the buttons on the property bar should look familiar now. You can do most of the same things to text in your box that you can do to text in the rest of your document. As you get to the edge of the box you drew, WordPerfect wraps the text around to the next line, and the box gets taller.

TextArt?! Text by Artists

Ever see that painting by Salvador Dali, with the clocks melting all over the landscape? Well, TextArt enables you to do that to your text. Sound like fun? Actually, it can be kind of nice to add an accent to a graphic or a document.

TextArt can go in its own box directly in your document or in a box inside a drawing box. In either case, all the same box-ish things, such as borders and fill, apply. Unlike most other places in WordPerfect, where you type your text directly into the document, in TextArt you get a dialog box, like the one shown in Figure 11-9.

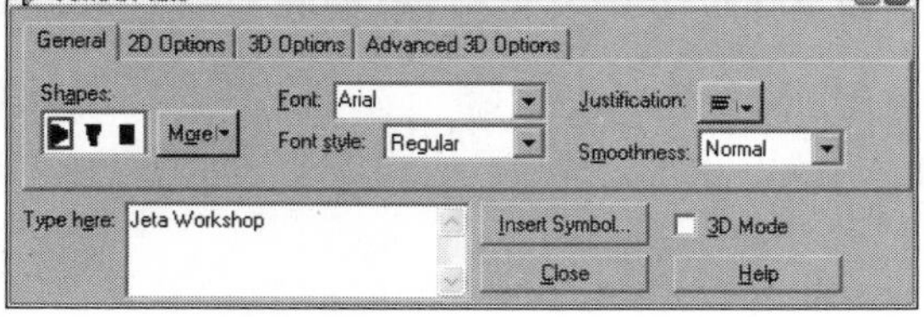

Figure 11-9:
Being artsy
in the
TextArt
dialog box.

To create TextArt, follow these steps:

1. **Move your cursor to the place where you want to insert TextArt.**

   As with all WordPerfect boxes, you can move it later.

2. **Choose Insert⇨Graphics⇨TextArt.**

   The TextArt dialog box appears.

3. **Decide what you want your TextArt to say, and type it in the Type Here box.**

   If text was highlighted when you choose Insert⇨Graphics⇨TextArt, that text appears in the Type Here box.

   Short phrases are better than long sentences; single letters don't show TextArt effects well.

4. **Now, the fun part — click the More button.**

   You see a bunch of black blobs of different shapes. Each of those shapes tries to describe the shape your text will take if you select it. The only way you can really tell what each shape will look like is to try it. You'll soon develop a short list of favorite shapes.

5. **Get into the particulars of how your TextArt looks.**

   You may find that TextArt has chosen some peculiar colors for your text. Click the 2D Options tab, and you can begin to straighten this out. (Make sure the 3D Mode check box is *not* checked. After you understand the 2D options, most of the 3D options will make sense.)

   You can use up to four colors to draw your 2-D TextArt:

   - **Text color:** This is the simplest color. It's the one that your letters are drawn in.

   - **Outline color:** Because so many TextArt effects can make it difficult to see the edge of your letters, TextArt outlines your letters after drawing them. This is the color it uses for the outline. Just to make things confusing, you can also change the text color when you click this button.

   - **Shadow:** You specify the direction in which the shadows will fall from your letters and the color of the shadows.

   - **Pattern:** You can draw a pattern on the face of your letters, inside the outline. After clicking this button, you can specify the pattern and the color.

6. **Click Close to finished editing your TextArt.**

   Figure 11-10 shows you an example of some simple TextArt.

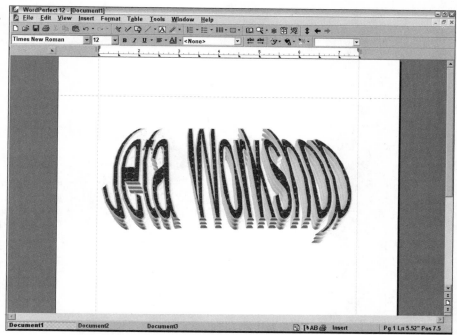

Figure 11-10:
Some
TextArt
formatted
with a cool
effect.

Using Graphs and Charts

Using the graph/chart tool, you can create a variety of data charts, such as pie charts, bar graphs, and line graphs. To create a chart in your document, choose Insert⇨Chart. A chart obligingly appears in a box in your document, and a separate window, called the *datasheet,* gets splatted across the top of your document (see Figure 11-11).

The datasheet is a sort of spreadsheet or table where you put the data that you want to chart. WordPerfect draws the chart automatically from the data.

When you use the WordPerfect charting feature, the menu bar, toolbar, and property bar change appearance to offer you chart-specific options. To exit the charting feature and return to the text of your document, just click anywhere in the text. The menu bar, toolbar, and property bar return to normal. To return to the charting feature, double-click the chart.

WordPerfect gives you a bar chart example to begin. You can easily change to another kind of chart and then substitute your own data for the example data.

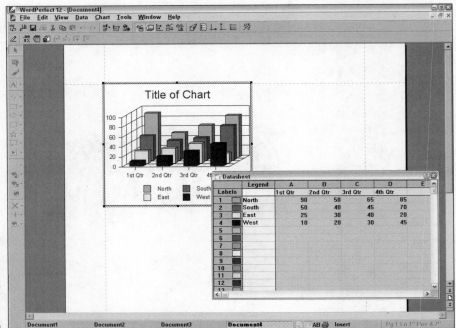

Figure 11-11:
Creating a
data chart
in Word-
Perfect.

You can find out a lot about how WordPerfect charts data by examining the datasheet and the chart. Notice that Labels (the top row of the datasheet) places labels along the horizontal axis in the chart. Also notice that each row of data in the datasheet has its own color, which matches the color of the data in the chart. Observe that the words in the Legend column (the leftmost column in the datasheet) appear in the Legend box in the chart.

To make the sample chart into *your* chart, follow these steps:

1. **Change the chart to the type that you want.**

   Click the toolbar button with the tiny pictures of the bar chart, pie chart, and line graph on it. Alternatively, you can choose Chart⇨Gallery. In either case, click a chart type in the menu that drops down.

2. **Delete the sample data.**

   Click the title bar of the datasheet window (which says *Datasheet*). Each little rectangle in the datasheet that contains a word or number is a *cell*. Delete the values in individual cells by clicking them, pressing the Delete key, and clicking OK in the Clear dialog box that appears.

To delete a rectangular group of cells, click the cell in the top-left corner of the data to be deleted. Then hold down the mouse button, drag the mouse to extend the highlight to the bottom-right corner of the data, and release the mouse button. Press the Delete key on your keyboard. Click OK again in the Clear dialog box.

3. **Click individual cells and type your own data, legends, and labels.**

   Expand the datasheet window, if you need to, by clicking and dragging its edges.

4. **To put your own title on the chart, double-click the title (which initially reads *Title of Chart*).**

   In the Title Properties dialog box that appears, click in the text box that contains the words *Title of Chart,* change the text there, and then press Enter.

The toolbar, property bar, and menu bar have selections that enable you to change the chart type (to, say, a line chart or a pie chart), the style (3-D versus 2-D, for example), and other appearances. As always, if you position your mouse pointer on any button, WordPerfect displays the button's name and description. If you want to change the way something looks in the graph, the first thing that you can try is to double-click it. This works particularly well for things such as the *axis lines* (the horizontal and vertical lines that label the numbers in the graph). You get a dialog box with about a million options that allow you to control every aspect of the axis. Happy exploring!

There are more straightforward ways of changing one thing or another in the graph, in case you don't want to wrestle with each and every option. Try these:

- **Change the chart type:** Click the property bar button that says Data Chart Gallery if you pause with the mouse pointer over it. As you pause over the many different chart types, WordPerfect gives you a preview of what your chart would look like if you clicked here. When you see one you like, click it.

- **Change from 3-D to 2-D:** Click the button on the toolbar that has a cube icon on it. (This is the 3-D Chart button.)

- **Change the line color and style, fill color and pattern, text color, or legend box appearance:** Double-click the line, bar, or text. Dialog boxes with many tabs and settings appear. Do some more exploring — remember, you can always click the Cancel button or choose Undo if you change your mind.

- **Change the font:** First click the text. Then the Font Selection button (initially labeled Arial) on the property bar to choose a font. Click the Font Sizes button to choose a size. Click the **B**, *I*, or U button on the toolbar to choose a style.

✔ **Change the axis range and intervals:** Choose Chart⇨Axis⇨X or Chart⇨ Axis⇨Primary Y to display the Axis Properties dialog box for the X or Y axis, respectively. Double-clicking the axis line you're interested in also shows you the appropriate dialog box full of options.

In general, you can change something in a chart by right-clicking it. Word-Perfect then presents a menu enabling you to see any one of a number of dialog boxes with settings controlling whatever it was you just right-clicked.

As with all boxes in WordPerfect, you can change the size of your chart by dragging the black handles while the chart is active (that is, while it has the hashed black-and-white stripe around it). WordPerfect redraws your chart in the amount of space that you gave it.

Chapter 12

Working with Templates and OfficeReady

Free Inside. As children, those words were precious indeed when we saw them on the cover of a cereal box. They promised the excitement of a new toy to be found at the bottom of the cereal contents. Rarely did those freebie toys live up to their appeal on the box cover, but that didn't dissuade us much: We always looked forward to the next visit to the grocery store.

The WordPerfect Office box may not have a *Free Inside* sticker on it, but it does have a lot of hidden goodies, called templates, that will make your life easier when creating many popular types of documents. In this chapter, we talk about what a template is and how to use one to create crowd-pleasing documents. And best of all, you don't need to pour all the cereal out of the box to get to it!

What Are Templates?

Templates are prototypes for different types of documents. Templates are sort of like blank forms. They don't necessarily contain text, though. A template might contain only a collection of the particular fonts and format styles for a particular type of document, or it might contain all the text of, say, your boilerplate contract.

Whenever you create a document, WordPerfect uses a template. The blank document that you see when you start WordPerfect is based on a template called `wp12us.wpt`. If you create a document by clicking the New Blank Document button on the toolbar (the one that looks like a blank page with the corner turned down) or by pressing Ctrl+N, WordPerfect again uses that standard template. If you start a new document by choosing File⇨New from Project, however, WordPerfect explicitly asks you what kind of template to use.

If you don't care for any of the several dozen WordPerfect templates, you can create your own. For example, you may want a template for letters that specifies the use of 10-point Times Roman font. A template for product announcements might use 14-point Helvetica for titles and 12-point type for other text. A template for a newsletter, however, might contain title text, a graphical logo, and three-column formatting, in addition to specified fonts.

For most practical purposes, though, you can't do much more with a template than you can do by creating an ordinary document as a prototype, reusing it when you want to write a similar document (by opening it and changing the text), and being careful to use File⇨Save As to save your new documents with new names. The care and feeding of templates has become convoluted as WordPerfect has evolved, and templates are now all tied up with projects and experts. In fact, unless you're going to use a document type over and over, you may be better off sticking with this save-the-prototype-document-file method.

Using Templates

When you talk about using templates in WordPerfect, it's a lot like talking about breathing air; you don't have much choice in the matter. All documents use templates.

As we mention earlier in this chapter, you use something called the *standard template* every time you create a new document. There's not much in the standard template — at least, not much as it comes out of the box from Word-Perfect (you can change it, though). Mostly, the standard template contains the initial paragraph, character, and page formatting that WordPerfect uses for your documents. If you're having to change your fonts and other formatting every time you create a new document, you probably should edit the standard template.

Here's how to use a template other than the standard one:

1. **Choose File➪New from Project.**

   You see the PerfectExpert dialog box, as shown in Figure 12-1. Word-Perfect has so many templates that they're divided into categories.

Figure 12-1:
Choose the kind of document you want to create.

2. **In the pull-down list at the top of the dialog box, click a template category.**

   We recommend that you stick with WordPerfect's standard list. So if `WordPerfect` doesn't show up in this box, click the down arrow and scroll up and down the list until you find it. It's usually close to the top.

3. **In the list of templates just below the pull-down list, click the template that you want to use.**

   Each template has a brief description at the bottom of the dialog box.

4. **Click the Create button.**

   Some templates kick off a PerfectExpert to guide you through creating a document. If nothing appears to happen when you click Create, that's probably what's going on. Arousing and invoking Experts takes some time. Look in the section called "Getting WordPerfect to write your letter for you" for a description of how to get along with PerfectExpert.

   Some of the templates contain PerfectScript macros to provide an added level of customization. Because macros can sometimes be used to spread viruses, WordPerfect warns you before you create the new document. In fact, based on dire warnings in the message box, you may think it's crazy not to disable the macros before continuing. However, if you know that the template came from WordPerfect and is not something you or some-one added, you should feel comfortable clicking the No button (to not disable the macros). If you decide to disable the macros, automated tasks that the template would normally do probably won't operate correctly.

Creating Your Own Templates

In addition to using prebuilt templates, you can create your own. Perhaps they won't be as fancy as the WordPerfect ones, with dialog boxes and Perfect-Experts and stuff, but they can end up pretty fancy and customized for your needs. In this section, we talk about the two ways to make a template.

Creating a normal template

To create a regular template, follow these instructions:

1. **Choose File⇨New from Project.**

2. **Click the Options button in the PerfectExpert dialog box.**

3. **Choose the Create WP Template item in the list.**

   A template is created that will look just like a document. If you have a prototype document that you've already created, you can include it in your document by choosing Insert⇨File.

4. **Customize the template.**

   Consider the following ways to set up your template:

   • Add or modify styles in the template, so that any documents you create from the template have those same style settings. See Chapter 9 for more on styles.

   • Set up headers or footers, margins, or any custom page layout setting. See Chapter 8 for more on page-level settings.

   • Add boilerplate text or graphics, such as a letterhead or a signature line, that will appear in each document you create based on the template.

5. **Choose File⇨Save.**

6. **Type a description and name for your template and select a category.**

   The Template name is the name your template will have on disk. The Template category is where your template will live in the PerfectExpert dialog box's template groupings; those are the names in the drop-down list at the top of the PerfectExpert dialog box.

7. **Click OK to save the template.**

Editing templates works the same way: Select the template, but instead of clicking Create WP Template in the PerfectExpert dialog box (Step 3), click Options and select Edit WP Template. Edit to your heart's content. When you're finished, choose File⇨Save.

Creating a pseudo template

A second, unofficial way to create a template is to use a prototype document instead. A prototype document is a plain old WordPerfect document that you want to reuse. The trick is to make sure WordPerfect doesn't allow you to write on top of the document. That way, when you customize the document and forget to use Save As, and use the Save command instead, WordPerfect complains that you're not allowed to write on your prototype document. Those of us who are a little absent-minded find this reminder very useful.

To create a pseudo template, follow these steps:

1. **Create your document and save it normally.**

2. **Choose File⇨Save As.**

3. **Find your file in the dialog box, right-click it, and choose Properties (usually the last command).**

   The properties for your file appear.

4. **In the Attributes section, click the Read-Only attribute.**

5. **Click OK.**

   In the future, if you try to save on top of this file, WordPerfect complains. If you find that you want to modify the document, just deselect the Read-Only attribute before you try to save the file.

Creating Letters

Chances are, you'll do a lot of letter writing with WordPerfect. After all, a word processor makes tasks like that quick and easy.

Word processing should enable you to concentrate on your sterling prose and not on the position of the inside address. So look through the following pointers on how to get WordPerfect to lay out a letter the way you like it. Then save your work as a template so that you don't have to do it all again.

Getting WordPerfect to write your letter for you

We used to say that, with all the wonders of word processing, you still have to choose what words you're going to process. Well, at least for letters, Word-Perfect is willing to take a crack at letter writing for you. (Now, if we could just get it to write books. . . .)

WordPerfect ships with more than 100 sample letters. Admittedly, most of them aren't profound or eloquent, but if you go into gridlock at the sight of a blank sheet of paper, they might serve to get you started. Even if you don't use the words in the letter, you can let WordPerfect set up the letter for you, with nice headers and footers containing the date and page number. You can then modify the letter to suit your fancy.

Here's how to get WordPerfect writing and formatting for you:

1. **Choose File⇨New from Project.**

   Yes, we know, you're already looking at a blank unmodified document, so why bother. This is the only way to get WordPerfect to show you its list of templates.

2. **Use the scroll bar to move down the list of templates until you see** `Letter, Business`.

   We're *not* talking about the drop-down list with the little arrow beside it at the top of the dialog box. Or, for personal letters, you can choose the `Standard Letter` as an option.

3. **Click the Create button.**

4. **If you see a PerfectScript dialog box that asks whether or not you want to disable macros for this document, respond Yes or No.**

   WordPerfect provides this warning for any document that contains macros as a way to prevent potentially harmful viruses. As long as you are sure that the template is from WordPerfect, feel comfortable in running the macros and click No.

5. **If this is your first time running the letter template, decide whether you want to personalize your template by specifying your contact information**.

   WordPerfect allows you to specify this information from your Address Book. You can do so, if you want, or click Cancel to enter the information yourself. After you do so, PerfectExpert appears on the left side of your screen, chock-full of helpful hints about how to write your letter, as shown in Figure 12-2. (If this PerfectExpert stuff is foreign to you, see Chapter 1.)

6. **Select each item in the PerfectExpert window, and fill in the requested information.**

   Some of the selections in PerfectExpert ask you to specify information, such as the recipient of your letter. Other selections change the overall appearance of your letter. Still others have a little arrow you can click to choose from a list of options.

   While you're working on the letter, you may find it useful to click the Zoom button and zoom out to full-page view. The box is too small to work in, but at least you can see what PerfectExpert is doing as it reformats your letter.

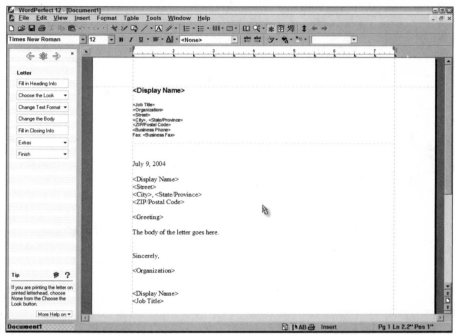

Figure 12-2:
Perfect-
Expert,
at your
service.

7. **When you're ready to type the body of your letter, click the Change the Body button.**

   Those 100 letters we talk about at the beginning of this section are separated into categories. You'll see Accepting Requests as the initial category and the various letters in that category. You can choose another category and then choose an individual letter from among those listed under the category name.

   If the letter you select contains any words surrounded by 〈 and 〉, you need to fill in that information. For example, our donation letter had 〈amount〉 to indicate where the dollar amount was supposed to be. We deleted 〈amount〉 and typed $25.00.

8. **When you're satisfied with how your letter looks, click Finish.**

9. **Select Save, give your letter a filename, and that's it!**

   Close the letter window and the PerfectExpert window to clear your screen.

Congratulations: You've written a letter (with a little help from WordPerfect). Take a look at the following tips to tweak your letter so that it's just right.

Printing your own letterhead

Now that you're looking at a tasteful letter, you may decide that you want WordPerfect to print letterhead for you directly on your letter. Using the many fonts, lines, boxes, and other effects in WordPerfect, you can create a pretty snazzy letterhead; you can even include graphics. Take a look at Chapters 10 and 11; most of what's in those two chapters makes good material for letterhead.

After you create a letterhead that you like, consider using it as part of a template so that all your letters can include it automatically. See the "Creating Your Own Templates" section for more.

Skipping space for the letterhead on stationery

If you are printing on stationery, you have to leave a bunch of space at the top of the letter so that your text doesn't print on top of the letterhead. Use the following steps:

1. **Get out a ruler and measure how far down the page you want your letter to start.**

   That place is where you want the first piece of text (usually, the date) to appear.

2. **Choose View⇨Guidelines so that guidelines appear on your editing screen.**

   Some of us like to have all the guidelines on all the time so that we can see what WordPerfect thinks it's doing to our documents.

3. **Click the guideline at the top of the page and drag it down to where you want the first text to appear.**

   As you drag, a little yellow box appears, telling you exactly where your top margin is going to be. When this box indicates that you've reached the correct position, release the mouse button.

This method works fine for one-page letters. But what if you are creating a letter that is two or more pages long? All that white space at the top of the second and subsequent pages would just waste space and look silly. No problem! The quick we're-using-this-document-only-once approach is to drag the guideline back up to where you want it when you get to the top of the second page. However, we don't like this solution because the spacing will probably get messed up if you edit the letter.

Here's a better way to leave space for a letterhead on the first page of your letters: Tell WordPerfect that the spacing on the first page is different than the spacing on the second page. To do that, use the WordPerfect Advance feature. With your cursor at the top of the first page, choose Format⇨Typesetting⇨ Advance (don't ask us what advancing down the page has to do with typesetting). WordPerfect displays the Advance dialog box. For the Vertical Position option, choose From Top of Page, and fill in the Vertical Distance box with the number of inches (or centimeters) that you want to move down the page. When you click OK, WordPerfect inserts an Advance code (VAdv) that moves down to the position you specified.

Dating your letter and numbering the pages

If you'd like to have WordPerfect enter the current date rather than type it yourself, press Ctrl+D. For multiple-page letters, you should number the pages. Use the page-numbering, header, or footer feature in WordPerfect (described in Chapter 8). Be sure to tell WordPerfect *not* to number the first page.

Saving your letter as a prototype document

When you've finished your letter, you may want to save a copy to use the next time you write a letter. If so, here are a few things to keep in mind to make the process easier:

1. **Delete all the text from the letter.**

   Unless you're saving this as a particular kind of letter (order confirmation, for example), you'll want to type new text every time.

2. **Delete the name of the person to whom you sent the letter.**

   To keep the formatting of the address, don't simply delete it. Instead, highlight it and type something like **<Address goes here>** to remind yourself to enter the address in that location.

3. **Do the same thing for the salutation.**

   Nothing is more embarrassing than sending a letter to Helen with the salutation *Dear Fred.* So highlight the *Dear Fred* salutation and replace it with something like **<Salutation goes here>**. That's all there is to it.

4. **Save your prototype letter for future use by choosing File⇨Save As.**

Don't forget the trick we mention earlier in this chapter. After you've saved your prototype, choose File⇨Save As again. Right-click your document and set its properties to Read-Only to prevent yourself from accidentally writing over your prototype. (The details are in the "Creating a pseudo template" section, earlier in this chapter.) *Voilà!* You have a prototype document to use, with all the formatting already set up.

Creating Envelopes

After you write the world's most clear and cogent letter, you need an envelope to put it in. (We have stooped to using window envelopes because we're too lazy to print envelopes, but we suspect that you haven't fallen that far.)

The folks at WordPerfect created a command that formats a document (or one page of a document) as an envelope. Wow — we're talking *convenience.* Word processing takes a major step forward.

Printing the address on the envelope

To print an address on a regular #10 (business-sized) envelope, follow these steps:

1. **If you've already written the letter that will go in the envelope, open that document.**

   If not, no big deal.

2. **Choose Format⇨Envelope.**

   WordPerfect displays the envelope as it will be formatted for print, as shown in Figure 12-3. If the current document contains a letter in a fairly normal format, WordPerfect — get this — *finds* the name and address at the top of the letter and displays it in the envelope format on your screen. This feature is really cool; you don't have to type the address again.

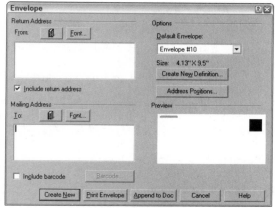

Figure 12-3:
Creating an
envelope.

3. **Enter your address in the return address spot, if it's not there already.**

4. **Decide whether to print the envelope now or as part of the document:**

   - To print the envelope by itself, click the Print Envelope button.

   - To print the envelope as part of your document, click the Append to Doc button. If you have a one-page letter, your envelope is page two. Then print the entire document. WordPerfect adds the envelope as a separate page at the end of your document, along with all the formatting you need to make it print correctly. This feature is great when the current document is the letter that goes inside the envelope. Whenever you print the letter, you print an envelope, too. However, your printer must be equipped with at least two paper feeds for this option.

TIP

Printing barcodes

If you want to make the U.S. Postal Service happy (and who wouldn't?), print a USPS POST-NET barcode. To do so, check the Include barcode box in the Envelope dialog box. Then click the Barcode button. In the POSTNET Barcode dialog box, enter the barcode digits (Word-Perfect defaults to the addressee's zip code) and choose whether you want to position the barcode above or below the address. Finally, click OK to close the dialog box. When you print the envelope, a tasteful row of little vertical lines appears above or below the address. If you enter a 9-digit zip code, the lines will be longer. Some machine at the post office knows what the lines mean.

Creating Mailing Labels

Zillions of kinds of labels exist — sheets of mailing labels, continuous rolls of mailing labels, disk labels, you name it. This section shows you how to print addresses on them. WordPerfect can handle an amazing variety of formats.

Printing addresses on mailing labels

To print addresses on mailing labels, follow these steps:

1. **Begin with a new, blank document.**

2. **Choose Format⇨Labels.**

   The Labels dialog box appears, as shown in Figure 12-4. WordPerfect already knows about an amazing variety of labels, including most of the ones manufactured by Avery. Most label definitions listed in the Labels section of the dialog box are identified only by their Avery part number. This number is useful because most often label manufacturers now include the equivalent Avery number on their packages.

   You can filter the Labels list by selecting the appropriate option in the List Labels For area: Laser Printed, Tractor-Fed, or Both. Unless you have an old dot matrix or a special printer, choose the Laser Printed option.

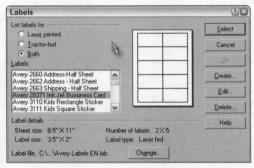

Figure 12-4: Sheets, rolls, or stacks of labels.

3. **Tell WordPerfect the kind of labels you're using.**

   In technical jargon, you're providing a *label definition*. In case you're not sure which kind you have, WordPerfect displays a little diagram of the labels that you select. Avery 5159 Address labels, for example, come in sheets of two across and seven rows per page. The Label Details area of the dialog box describes the size and shape of the sheets and individual labels that you selected.

4. **Click Select.**

   The dialog box closes, and your document now looks truly weird. An area the size of a label stays white (or whatever background color you use for WordPerfect documents), and the rest of the page is draped in shadow, as shown in Figure 12-5.

5. **Type the addresses.**

   Or type whatever it is that you want to print on the labels. WordPerfect allows you to enter only as much information as fits on a label. To move to the next label, press Ctrl+Enter. After you enter a bunch of labels, you can press Alt+PgUp and Alt+PgDn to move from label to label. (If you can't remember these arcane key combinations, just use your mouse.)

6. **Save the document.**

7. **Print the labels.**

   Put the labels in your printer. If you have a sheet-fed printer, be sure to insert the label sheet so that you print on the front, not on the back.

   We recommend that you do a test run on the first page to make sure everything fits as you expect.

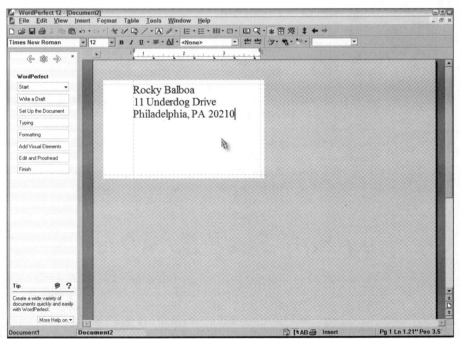

Figure 12-5:
Typing addresses for your mailing labels.

Selecting which labels to print

You don't have to print an entire page of labels at a time. To print selected labels, you can refer to them by number. WordPerfect thinks of each label as a separate miniature page. On the application bar, in fact, the Pg number is the number of the label.

When you know which labels you want to print, choose File⇨Print and then choose Multiple Pages. Click the Multiple Pages tab and select which labels you want to print. For example, enter 3 to print the third label, 5–12 to print a range of labels, or 15– to print from the fifteenth label to the end.

Tips for printing labels

You can use for labels all the usual formatting you use for any document, such as font typeface, font size, and alignment.

WordPerfect's list of label definitions is awfully long. To make it shorter, choose the Laser Printed or Tractor-Fed option in the List Labels For section of the dialog box. WordPerfect lists only labels of that type. If you use an ink jet printer, choose the Laser Printed option.

If you've used WordPerfect's merge feature to enter a list of addresses for creating junk mail (refer to Chapter 15), you can print the same addresses on mailing labels. Create a new *form file* (the merge term for the document that contains the form letter), and choose Format⇨Labels to format it for labels. In the first mailing label, enter merge codes for the parts of the address. Then choose Tools⇨Merge to fill in the labels.

If you're using a type of label that WordPerfect doesn't know about, you can create your own label definitions. Click Create in the Labels dialog box, and tell WordPerfect all about the size and arrangement of your labels. You can also cheat, and look for a label on the list that matches the labels you bought.

Creating Half-Sized Booklets

One common typing job is a pain in the neck with most word processors: creating a little booklet consisting of regular sheets of paper folded in half. Fortunately, WordPerfect comes to the rescue with its special booklet feature for making just this kind of document. This feature is a cool one that makes us want to take back all the snide things that we've said about the software.

Creating a booklet document

These steps show you how to make a 5½x8½-inch booklet that consists of folded sheets:

1. **Type the text for your booklet.**

   Do all the character and line formatting, including fonts, bold, and centering. Set up page numbering, headers, and footers as you want them.

2. **Save your document.**

   Whatever else happens, it would be a pain to have to type the text again! The next step is to tell WordPerfect to print sideways (landscape orientation) on the page and to print two pages of your booklet on each sheet.

3. **Make sure that your cursor is at the beginning of the document so that the formatting affects the entire document.**

   Press Ctrl+Home to get to the tippy-top.

4. **Choose Format⇨Page⇨Page Setup.**

   The Page Setup dialog box appears.

5. **Click the Page Setup tab, if needed.**

6. **In the Page Definition list, choose Letter 8.5" x 11".**

   That's a regular-sized piece of paper. If you want to get fancy, you could try some other paper size. If you're in Europe or were playing Bingo at the office supply store, choose the A4 paper size.

7. **Click the Landscape option.**

   Now you're set to print sideways on the paper. Take a look at the beginning of Chapter 8 for a review of selecting paper.

8. **Click the Layout tab.**

9. **In the Divide Page section, enter 2 in the Columns box.**

   WordPerfect will treat the columns like separate pages. If you don't see your text in two columns, choose View⇨Page.

10. **Create a front cover, if you want one.**

    At the beginning of the document, enter the title or other material you want to appear on the cover. Press Ctrl+Enter to insert a page break between the cover text and the next page. You can center the cover text on the page by using the Format⇨Page⇨Center command.

Now your document looks like a booklet, with two pages per sheet of paper.

Printing your booklet — the magic part

Now comes the tricky part: telling WordPerfect to shuffle the pages so that they're in the right order when you fold your booklet in half. Luckily, Word-Perfect does almost all the work. Just follow these steps:

1. **Tell WordPerfect to print your document on both sides of the page (*duplex*).**

   If your printer supports two-sided printing automatically, choose one of the options under the Automatic (printer supports two-sided printing) heading. If your printer doesn't print duplex, you can click Step 1: print odd pages on the Layout tab of the Print dialog box.

2. **Choose Print as Booklet by clicking the check box in the lower-right corner of the dialog box.**

   This step tells WordPerfect to switch the order of the pages so that when the sheets of paper are folded, the booklet pages are in order.

3. **Click Print.**

   Many minutes later, the printer spews out your booklet. If you have a printer that automatically prints both sides, you're finished. If you're manually printing both sides, WordPerfect prints half the pages.

4. **For manual double-sided printing:**

   a. **Reinsert the pages so that the first sheet of paper that was printed last time will be the first printed this time — make sure that the blank side is set to print.**

   b. **Choose File⇨Print.**

   c. **On the Layout tab, select Step 2: Print Even Pages.**

   d. **Click Print.**

Working with Master Documents

Sometimes you may want to use WordPerfect to handle really large documents. In cases like this, WordPerfect allows you to avoid putting all the pages inside one behemoth, mega-sized document and instead break it up into smaller chunks. These smaller pieces — perhaps chapters or parts — are documents that you can connect through a master document.

A *master document* is a WordPerfect document that contains secret codes that link it to other documents. These other documents are called *subdocuments*. Take, for example, this book. We could create a subdocument for each chapter. The master document contains a secret reveal code for each chapter document, in addition to introductory text, the table of contents, and the index.

To go about creating your own version of *WordPerfect 12 For Dummies* or some other really big document, create the subdocuments first. Then create the master document. Finally, set up the table of contents. Don't worry; in this section we step you through the process.

Master documents and subdocuments

To create the master document and its subdocuments, get the text of the book organized. Follow these steps:

1. **Create a document for each chapter.**

   Because you want all the chapters to be formatted the same way, consider creating a template that contains the formatting. Alternately, create a prototype chapter with some section headings and other elements you expect to use in each chapter. Don't worry about page numbering, headers, or footers in the subdocuments; those elements are controlled by the master document. Give the documents names such as `Chapter1.wpd` and `Chapter2.wpd`.

2. **Type the text in each chapter document or copy the text from existing documents.**

3. **Create the master document.**

   Open a new document, and type the title page and other front matter. Skip the table of contents for now (we get to it in the following section). If the introduction and preface (or whatever) are short, you can include them in this document. If they're long, store each one in its own document, as you do chapters. Save the document with a name such as `MyBestseller.wpd`, `Book.wpd`, or `Report.wpd`.

4. **For each chapter, create a reveal code in the master document:**

   a. **Move your cursor to the spot in the master document where you want the chapter to appear.**

   b. **If you want the chapter to begin on a new page, insert a page break by pressing Ctrl+Enter.**

   c. **Choose File⇨Document⇨Subdocument.**

A faster way to issue the File⇨Document⇨SubDocument command is right-click in the left margin of the document and choose Subdocument from the QuickMenu.

d. In the Include Subdocument dialog box, select the filename of the chapter, and click Include.

Not much happens at this point. If you're in Page view, you see a little subdocument icon in the left margin of your master document. If you're in Draft view, you see `Subdoc: MyBestseller - Chapter 1.WPD` or whatever you named the subdocument.

To find out which document the little subdocument icon refers to, click it.

Expanding the master document

WordPerfect can display (and store) a master document in two ways: expanded or condensed. When a master document is *expanded,* WordPerfect retrieves the text of each subdocument and sticks it into the master document right where it belongs. When a master document is *condensed* — you guessed it — the text of each subdocument is stored in its separate file, and you see only subdocument icons.

To expand a master document, choose File⇨Document⇨Expand Master (or double-click one of those subdocument icons). WordPerfect displays the Expand Master Document dialog box, which lists all your subdocuments. To expand them all, click OK. If you want to skip expanding any, click their check box so that no check mark appears in it.

When you expand a master document, you still see the subdocument icons. You see twice as many, in fact — they appear at the beginning and the end of each subdocument.

Saving a master document

When you save a master document, WordPerfect wants to know two things about each of its subdocuments:

- ✔ Do you want to *save* the text of the subdocument back in the subdocument's file?

- ✔ Do you want to *condense* the subdocument so that only its icon appears in the master document?

You answer both of these pithy questions in the Condense/Save Subdocuments dialog box. When you want to save your master document, follow these steps:

1. **Choose File⇨Save, press Ctrl+S, or click the Save button on the toolbar.**

   WordPerfect displays the Save File dialog box. If you haven't expanded your master document or if you've condensed it, WordPerfect saves the document with no comment.

2. **If WordPerfect asks whether you want to condense the document, click No to save the document as is or click Yes to save each subdocument in its own separate file.**

   If your master document is expanded, WordPerfect displays the message `Document is expanded. Condense?`.

   If you click No, WordPerfect saves the master document with the text of all the expanded subdocuments, too. It *doesn't* save the text of the sub-documents back to the separate subdocument files. If you edited the text of your chapters in the master document, therefore, your edits are not saved in `MyBestseller.wpd - Chapter 1.wpd`, `MyBestseller.wpd - Chapter 2.wpd`, and so on — they're saved only in `MyBestseller.wpd`.

   If you click Yes, WordPerfect displays the Condense/Save Subdocuments dialog box. Each subdocument is listed twice: once so that you can condense it (remove the text from the master document) and once so that you can save it in its own file. We always leave all the boxes checked. Go for the gold, we say.

3. **Click OK.**

You can condense a master document also by choosing File⇨Document⇨ Condense Master.

Editing a master document

After you set up the master document, what do you do when you want to edit a chapter of your book? What if you suddenly remember the time you arm wrestled the President and decide that would be a good anecdote to include? You have two choices:

✔ **Edit the chapter file.** In this case, make sure that your master document is condensed to ensure that the text of your chapter is stored in the sub-document file, not in the master document. Make your changes, and save the chapter file. The next time you open and expand the master document, the updated chapter appears.

✔ **Edit the master document.** In this case, make sure that your chapter file is closed. Open the master document and expand the subdocuments (or at least the one that you want to edit). Make your changes and save the master file. You probably want to save the changes back to the subdocuments when WordPerfect presents you with the Condense/Save Subdocuments dialog box, as we just described.

This process can get confusing when you try to remember where the text of your chapters is *really* stored. We recommend that you always do your editing the same way and always store your master document the same way (either expanded or condensed).

Creating a Table of Contents

Whether you're using master documents or not, WordPerfect can automatically generate a table of contents for you. In fact, WordPerfect will take any old document you have and create a table of contents by using the headings in the file. These steps show you how:

1. **Open your document and expand it.**

   You want to be able to see all your lovely chapters so that you can decide which ones should appear in the table of contents.

2. **Choose Tools⇔Reference⇔Table of Contents.**

   More lovely buttons appear, mostly named Mark (see Figure 12-6).

   Unlike most other dialog boxes, you can keep the Reference Tools dialog box open while you continue to work with your document. Feel free to move it off to the side so you can work on your document at the same time.

Figure 12-6:
Marking the headings that you want to appear in your table of contents.

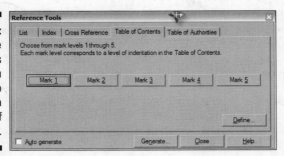

3. **Mark the lines of text (headings) you want to use in the table of contents.**

   Your table of contents can have several levels (chapters and sections within chapters, for example). To mark each heading, select it and then click the appropriate Mark button. Mark each chapter title by using Mark 1, for example, and each section within the chapters by using Mark 2.

   When you perform this step, nothing seems to happen. However, Word-Perfect secretly inserts reveal codes at the beginning and end of each selected heading (the Mrk Txt ToC code, if you were wondering).

4. **Create a new page where you want the table of contents to appear.**

   For most books, you want the table of contents to be on a page by itself, right after the title and copyright pages. Press Ctrl+Enter to insert a page break.

5. **Beginning with the first page of the master document, tell WordPerfect to number the pages with small roman numerals.**

   Most books number the front matter (including the table of contents) with roman numerals and then start the page numbers again with arabic numerals at the beginning of the introduction or first chapter. (Confused? Check out the beginning of this book.)

   Move your cursor to the beginning of the master document, and choose Format⇨Page⇨Numbering. Set the Position option to Top Inside Alternating or Bottom Inside Alternating so that the numbers appear on the right side of left pages and on the left side of right pages. Select one of the roman numeral options (iv, -iv-, IV, or -IV-). Then click OK to finish page numbering.

   You may want to suppress page numbers on the title pages and some other front matter pages. To do so, choose Format⇨Page⇨Suppress.

6. **Go to the first page of the introduction or Chapter 1 and reset it to be page number 1, in arabic numerals.**

   With your cursor at the top of the page that you want to be page 1, choose Format⇨Page⇨Numbering. Click Set Value, set the page number to 1, and click OK. Back on the Select Page Numbering Format dialog box, set the Page Numbering Format option to 1. Then click OK to finish page numbering. We go through this in gory detail in Chapter 8.

   Now WordPerfect knows which page numbers should appear on every page. You are ready to create the table of contents (and not a moment too soon!).

7. **Move your cursor to the location where you want the table of contents to appear and click the Define button (on the Table of Contents tab of the Reference Tools dialog box).**

   WordPerfect displays the Define Table of Contents dialog box.

8. **Tell WordPerfect the number of levels and which style to use for each level (whether to include page numbers and dot leaders), and then click OK.**

   WordPerfect inserts an invisible code and the text `<<Table of Contents will generate here>`.

9. **Click the Generate button in the Reference Tools dialog box to display the Generate dialog box.**

   WordPerfect gives you the option of saving your subdocuments. To do so, click the Save documents box in the Generate dialog box. We think this is a good idea. You can also build hyperlinks by checking the appropriate box, but don't worry about that now. (We talk about hyperlinks in Chapter 13.)

10. **Click OK.**

If you update your book and make chapters shorter or longer, WordPerfect will update the table of contents and correct the headings and page numbers when you click the Generate button again.

After you finish fooling with the table of contents, click the Close button on the Reference Tools dialog box.

Using WordPerfect OfficeReady Templates

WordPerfect 12 comes with a separate application called the WordPerfect OfficeReady browser. This handy utility allows you to organize and preview your templates visually. When you install WordPerfect OfficeReady, it also provides 40 additional templates for WordPerfect (as well as for Quattro Pro and Presentations).

The WordPerfect OfficeReady browser is not installed as part of the normal installation. You can find it on CD 2 of your WordPerfect Office 12 disc set. You can also download it for free from the Corel Web site at `www.wordperfect.com`.

After you install WordPerfect OfficeReady, launch it by choosing All Programs⇨ WordPerfect OfficeReady⇨Start WordPerfect OfficeReady from the Windows Start menu. The WordPerfect OfficeReady browser is shown in Figure 12-7.

The left pane organizes the templates into categories. Click to select the category of your choice, and the top-right pane displays a thumbnail list of WordPerfect, Quattro Pro, and Presentations templates. Click a template thumbnail to preview the template in the bottom-right pane. Or double-click the thumbnail to create a new document based on that template.

Unlike the WordPerfect templates discussed in the "Using Templates" section earlier in the chapter, the WordPerfect OfficeReady templates are *not* integrated into WordPerfect's PerfectExpert feature. You can access them only by using the WordPerfect OfficeReady browser.

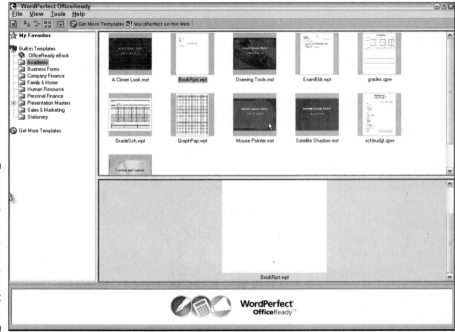

Figure 12-7: Access many handy-dandy, time-saving templates in Word-Perfect OfficeReady.

Part IV

All the World's a Page: Going Beyond Your Desktop

The 5th Wave   By Rich Tennant

"I'm just not sure it's appropriate to send a digital resume to a paper stock company looking for a sales rep."

In this part . . .

Ahhh, when life was simple. In the past, when you created a document with a typewriter or a word processor, you invariably printed the document and handed it to
someone or mailed it. But, in the 21st century, life had to
go and get complicated.

Yes, you can still use WordPerfect for printing documents,
but the ways in which people communicate are far more
complex than ever before. Fortunately, WordPerfect rises
to the challenge and allows you to communicate with
others in many different ways. You can create Web pages,
Adobe Acrobat documents, XML files, and even Microsoft
Office documents. What's more, if you ever need to send a
similar document to a whole bunch of people (that's a
nice way of saying "junk mail"), look no further than
WordPerfect.

Read this part and you may feel ready to conquer the
world, all by sitting behind your computer desktop. And
even if you don't feel like conquering, you'll at least be
able to communicate effectively with your coworkers,
business contacts, and family.

Chapter 13

Publishing for the Web

● ●

In This Chapter

▶ Getting Internet basics

▶ Creating hyperlinks in your documents

▶ Publishing your document as a Web page

▶ Exploring the differences between WordPerfect and HTML documents

▶ Publishing your document as an Adobe Acrobat file

● ●

*O*ne of the little-known provisions of the recent U.N. Treaty on the Internet and Other Really Cool Stuff made it illegal to market any product in the world unless it could connect to the Internet. Thus, we have Internet-enabled word processors, databases, spreadsheets, toaster ovens, and guacamole dip.

Okay, okay . . . we're kidding around. There's no U.N. treaty, but there might as well be. Any software you use these days invariably has some tie-in to the Web, and WordPerfect is no different. In this chapter, we do several things to help you become a Web-savvy WordPerfect user. We start by talking about hyperlinks and bookmarks, which WordPerfect uses to link information from one document to another. Using WordPerfect bookmarks and links is a good way for you to get started working with hyperlinks. Rather than dealing with the peculiarities of hypertext formatted documents, you can concentrate on the content and the organization of that content.

Next we talk about how to publish your WordPerfect documents as HTML Web pages and Adobe Acrobat PDF documents. And in the process, we explain what these funny acronyms mean, too.

We don't spend much time talking about the basics of the Internet and the Web, but if you'd like more information, one of us helped write an entire book about the subject. Check our *The Internet For Dummies*, 9th Edition, by John Levine, Carol Baroudi, and Margaret Levine Young (published by Wiley).

Creating Hyperlinks and Bookmarks

If you've spent any time on the Web, you know what hypertext is, even if you don't know it by name. Hypertext is like regular text, really, except for one thing: When you click certain words or phrases, you're magically transported to different text, either in the same document or to another document located somewhere else. Using hypertext, you can follow related ideas in a way that would be difficult if you had to skip around from page to page in a book, or from book to book. Much like an automobile's dependency on gasoline, hypertext is the fuel for the rapid popularity of the Web.

As a first step in Web pages in WordPerfect, you'll want to add hyperlinks to your document. To do so, you create bookmarks in your document and then link to them. Then, once you have those techniques mastered, you'll be able to quickly turn your WordPerfect document into a snazzy Web page.

Creating a bookmark — a place you jump to

Bookmarks within a single document work pretty much the way their name implies — they enable you to mark a position in a document and go back to it quickly. Suppose, for example, that you've written *Of Chocolate and Chocoholics,* a 500-page WordPerfect master document with 30 chapter subdocuments (for more on master and subdocuments, see Chapter 12). If you're working on Chapter 23, "Ceremonial Uses of Chocolate," and want to check what you said about that topic in Chapter 1, "A History of Chocolate," you have several options (of course you do; this is WordPerfect):

- ✔ **Press the PgUp key on the keyboard until you get to Chapter 1.** This method will make your finger sore and will take a long time.

- ✔ **Choose Edit⇨Find and Replace to search for the text *A History of Chocolate*.** The problem with this method is that WordPerfect stops at every occurrence of *A History of Chocolate* in the entire book up to this point. This method also will take a long time.

- ✔ **Use a bookmark.** After you set a bookmark on the text of *A History of Chocolate,* you can get back there anytime by displaying the Go To dialog box and selecting the name of the bookmark. No matter how far away you are, WordPerfect takes you there as though you were on a magic carpet. After you check out what you want to see, you can use Go To to take us back to your last position in Chapter 23.

Setting bookmarks and going to them may seem like a lot of work — and it is. It's worth the trouble only if you plan to go back to that bookmark often or if you plan to use some of the *really* obscure features of WordPerfect. (That's why we haven't explained bookmarks until now.) Now, with the advent of hypertext and the Web, everyone wants to know about bookmarks.

To create a bookmark, follow these steps:

1. **Highlight the text that you want to appear inside the bookmark.**

2. **Choose Tools⇨Bookmark.**

   The Bookmark dialog box appears.

3. **Click the Create button.**

   A little dialog box appears, and it suggests that text as the name for your bookmark based on your highlighted text. If you didn't highlight some text, type a name for your bookmark. The Create Bookmark dialog box is shown in Figure 13-1.

Figure 13-1: Creating a bookmark.

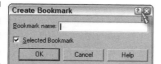

The extremely observant among us will have noticed that the right end of the property bar changes when a word or other block of text is selected. The rightmost button changes to look like a spider web with a chain link underneath. Click this button, and you get a little two-item menu; click Insert Bookmark, and you get the Create Bookmark dialog box.

4. **Click OK to create the bookmark.**

   Poof! Nothing happens. Well, the dialog boxes go away, but nothing looks different in your document. But now the fun begins!

Now that you've created a link destination, you need to know how to jump *to* it.

Creating a hyperlink — a way to jump somewhere

Consider Chapter 23, "Ceremonial Uses of Chocolate," in the hypothetical book you're writing. In a traditional book, you might say something like, "The first known ceremonial use of chocolate occurred in Aztec society long before the European discovery of America (see Chapter 1)." The reader then flips to Chapter 1 and skims it to see whether it says anything about Aztecs. This works fine on paper but is a little awkward on a computer screen, especially the flipping part.

As a result, word-processing scientists have found a way to create document features that can't even be put on paper: hyperlinks. (For example, if we asked you to go look at a figure in Chapter 2 of *Windows XP For Dummies*, you would have to go out to the bookstore and buy the book to continue. What a pain in the neck. But you've probably clicked those little links on the Web before. And *that's* why hypertext is a good idea.) You can create a link to Chapter 1 in your book on chocolate. Follow these steps:

1. **Create a bookmark at the place *to which* you want your reader to be able to jump.**

   In our example, we just finished creating a bookmark on the word *Aztec* in the document `Chap1.wpd`.

2. **Open the document that contains the place *from which* you want your reader to be able to jump.**

   In this case, that's `Chap23.wpd`.

3. **Highlight the word(s) that you want the user to be able to click.**

   In this case, choose a reference to the Aztecs at the beginning of Chapter 23.

4. **Choose Tools⇨Hyperlink.**

   The Hyperlink Properties dialog box appears (see Figure 13-2). In this box, you tell WordPerfect what you want to happen when someone clicks the link you're creating.

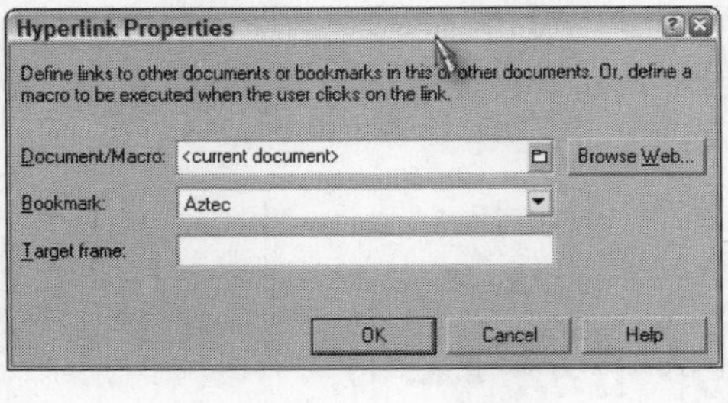

Figure 13-2:
Creating a link to a Word-Perfect bookmark.

5. **In the Document/Macro box, type the name of the document that you want to link to.**

   In this case, it's `Chap1.wpd`. If you're lazy or can't remember, click the little file folder icon. You see the WordPerfect standard file-browsing dialog box, and you can select the file there.

If you'd like to create a hyperlink to a Web page, click the Browse Web button. Your default browser appears. Go to the page of your choice, select the address in the browser window with your mouse, and press Ctrl+C to copy the address. Then, click in the Document/Macro box to paste it in there.

6. **In the Bookmark box, type the name of the bookmark you want WordPerfect to take the user to.**

   In this case, it's Aztec. If you've forgotten the name of the bookmark in the document that you just selected, you can click the down arrow at the end of this box. You see a list of all the bookmarks in that document. If you specify a Web address, the Bookmark list box is empty.

   You don't have to specify a bookmark, and with Web addresses, you usually don't. If you leave the bookmark box blank, WordPerfect just takes the user to the top of the target document.

7. **Click OK.**

   This time, you actually see a change in your document. The word (or phrase, or character) that you highlighted is now underlined and blue.

Do yourself a favor: Save the document now. Congratulations; you've created your own hyperlink. Creating hypertext is nothing more than creating lots and lots of these links.

To test your link, click it. If the Activate Hyperlinks setting is on (see the "Activating and deactivating links" sidebar), WordPerfect will take you to the document you just linked to.

Using the Hyperlink property bar

When you're ready to work with the hyperlink text, turn off the Activate Hyperlinks setting (see the "Activating and deactivating links" sidebar). Then click a word inside your hyperlink. When you do so, the Hyperlink property bar is displayed.

Letting WordPerfect create links for you

WordPerfect makes it easy to add Web-based links to your document. To do so, type the Web address of the page you want to link to in your document text. WordPerfect recognizes it as a Web address and automatically turns it into a link. You can add links to Web addresses that start with http: (those are links to other Web pages) and e-mail addresses that start with *somename*@someisp.com (or .net, or .org).

Activating and deactivating links

Normally when you click a hyperlink (that's the word in blue) in your document, WordPerfect puts on its browser hat and attempts to take you to the document that the link is associated with, just like your Internet Explorer or Netscape Navigator Web browser. Although that functionality may be helpful when you want to test or view the links, it's a pain to edit the text inside the link. Why? Because each time you click any of the text inside the link, WordPerfect forgets about being a word processor and becomes Mr. Browser again so it can navigate the link. To deactivate this functionality, so you can more easily edit the hyperlink text, follow these steps

1. **Choose Tools⇨Settings.**

   The Settings dialog box appears

2. **Click the Environment button.**

   The Environment Settings dialog box appears.

3. **Click the General tab if it's not already selected.**

4. **Click the Activate Hyperlinks check box to remove the check mark.**

5. **Click OK.**

You can also use the Hyperlink toggle button on the Hyperlink property bar (see the section "Using the Hyperlink property bar") to activate and deactivate links.

Alternatively, you can edit the hyperlink text with the Activate Hyperlinks option on if you use the keyboard and avoid the mouse. To do so, use the keyboard arrow keys to position the text cursor inside the link text, and then use the keyboard to edit or remove the hyperlink text. You can also right-click and choose Edit Hyperlink from the QuickMenu.

The property bar is the easiest way to care for and feed your hyperlinks, so it's worth getting to know its buttons. Figure 13-3 illustrates the property bar when its mind is on hyperlinks:

- **Font selection box:** Why the font is a property of your hyperlink but its other text properties such as bold and italic aren't is a mystery to us. We prefer to format our text using the Format⇨Font command.

- **Font size box:** Works just like the font size box on the regular property bar. We still prefer the Format⇨Font command.

- **Hyperlink Perform:** Clicking this button is the same as clicking a link, though links don't work when they've been deactivated (see Links on/off, later in this list). The Hyperlink Perform button lets you test your links even if you've cleared the Activate Hyperlinks check box or turned links off. It's useful for testing your links while you edit them.

✔ **Previous:** This button finds the last hyperlink before your current position in your document.

 ✔ **Next:** You guessed it — this button finds the next hyperlink after your current position in the document.

 ✔ **Delete:** This button deletes the hyperlink associated with the highlighted text, turning it back into regular text. Because it's regular text now, the Hyperlink Tools property bar disappears, and the familiar old text properties take its place.

 ✔ **Edit:** Clicking this button displays the Hyperlink Properties dialog box, in case you want this link to go somewhere else. It's the same as choosing the Tools⇨Hyperlink command.

 ✔ **Toggle hyperlinks:** Allows you to quickly turn off or on the Activate Hyperlinks setting (see the "Activating and deactivating links" sidebar).

 ✔ **Style:** Clicking this button enables you to change the way that links are displayed. For more information, take a look at Chapter 9.

Figure 13-3:
The
Hyperlink
property
bar.

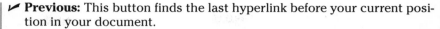

Now you have all the tools you need to create hypertext documents.

Publishing Your Documents as Web Pages

If you know how to use WordPerfect to create documents, you pretty much know how to create a Web page. After all, a Web page contains text, graphics, and hyperlinks, which amazingly enough, is what WordPerfect documents contain.

To publish your WordPerfect document as a Web page, you need to save it as an HTML (HyperText Markup Language) file. HTML is the standard document format used on the Web.

To publish to HTML, follow these instructions:

1. **Choose File➪Publish To➪HTML.**

   The Publish to HTML dialog box is displayed, as shown in Figure 13-4.

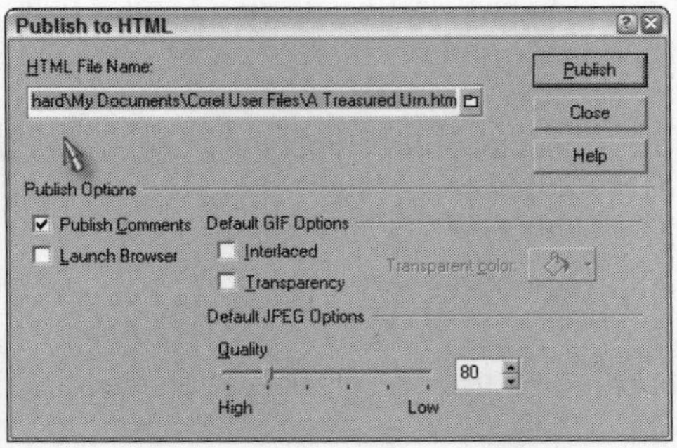

Figure 13-4:
Publish like
a Web
master right
from Word-
Perfect.

2. **In the HTML File Name box, specify the name of the Web page.**

   WordPerfect suggests a name for you, placing the Web page in the same folder as your existing document but adding an `.htm` extension instead.

3. **Click Publish.**

   WordPerfect converts your document to HTML format and, if the Launch Browser box is checked in the dialog box, your default browser displays the Web page.

If your document contains images, be sure to see the picture embedding information in the "Stuff that WordPerfect and Web pages do differently" section.

If you try to open the HTML file you just published using File➪Open, you'll notice that WordPerfect converts the HTML file into a WordPerfect document and renames it something like `Document1`. Therefore, we recommend that you don't try to edit the HTML file you just published if any changes need to be made. Instead, go back to your original WordPerfect document, make the necessary edits, and then republish.

Previewing your document in a browser

No matter how hard WordPerfect tries, your document is likely going to look different in your Web browser than the way it does in WordPerfect. If you'd like to see what your WordPerfect document will look like as a Web page before you publish, choose View➪Preview in Browser.

Stuff you can do in WordPerfect that you can't do on a Web page

Following are the features that don't convert to a Web page, roughly in the order in which we think you might care about them:

- **Margins (left or right):** Web pages take their margins from the size of the user's window.

- **Page numbering:** What's a page? Numbered relative to what? We're talking about hypertext on the screen here.

- **Columns:** Any columns in your document will be removed.

- **Headers and footers:** These elements don't apply to Web pages.

- **Vertical lines:** Use tables instead.

- **Watermarks:** A watermark image will be removed.

Stuff that WordPerfect and Web pages do differently

One of the more useful things about using WordPerfect to create Web documents is that you can use those documents on the Web. You probably already have a bunch of WordPerfect documents. Presto — instant content for your Web site. The only problem is that the documents are not formatted as Web pages, and they probably use all sorts of features that work differently on Web pages. Here are some important differences to consider:

- **Fonts:** If you read Chapter 6, you discovered how great it is to add a variety of nice-looking fonts to your document. The problem when creating a Web page is that there's no guarantee that the computer halfway around the world displaying your Web page has ever heard of the font that you chose. If you choose a font that a particular computer doesn't know about, the computer will choose something it thinks is reasonable, but the substitute is not always a good one.

   Stick with well-known (and easy-to-read) fonts, such as Times New Roman, Arial, Courier New, Tahoma, and Verdana.

- **Picture embedding:** When you add a picture to a WordPerfect document, WordPerfect stores the graphic in the .wpd file. Therefore, if you copy or e-mail the document to give it to others, people can view the graphic in the document just as you intended. However, HTML documents store just your text and simply link to images stored in their own files. Therefore, when WordPerfect publishes to HTML, all the images on your page are placed in a subfolder in the folder you're publishing to. The name of the subfolder is the name of the HTML document (minus the `.htm` extension).

If you copy the HTML document to another location, make sure you take the images subfolder along with it. Otherwise, your images will no longer be displayed properly in your Web page.

✔ **Picture wrapping:** We talked about how to add pictures to your document in Chapter 11. Web pages also allow you to have graphics added to them. However, HTML is much more limited in its capabilities for text wrapping around the images themselves. No matter what the text wrap setting is for your image, when WordPerfect publishes it as an HTML page, the Neither Side setting is used. Text is wrapped only above or below the text, not on the left or right side of the image.

To create the look of a picture alongside text, you can create a table and add text in one cell and the picture in the cell beside it. See Chapter 10 for more on tables.

✔ **Picture format:** As we discuss in Chapter 11, WordPerfect allows you to add clipart, photos, and virtually any other graphic you can think of to your document. However, although WordPerfect may be smart enough to know how to work with all those types of graphics, your Web browser isn't. When you publish a document, WordPerfect has to convert it into one of two types of formats: GIF or JPG. WordPerfect uses GIF format unless you specify differently for a graphic.

In general, GIF format works best for general use, clipart, and images containing text. JPG format is often preferred for photos and other high-resolution graphics. To change the format of a graphic:

1. **Right-click the graphic in your document and choose HTML Properties.**

2. **Click the Publish tab in the HTML Properties dialog box.**

3. **In the Output format section, click the appropriate format.**

4. **Click OK.**

Publishing in Adobe Acrobat (PDF) Format

Because of the formatting limitations of HTML (see the "Stuff that Word-Perfect and Web pages do differently" section, earlier in this chapter), Adobe Acrobat has become increasingly popular as a way to distribute a document in a read-only format that preserves the document's formatting. Because

Adobe Acrobat has free reader software available, nearly everyone who has a Web browser and can read HTML pages can read Adobe Acrobat (PDF) files as well.

WordPerfect provides the ability to publish your document as an Acrobat file in a seamless fashion. When you publish your document as a PDF file, people who don't even have WordPerfect on their PC will be able to view your document.

To publish to PDF, follow these instructions:

1. **Choose File⇨Publish To⇨PDF.**

   The Publish to PDF dialog box is displayed, as shown in Figure 13-5.

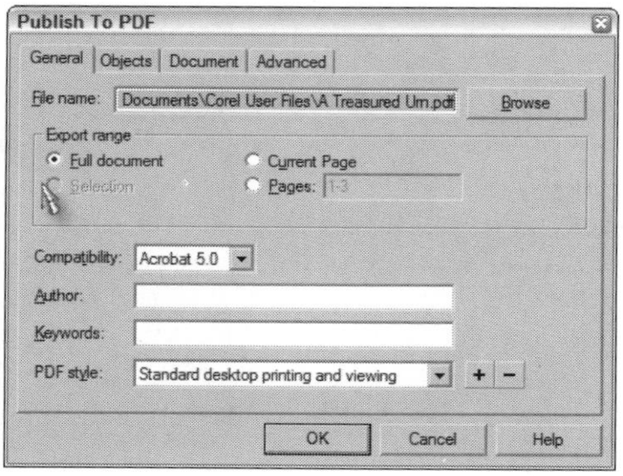

Figure 13-5:
Do
acrobatics
around your
office with
the Publish
to PDF
dialog box.

2. **In the File Name box, specify the name of the PDF document.**

   WordPerfect automatically suggests a name for you, placing the Acrobat file in the same folder as your existing document but adding a .pdf extension instead.

3. **Click OK.**

   WordPerfect converts your document to PDF format. Unlike HTML, Adobe Acrobat maintains your fancy-schmancy formatting, such as columns, headers, and page numbers.

When you take a look around the Publish to PDF dialog box, you notice a lot of options. Most of them are technical, but here are some options that you may find useful:

- **Export range area:** This section allows you to publish the entire Word-Perfect document or only part of it.

- **PDF Style:** The PDF Style box at the bottom of the General tab allows you to automatically adjust the other settings on the Objects, Document, and Advanced tabs by specifying the purpose of the Acrobat file. If you're going to publish the PDF file to the Web, for example, choose the PDF for the Web item. Or, if you're going to be distributing the PDF file in your office, choose PDF for Document Distribution.

- ✔ **Bookmarks:** If you created bookmarks or hyperlinks in your document (see the "Creating Hyperlinks and Bookmarks" section), you can have these enabled in your Acrobat file as well. To do so, click the Document tab and then click the Include Hyperlinks and Generate Bookmarks boxes.

Chapter 14

Using WordPerfect in a Microsoft Office World

*U*nless you "think different" and use a Mac, we can safety predict that the computer you have sitting on top of your desk runs Microsoft Windows and a few other Microsoft applications, too. Indeed, for many years now, Microsoft Windows and Microsoft Office have dominated the world of software. And in the category of word processing, Microsoft Word is the current King of the Hill. Therefore, if you ever share documents with friends or coworkers, chances are you're going to be forced into working with Microsoft Word files in WordPerfect.

On the surface, you may think that using WordPerfect in a Microsoft Office world will leave you feeling like a square peg trying to fit into a round hole. However, as you explore in this chapter, WordPerfect is a crafty, little ol' application that adapts itself well to its surroundings. In fact, you can use WordPerfect to open and save Microsoft Word files as well as access Microsoft Outlook information inside of your documents. Finally, for all those former Microsoft Word users out there, WordPerfect also has an option available to simulate the look and feel of Microsoft Word in its workspace.

Sharing Microsoft Word Documents

Back in the Stone Age years of word processing, converting a document from one file format to another was a giant pain in the neck. First off, some software companies would make it cumbersome to work with documents generated by their competitors. Second, even when you could convert between formats, you usually had to use a utility outside your word processor to do the conversion. Fortunately, we've come a long way since those early days. In fact, WordPerfect 12 allows you to open a Microsoft Word document as seamlessly as you would a WordPerfect one, and makes it almost as easy to save your file back into Microsoft Word format.

Opening Microsoft Word documents

To open a Microsoft Word file, simply select the document from the Open File dialog box. WordPerfect converts the document behind the scenes and presents it in your WordPerfect workspace. It's so simple, we don't need to write any more about it!

Preserving Microsoft Word format when you save documents

In a very cheeky move, when you attempt to save a Microsoft Word document you've opened in WordPerfect, WordPerfect wants to save the original DOC file in WordPerfect format rather than preserving the original Microsoft Word format. The problem is that, without realizing it, you can make it difficult or even impossible for Microsoft Word users to open the file after you've done this. (It depends on whether or not they have a WordPerfect file conversion utility installed.)

To prevent this snafu, you can preserve the original Microsoft Word format in two ways. When you choose File➪Save, a Save Format dialog box is displayed, as shown in Figure 14-1. Rather than keeping the default option, make sure you select the MS Word 97/2000/2002/2003 for Windows option and click OK. When you do this, WordPerfect saves the document as a Microsoft Word file.

Figure 14-1:
The default option in this dialog box converts a Microsoft Word document into Word-Perfect format.

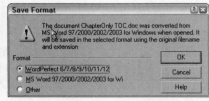

The second way — and the technique we recommend — is to change the system setting to prevent any possible problems. To always preserve the original format of documents when you save them:

1. **Choose Tools⇨Settings.**

   The Settings dialog box appears.

2. **Click the Files button.**

3. **If necessary, click the Document tab to select it.**

4. **Click the option titled On Save, Keep Document's Original File Format.**

5. **Click OK.**

Problems moving between WordPerfect and Microsoft Word

We'd like to say that you can open any Microsoft Word document in Word-Perfect, do anything you want to it, save the file, and no one but you will ever know the difference. Unfortunately, that perfect scenario doesn't exist with WordPerfect 12. WordPerfect will maintain all text and basic formatting, but we can't guarantee that all formatting will move easily between the two word processors.

In our experience, the formatting features of WordPerfect 12 and Microsoft Word are perhaps 90 percent compatible, but that remaining 10 percent can give you headaches, especially if you use a lot of borders, text boxes, tables of contents, and footnotes in your document. As a result, if you aren't careful, you could open a Microsoft Word document, unintentionally remove some formatting, and save over the original version. If so, we suspect you'll end up making other Microsoft Word users mad at you for changing the look of their documents.

The following list provides some of the most commonly used Microsoft Word formatting that is *not* preserved when you open the document in WordPerfect:

- ✔ All caps and strikethrough text
- ✔ Text, paragraph, and page art borders
- ✔ Custom footnote and endnote symbols
- ✔ Sections
- ✔ AutoShapes and certain drawing options
- ✔ Some wrapping of text and picture objects

Therefore, when you save the document back to Microsoft Word format, the original formatting is lost. Therefore, if a Microsoft Word user opens the document again, any of the formatting from the preceding list will have been removed from the document.

You should also be aware that some WordPerfect formatting is not supported by Microsoft Word, including the following:

- ✔ All justification alignment for paragraphs
- ✔ Column shading
- ✔ Color borders for boxes
- ✔ Some text wrapping options for boxes
- ✔ Table formulas
- ✔ Advanced features of footnotes and endnotes (custom numbering, styles, number formats)

If you're certain that the Microsoft Word document you're working with isn't using incompatible formatting features, we recommend that you use only WordPerfect as your word processor.

Automatically Saving Your Documents in Microsoft Word Format

No matter how much we love WordPerfect, the fact is that Microsoft Word has the lion's share of the word-processing market. As a result, the Microsoft Word format is the default document format for most purposes. However, just because the Microsoft Word format dominates, that doesn't mean you can't use WordPerfect for creating and editing your documents.

WordPerfect enables you to specify the default document format for saving your files. If you'd like to save your files in Microsoft Word format by default, simply follow these instructions:

1. **Choose Tools⇨Settings.**

2. **Click the Files button.**

3. **On the Document tab, click the down arrow next to the Default Save File Format box.**

   A list of file formats is displayed in alphabetical order.

4. Select MS Word 97/2000/2002/2003 for Windows from the list.

5. Click OK.

Using Microsoft Outlook Contacts in WordPerfect

If you have a large database of contacts that you work with, hardly anything is more annoying than being forced to re-enter that information for each application. If you use Microsoft Outlook to maintain your contacts, you're in luck. WordPerfect can access that information for you when you're creating bulk mail letters, envelopes, or labels.

To enable Microsoft Outlook support, follow these directions:

1. **Choose Tools⇨Settings.**

2. **Click the Environment button.**

3. **On the General tab, click the Use Outlook Address Book/Contact List option.**

4. **Click OK.**

After you enable this option, you can fetch address information from Outlook each time you create a letter, an envelope, or a label. For more information on how to create these documents, see Chapters 12 and 15.

Making WordPerfect Look (Kinda) Like Microsoft Word

If you're a newcomer to WordPerfect 12 but already know how to use Microsoft Word, we're guessing that you'd prefer to not have to learn a new user interface. WordPerfect wants to make it easy for former Microsoft Word users to use their word processor. One way they do this is by allowing WordPerfect to simulate the toolbar icons and menu naming of Word. Figure 14-2 shows Word-Perfect with this feature turned on.

Okay, we admit that the simulation goes only so far; you'll never mistake the WordPerfect workspace for Microsoft Word. But let's give WordPerfect some credit for dressing up as its competitor. To enable this functionality, use Workspace Manager, which we discuss fully in Chapter 18.

Figure 14-2:
A Word-
Perfect
wolf in
Microsoft
Word
clothing.

Chapter 15

Mail Merge: Printing to the Masses

*I*n this modern world, it seems like everyone likes to tweak words to suit his or her particular needs. If we get fired from our job, we prefer to say we were "let go." If a child fails every subject in school, he was "held back." If we receive a bulk rate letter in our box, we get "junk mail." But if we're the ones who sent the junk mail, we think of it as simply sending out a bountiful supply of amazingly similar-looking personalized letters.

In this chapter, you'll discover how you can create *merge documents*. We'll show you all about how you can do this in WordPerfect, but we'll let you decide whether you want to call them "junk mail" or "amazingly similar-looking personalized letters."

Exploring the Everyday Uses of Merge

At first glance, creating junk mail (er, we mean merging documents) seems like a job performed only by a sinister team of crackpots working in an obscure industrial complex in New Jersey. But even if that description doesn't fit you (we promise it doesn't fit us, either), you might be surprised at how useful merging documents can be in everyday situations. Consider the following scenarios:

- ✓ **You want to send a bunch of documents (newsletters, letters, or whatever) that are similar to each other.** Suppose you have a list of friends and contacts, items, or part numbers. You'd like to send a newsletter or letter to each person, print a label for each item, or print a sheet for each part number, respectively. We're assuming that you want to do the job only once, but many documents need to be done in the same way.

- ✓ **You want to maintain *one* list — make all your address changes, product updates, or whatever, in *one* place — and still create a variety of printouts.** Suppose you're maintaining a list of your friends and family, but you'd like to use the address list to print the list for a variety of purposes: labels for Christmas card envelopes, invitations for your dog's first birthday, and a fund-raising letter for that flat-screen HDTV television you have your eye on. You keep an address book of contacts and every so often, when that holiday rolls around or that new electronic goodie comes out that you have to find money for, you can create multiple documents based on the same set of names.

Document merge does require a fair amount of setup, so it may not be worth the trouble if you need to create only a handful of letters. For small jobs, type one letter and print it; then edit the address and print it again; and so on.

How Does Document Merge Work?

To create personalized junk mail (sorry, we have to stop that bad habit — document merge mailings), you begin in the Merge dialog box (see Figure 15-1), which is accessed by choosing Tools⇨Merge.

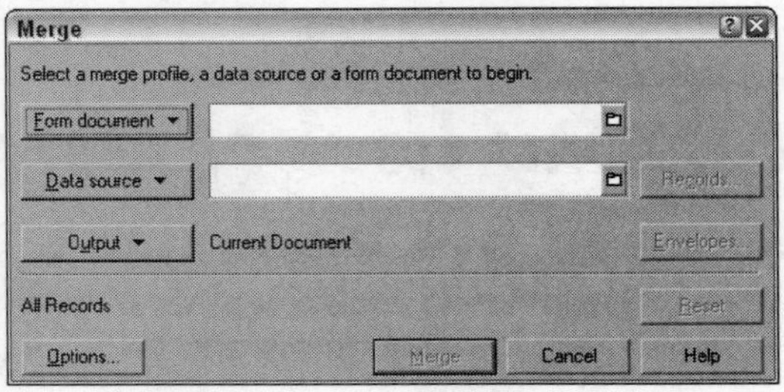

Figure 15-1:
The Merge
dialog box
serves as
Mission
Control for
creating
eerily
similar-
looking
personalized
documents.

Merge			? ✕
Select a merge profile, a data source or a form document to begin.			
Form document ▼		▣	
Data source ▼		▣	Records
Output ▼	Current Document		Envelopes
All Records			Reset
Options...		Merge	Cancel	Help

To perform a merge, you first need two documents: a data source and a form document:

- **Data source:** The *data source* contains the stuff that you plan to put in each of your documents. Your data file can be in a variety of formats, such as a special WordPerfect Data file, Windows address book, or Quattro Pro file. Each data file contains a single database table of records.

- **Form document:** The *form file* contains the form letter. In place of a name or address, the form file contains *merge codes* that tell WordPerfect to use information from the data file.

    One of the most useful aspects of data files and form files is the fact that a single data file can feed several different form files. That way, the same data can appear in several different printouts. When someone's address changes, you don't have to change it on the mailing label, *and* the address list, *and* the family-tree listing, for example.

When you perform the merge, you tell WordPerfect to create one copy of the form file for each person in the data file. You can send this combined file directly to the printer or store it as a new third document.

Your first objective is to get the data file in order before you continue. Exactly how you proceed next depends on whether or not you have data:

- If you're creating the data file from scratch, read the following section, "Creating a WordPerfect Data File." After you've a defined data file, continue on to the "Creating a Form Document" section.

- If you have addresses in a plain old WordPerfect document, read the section "Creating a Form Document," later in this chapter.

Creating a WordPerfect Data File

Before you begin creating a data file, you have to know what fields you want to put in it. *Fields* are the bits of information that will enable you to create the merged documents (that is, the junk-mail letters). These fields are things like a person's first and last names, street address, city, state, and zip. Or a list of part numbers and prices. Or a list of relatives and parents and children. The collection of fields you need for creating one merged document is a *record*.

Take some time to figure out what information you need; it will make the rest of the process much smoother. When you have a list jotted down, you're ready to start creating your WordPerfect merge data file.

Making the data file

Follow these steps to make a data file:

1. **Choose Tools⇨Merge.**

   You see the Merge dialog box (refer to Figure 15-1).

2. **Click the Data Source button and then select Create Data File from the list.**

   If you have a blank document, WordPerfect immediately displays the Create Data File dialog box, as shown in Figure 15-2.

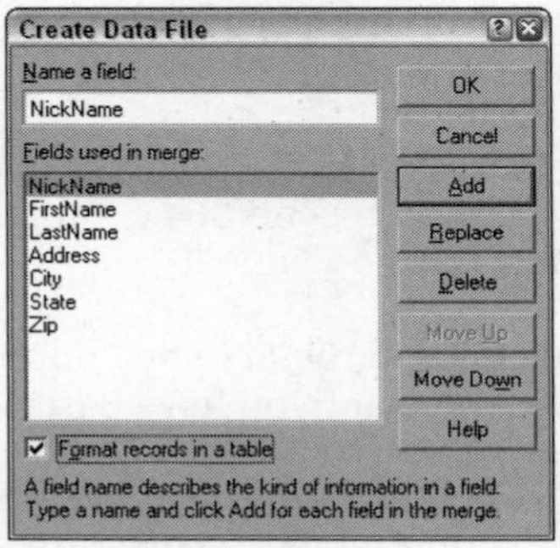

Figure 15-2:
Defining
your field
names in
the Create
Data File
dialog box.

If you have a document with text opened, WordPerfect displays a second dialog box that asks whether you want that file to be the data source or whether you want to create a new document for that purpose. Unless you've just converted an existing file full of data into a merge file, you should choose the New Document Window option. However, if you've created a data file by hand (see the "Creating a Form Document"), click the Use File in Active Window option.

3. **Decide which fields you want to store about each person or other type of information.**

4. **Enter the names of the fields.**

   For each field, type the name in the Name a Field box. When you choose Add (or press Alt+A or the Enter key), the field name appears in the Field Used In Merge list.

5. **Click the Format Records in a Table check box at the bottom of this dialog box.**

   This box determines which of two formats your data file will be in:

- **Tasteful:** If you check the Format Records in a Table check box, all the data file information is neatly arranged in a table, with one row of the table for each record and one column of the table for each field. We highly recommend using this option.

- **Ugly:** If you leave the Format Records in a Table check box unchecked, you get an ugly, techie-looking document that shows each piece of information in the data file on a separate line, with lots of weird-looking WordPerfect merge codes in various colors.

We show you pictures of these two formats a little later in this chapter. You should use whichever format you prefer, but we recommend the attractive format unless your data is already in a data file (in which case, you *must* use the ugly format).

6. **When you finish naming fields, click OK.**

WordPerfect does three things to prepare the data file for your use:

✔ **Creates the document:** WordPerfect puts information about your fields at the beginning of the document. If you chose the ugly method, you see special merge codes, which are visible even though you aren't using the Reveal Codes window. You can see FIELDNAMES and ENDRECORD codes at the top of the document window. If you choose the tasteful method, you see a table with one column for each field.

✔ **Displays the Quick Data Entry dialog box:** WordPerfect obscures your view of the document with a fill-in-the-blanks data-entry screen. Figure 15-3 shows the Quick Data Entry dialog box that WordPerfect created for a three-hour boat tour guest list.

✔ **Displays the Merge toolbar:** WordPerfect displays the Merge toolbar. We'll talk more about the Merge toolbar just ahead, in the next section.

Figure 15-3:
The Word-
Perfect
Quick Data
Entry
screen for
merge data.

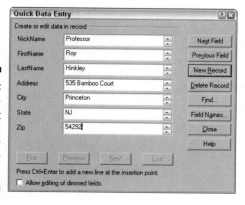

Now you're ready to enter data if you're creating a new file, or enter and edit data if you're converting an old file. Save your document when completed.

Entering your data

Before you can get WordPerfect to fill in the blanks and generate tons of letters, labels, address lists, or whatever, you have to tell it what to fill in the blanks with. If you're following along with us on our junk-mail saga, you should see the Quick Data Entry dialog box that appeared when you finished specifying the fields in your data file. If you're entering your data from scratch, follow these steps:

1. **If the data file isn't already open, open it.**

   If you just created the data file, it's still open.

2. **If the Quick Data Entry dialog box isn't visible, display it.**

   Click the Quick Entry button on the Merge toolbar, which is the row of buttons just above the top of your document. See Figure 15-4.

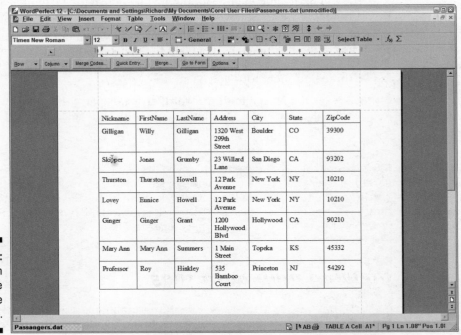

Figure 15-4: Records in a data file in a nice neat table.

3. **Fill in a value for each field to create one record.**

   Click the First button to see the first record. Wherever you are, you can fill in or review all the facts about one person (or record). To move down a field, press Tab, press Enter, or click Next Field. To move up, press Shift+Tab or click Previous Field.

4. **Click New Record to start the next record (the next person).**

   When you get to the last field in a record, pressing Enter is the equivalent of clicking this button.

5. **When you finish entering all the facts (field data) about all the people (record data), click Close.**

   WordPerfect asks whether you want to save the changes to disk.

6. **Unless you've been typing names just to see your fingers move, answer Yes.**

   If you are editing a file that was already saved to disk, WordPerfect updates it. If you started with a blank document, WordPerfect displays the Save File dialog box so that you can enter the filename.

7. **If WordPerfect displays the Save File dialog box, enter a filename and click OK.**

   You can type just the name part; WordPerfect adds the `.dat` extension for your file.

When you enter information in a data file, be sure to enter it as you want it to appear in your letters. In other words, don't enter the text in all uppercase or lowercase if that would look out of place in the document.

Viewing tasteful data files

If you chose to view data as a table (see the "Making the data file" section earlier in the chapter), you see a table like the one shown in Figure 15-4. As we discuss in the "Making corrections" section, you can view or edit the data directly in the table or else use the Quick Entry dialog box, shown in 15-3. For more information about using tables, refer to Chapter 10.

Viewing ugly data files

If you decided not to format the data file as a table (as discussed earlier in the chapter in the section "Making the data file"), you now see the data you entered with each field on a separate line. Between one record and the next are an ENDRECORD merge code and a page break. At the end of each field is the word ENDFIELD (another merge code). To see more than one record at a time, choose View⇨Draft so that page breaks appear as double horizontal lines; otherwise, with only one record per page, most of what you see is blank.

If you don't like your screen to be cluttered with these long merge codes, you can display them as little blobs instead. Click Options on the Merge toolbar (the rightmost button). A menu appears that probably has a check mark before the Display Codes command, which indicates that WordPerfect displays the names of merge codes in your document. If you choose Display As Markers, the code names are replaced by little red diamonds.

If you choose Hide Codes, the code names disappear. This idea may sound great, but it's usually a bad one. If you edit the records in the document, you should be able to verify that the ENDFIELD codes remain at the end of each field.

Making corrections

If your life parallels what happens to us, sooner or later you'll have to fix up the addresses that you entered or (in our example) delete the names of people who have decided not to come along on the three-hour boat tour. You can edit the data file as though it were a normal document, but if you created an ugly data file, you have to be careful not to mess up the ENDFIELD and ENDRECORD merge codes. And if you created a tasteful table data file, you may find the columns a bit too narrow to be useful.

A much better way to make your corrections is to use the Quick Data Entry dialog box, which you display by clicking the Quick Entry button on the Merge toolbar.

While you're using the Quick Data Entry dialog box (refer to Figure 15-3), you can do the following:

- ✔ **Find a record:** Click the Find button. (It doesn't matter which field your cursor is in when you do this; WordPerfect looks for the information in all the fields.) You see a Find dialog box that looks and works much like the familiar Find and Replace dialog box (refer to Chapter 3 if you don't recognize it).

- ✔ **Move between records:** Click the First, Previous, Next, and Last buttons near the bottom of the Quick Data Entry dialog box.

- ✔ **Move between fields:** Click the Tab key to move between fields in the dialog box. Or click the Next Field and Previous Field buttons.

✔ **Change field names:** If you'd like to tweak the names of the fields, click the Field Names button. The Edit Field Names dialog box is displayed so that you can make naming changes.

✔ **Delete a record:** Click the Delete Record button. But watch out — WordPerfect doesn't ask for any confirmation before blowing the record away. Click with care!

If you click this button accidentally and want your record back, click the Close button. A dialog box appears, asking whether you want to save your changes. Click No. Your precious record will be found.

✔ **Add a record:** Add more records by clicking New Record.

✔ **Edit a record:** To update the information in a record, find the record, move your cursor to the field that you want to correct, and edit it.

When you finish using the Quick Data Entry dialog box, click Close. Word-Perfect asks whether you want to save your work. Choose Yes. When you close the Quick Data Entry dialog box, the additions and corrections appear also in the document.

Creating a Form Document

After you create a list of recipients for your form letter, you can type the letter. The document that contains the form letter is called the *form document.* (In these steps, we're creating a letter but you can use these steps to create other documents as well.)

A form document is a regular old WordPerfect document. But in place of the name and address at the top of the letter, you enter funky-looking merge codes, as shown in these steps:

1. **Choose Tools➪Merge, click the Form Document button, and then select the Create Form Document item from the menu.**

   Unless the current document is blank, WordPerfect wants to know whether you want to create a new document to contain the form letter or whether you want to use the document that's on-screen.

2. **In the Form Document drop-down menu, choose Create Form Document. Or if you've already typed the letter and that letter is the current document, choose Current Document instead.**

   When you do make either choice, the Associate Form and Data dialog box (shown in Figure 15-5) is displayed. Use this dialog to specify which data file will provide the data for this form letter.

Figure 15-5:
Which
document
contains the
names and
addresses
for this form
letter?

3. Enter the name of your data file, and then click OK:

- Even if your data file is opened in WordPerfect, you still need to specify its filename in the dialog box. To do so, click the Associate a Data File option and then click the little file-folder button at the right end of the box, which allows you to choose the filename and directory. If WordPerfect can't find your file, click that button and browse around for the .dat file.

- If you're using your Windows Address Book as a data source, click Associate an Address Book.

- If you're using a Microsoft Access database or another outside database, click Associate an ODBC Data Source.

- If you haven't created the data file yet, choose No Association.

4. Click Cancel in the Merge dialog box after you've decided where your data will live.

We know, the natural thing to do is to click the Merge button, but clicking Cancel returns you to your Form Document.

WordPerfect opens a new document and displays the Merge toolbar just above it. The Merge toolbar contains different buttons depending on whether you're editing a form file or working on a data file.

5. Type any information that you want to appear before the date and the name of the addressee.

Type the text for your letterhead, for example, if you'll be printing on blank paper. For a letter, the next thing that you want to see is today's date.

6. If you want to add the date, click the Insert Merge Code on the Merge toolbar and choose Date from its menu.

WordPerfect inserts a colorful DATE code into your document. When you merge this form file with a data file, the current date appears here.

7. **Press Enter to start a new line, and press Enter again to leave a space before the name and address.**

8. **Choose Insert Field on the Merge toolbar.**

   WordPerfect displays the Insert Field Name or Number dialog box, as shown in Figure 15-6. The dialog box lists all the fields that you defined in the data file associated with this form letter.

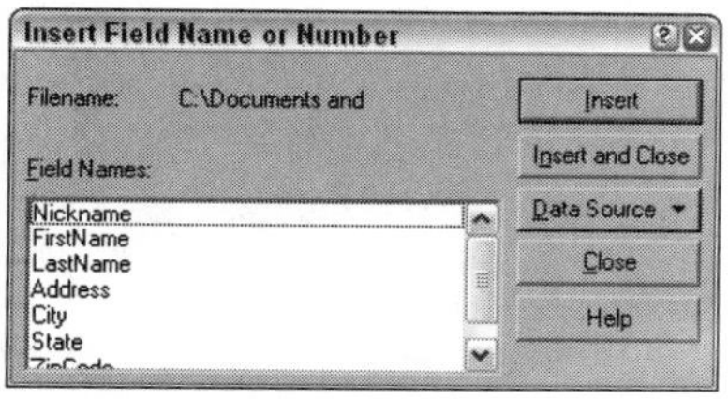

Figure 15-6:
Which
piece of
information
from the
data file do
you want
to use?

9. **Select the First Name field and then click Insert.**

   WordPerfect inserts FIELD(First Name) in color. You're looking at a WordPerfect merge code, which displays each person's first name when you print the form letters. The dialog box is still visible, which is nice because you have to use it a few more times.

10. **Type a space (to appear between the First Name and Last Name fields), select Last Name in the dialog box, and click Insert again.**

    Now codes for the First Name and Last Name fields appear in the form letter.

11. **Press Enter to start a new line.**

    Continue in this vein by inserting codes and typing spaces, pressing Enter, or doing whatever between the codes, until you have laid out the entire address. Check out Figure 15-7 for an example.

12. **Type any text that should appear before the first name, such as *Dear.***

13. **Type your letter.**

    You can use all the usual formats, fonts, and margins that you usually use in a letter. You can even include the contents of merge fields (Gilligan, for example) in the body of the letter for that personalized touch.

14. **When you've finished using the field codes, click the Close button to get the Insert Field Name or Number dialog box off your screen.**

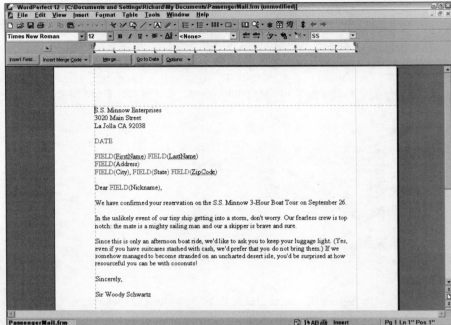

File   Edit   View   Insert   Format   Table   Tools   Window   Help

Times New Roman   12   B *I* U · ABC · *A* · <None>   SS

Insert Field...   Insert Merge Code ·   Merge...   Go to Data   Options ·

S.S. Minnow Enterprises
3020 Main Street
La Jolla CA 92038

DATE

FIELD(FirstName) FIELD(LastName)
FIELD(Address)
FIELD(City), FIELD(State) FIELD(ZipCode)

Dear FIELD(Nickname),

We have confirmed your reservation on the S.S. Minnow 3-Hour Boat Tour on September 26.

In the unlikely event of our tiny ship getting into a storm, don't worry. Our fearless crew is top notch: the mate is a mighty sailing man and our skipper is brave and sure.

Since this is only an afternoon boat ride, we'd like to ask you to keep your luggage light. (Yes, even if you have suitcases stashed with cash, we'd prefer that you do not bring them.) If we somehow managed to become stranded on an uncharted desert isle, you'd be surprised at how resourceful you can be with coconuts!

Sincerely,

Sir Woody Schwartz

PassengerMail.frm   AB Insert   Pg 1 Ln 1" Pos 1"

Figure 15-7:
Creating a
form file.

15. Save the document.

Choose File⇨Save As. It's best to type just the filename and let WordPerfect worry about the three-letter extension. (The extension WordPerfect uses is .frm.)

You can create several form files for one data file. If your data file contains a list of people who owe you money, for example, you can make one form file that contains a polite letter requesting payment. A second form file can contain a letter using firmer language, and a third form file can contain the letter that tells your buddy Rocky the Repo Man the names of the people he'll be visiting soon.

When it comes time to print, you can print envelopes to go along with your letters. You can even print envelopes but no letters, but that's a little more complicated. We explain how to do both before the end of the chapter.

What if you choose the wrong data file for this form letter? Or what if you create a new data file and want to use an existing form file? No problem. To associate a different data file with your form file, click the Merge button on the Merge toolbar. The original Merge dialog box is displayed. You can then link a new data file to your form document by entering the data filename in the Data File box and clicking Merge.

Merging and Printing Your Files

After you have a data file and a form document, you're ready to merge. Assuming that your form document is open, call the post office and tell them to get ready. Then follow these steps:

1. **Click the Merge button on the Merge toolbar.**

    WordPerfect displays the Merge dialog box, as shown in Figure 15-8.

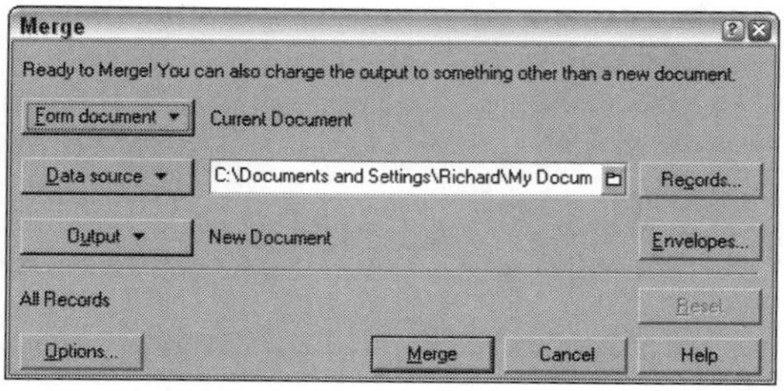

Figure 15-8: Making junk mail from a data file and a form file.

Merge dialog box:
Ready to Merge! You can also change the output to something other than a new document.

Form document ▾ Current Document
Data source ▾ C:\Documents and Settings\Richard\My Docum Records...
Output ▾ New Document Envelopes...
All Records Reset
Options... Merge Cancel Help

2. **If needed, select your data source.**

    Click the Form Document button and choose Select File from its menu. WordPerfect enables you to select the filename, and inserts the complete path name of the form file. This box is already filled if you already linked the data file with the form document.

3. **Tell WordPerfect where to put the resulting merged forms.**

    Click Output. We recommend the following choices:

    *   **<New Document>:** This is our favorite. WordPerfect makes a new document and sticks all the copies of your form letter in it for you to review before printing them.

    *   **<Printer>:** Choose this option to print the form letters without reviewing them. This choice is the "go for the gold" approach. You can waste a great deal of paper this way, however, if you discover a typo in your form file.

4. **Click the Envelopes button.**

   WordPerfect gives you the option of tacking a bunch of envelopes to the end of your form letter. This option is useful if you plan to mail your letters. The screen changes to a blank screen, where you can format your envelope.

5. **Click the Insert Field button to display the list of fields in your data file.**

6. **Select the first field from the data file to appear on the envelope (First Name, for example), and then click Insert.**

   For this example, WordPerfect inserts `FIELD(First Name)`.

7. **Type a space (to appear between the First Name and Last Name fields), and then insert the Last Name field.**

8. **Press Enter to start a new line.**

9. **Continue inserting codes and typing spaces, pressing Enter, or doing whatever between the codes until you have laid out the entire address, as shown in Figure 15-9.**

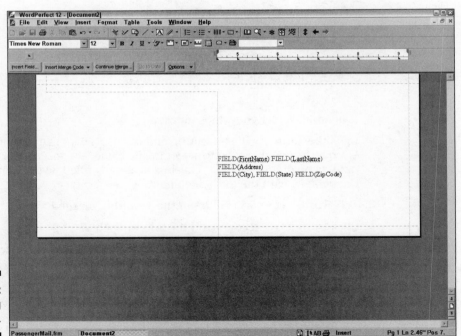

Figure 15-9:
Making
envelopes.

Sometimes you'll want to edit the return address or omit it (a useful technique to know when you use preprinted envelopes). Click the Return Address button while the envelope format is on the screen. If you created an envelope before, you see the last return address you used for a letter. You can edit this address on the screen or select Address Book from the Return Address button pop-up menu and choose an address from your book. Of course, the No Return Address option on the pop-up menu is the one you use when you have preprinted envelopes.

10. When you're finished with the envelope, click Continue Merge.

If you look carefully, you see that where the Merge dialog box used to say `All Records` in the bottom-left corner, it now says `All Records; Envelope`. This means that every time you do a merge with this form file, WordPerfect adds envelopes to the end of the letters that it creates. If you change your mind, click the Envelopes button again and select Cancel Envelope.

11. Click Merge.

WordPerfect makes one copy of your form file for each record in your data file and puts the results where you told it to put them.

Figure 15-10 shows a letter to our three-hour boat tour guests. All the letters are in this one new document, one per page. If you selected envelopes, all the envelopes come after all the letters.

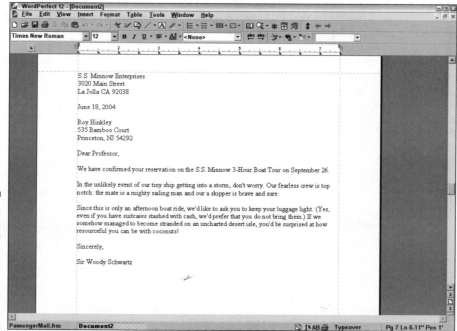

Figure 15-10: The grand results of our merging efforts. Each letter is on a separate page.

12. **If your merged letters are in a new document, print the document.**

   If you added envelopes to your merge document, this step can be a little tricky unless you have a printer with a separate bin that you keep stocked with envelopes or a printer clever enough to ask for envelopes when it needs them. For the rest of us mortals, scan down through your document until you see the first envelope. Click the envelope, and note the page number on the application bar (8, for example). Now print all the pages up to the first envelope (pages 1 through 7, in our example), put envelopes in the printer, and print pages 8 through 14, which are the envelopes.

You can look through the letters first to make sure that they are appropriately personal. You can even make changes in them so that they really are personalized. ("P.S. As you requested, in the event of being stranded on a desert isle, you will be able to room with Mary Ann.")

After you print your form letters, you can save the document that contains them or close it without saving it. After all, you can always create the letters again by repeating these merge steps.

Printing Your Data File

If you want to print an address list of the people to whom you sent letters, you can print the data file. If your data file is in tasteful table format, it looks rather nice.

If your data file is in ugly format, it looks fairly yucky with all those merge codes in there. To hide the merge codes in ugly format, choose Options on the Merge toolbar and then choose Hide Codes.

Part V
More Stuff You Can Do with Your Documents

The 5th Wave   By Rich Tennant

HANK ORDERS IDEAS FOR HIS MYSTERY/HORROR GAME.

Well shoot! This isn't a case of the willies, this is a case of the heebie-jeebies!

CREATIVE IDEAS INC

In this part . . .

If you yearn to wake up in the morning with the tune *I've Got the Power* buzzing through your ears, check out this part, where you discover the power side of WordPerfect. You start by checking out how to manage your many documents and then open up the hood to see the true power behind WordPerfect: reveal codes.

Chapter 16

Managing Your Documents

. . . .

In This Chapter

▶ Working with multiple documents

▶ Combining part or all of one document with another

▶ Finding files

▶ Moving, copying, and deleting files

. . . .

*P*reparing dinner for guests is inevitably a messy business. For one thing, you have to juggle the appetizer, main course, vegetables, dinner rolls, and dessert in a grand but futile effort to ensure that everything is ready to serve at the right time. Oh, in a perfect world, you could make each part of the meal in a steady sequence and have everything pipin' hot on the table the moment your guests ring the doorbell. But in the real world, by the time the doorbell rings, the appetizer is turning stone cold, the ham in the oven is getting dry from over-baking, and the veggies are being steamed to mush as we clean up the cake batter splattered on the kitchen floor.

Using WordPerfect can seem a lot like preparing that dinner. In a perfect world, you may be able to create a document, edit it, print it, and save it, and then close it so that you can move on to the next document. But the reality is that you're usually juggling several open documents, each of them in a different state of editing.

In this chapter, we welcome you to the world of document juggling and show you how you can use WordPerfect to work with multiple documents at the same time. We also touch on how you can combine and find files to get things better organized.

Working on Two Documents at the Same Time

As you're probably quite familiar with by now, you can work on a single document by clicking the Open button on the toolbar (or by choosing File⇨Open). WordPerfect displays the document in a window. This window occupies all of the WordPerfect *document area* — that is, the space between the property bar at the top and the application bar at the bottom.

If you've read the previous chapters in the book, you've been working with one document until this point. But you don't have to stop with just one. You can open another document without closing the first. WordPerfect keeps the first document open but covers its document area with a second window that contains the second document.

Switching between open documents

When you open more than one document, you'll see each document's name on the Document buttons on the left side of the application bar, as shown in Figure 16-1. (See Chapter 2 for more on the application bar.) You can click a document's button to make it visible.

If you like using the keyboard instead, cycle through the open documents by pressing Ctrl+F6 or Ctrl+Shift+F6. Or if you're menu kind of folk, choose Window from the menu bar. You see a menu that contains three commands (Cascade, Tile Top to Bottom, and Tile Side by Side) followed by a numbered list of the documents you have open. To switch to another open document, just choose its name from the menu.

Working with multiple documents

The most common reason for opening multiple documents is to refer to one document while you write another — or sometimes to borrow text from one document while you write another. WordPerfect makes this technique easy: You can use all the WordPerfect cut-and-paste commands to move or copy text from one document to another.

If you wrote a truly stellar paragraph in one document and want to use it in another one, for example, follow these steps:

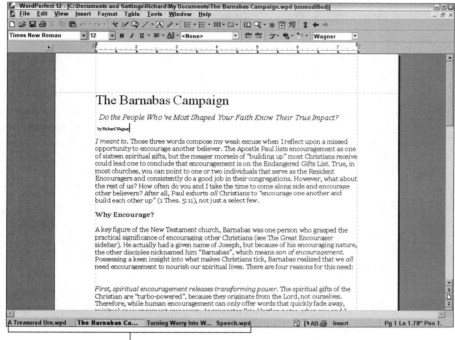

Figure 16-1:
The application bar displays the documents you have open.

Document buttons

1. **Open both documents.**

   Click the Open button on the toolbar (or choose File⇨Open). If the two documents are in the same directory, you can open them both at the same time. To do so, hold the Ctrl key down while you select each and then click OK. If the documents are located in different locations, open them one at a time and then proceed.

2. **In the original document, select the text that you want to copy.**

   See Chapter 3 for more on how to select text.

3. **To copy the paragraph to the Clipboard, click the Copy button on the toolbar.**

   Or press Ctrl+C or choose Edit⇨Copy.

4. **Switch to the other document by clicking its button on the application bar.**

5. **Move your cursor to the point where you want the paragraph to appear.**

6. **To paste the paragraph from the Clipboard, click the Paste button on the toolbar.**

   If you prefer, you can press Ctrl+V or choose Edit⇨Paste.

Maxing out

You can keep opening additional documents until nine are open. Then Word-Perfect puts its foot down and prevents you from opening any more by disabling the File⇨Open command and the Open and New Blank Document buttons on the toolbar.

To open another document, you must first close one of your nine open documents. We rarely encounter a situation in which we need to refer to more than nine documents at the same time; maybe your brain cells have more capacity than ours do.

Closing the curtains

When you finish working on a document, we recommend closing it. This way, you won't accidentally edit it. Also, multiple opened documents can slow WordPerfect just a tad on less powerful computers.

To close the window that contains a document, click the document's Close button (the X in the top-right corner of the document window), choose File⇨ Close, or press Ctrl+F4.

If the document you're closing has been changed since you last saved it, Word-Perfect gives you the chance to save it before closing it so that you don't lose your work. You can click Yes (so that WordPerfect saves the document before closing it), No (so that WordPerfect closes it without saving your changes), or Cancel (so that WordPerfect abandons the idea of closing it).

Combining Documents

Each WordPerfect document lives in its own cozy little file on your hard drive But sometimes you want to break down the walls between your documents and get them together, throw a little party, or whatever.

Suppose that one of your documents contains a standard description of the product you sell — chocolate-belly futures. Then you create a new document in which you begin a letter to a prospective client. You realize that you want to include the product description in your letter.

Inserting one document into another one

Follow these steps to insert one document into another:

1. **Move your cursor to the location where you want the text from the other file to appear.**

   For example, move the cursor to the point in your letter where you want to wax eloquent about chocolate-belly futures.

2. **Choose Insert➪File.**

   WordPerfect displays the Insert File dialog box, which looks suspiciously like the Open File dialog box and half a dozen other dialog boxes that have to do with files.

3. **Find the name of the file you want to insert in the current document.**

   To find the file, use the Look In drop-down list and search in the folders that appear.

4. **Click Insert or double-click the filename.**

   WordPerfect opens the file, sticks its contents into the current document right where your cursor is located, and pushes down any text that comes after the cursor.

You can insert more than one document into the current document. Word-Perfect has no limit to the number of other documents you can stick into the current one, but you are limited by the amount of hard drive space and memory you have in your computer.

WordPerfect doesn't keep track of where inserted text comes from. For example, after you insert Document A into Document B, its text is now considered part of Document B. Therefore, if you change the text of Document A in its original location, that change does not ripple to Document B. If you want the inserted text to change with its source document, you want *linked documents*. WordPerfect can do that; you choose File➪Document➪Subdocument, as we discuss in Chapter 12.

Saving a chunk of text as a separate document

You can also do the reverse of inserting text — you can save part of the current document in a new, separate file. Suppose that you write a letter that contains a terrific explanation of how to make gooseberry pie (your specialty). Now you want to save your recipe in its own file, as shown in these steps:

1. **Select the text that you want to save separately.**

   Chapter 3 shows you ways to select text.

2. **Click the Save button on the toolbar.**

   Or press Ctrl+S or choose File⇨Save. WordPerfect notices that some text is selected and displays the Save dialog box, as shown in Figure 16-2.

Figure 16-2:
Saving
some text in
its own file.

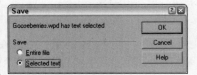

3. **To save the selected text in its own file, click Selected Text and then click OK.**

   WordPerfect displays the usual Save File dialog box so that you can tell it the filename you want to use for the selected text. You might call the selected text `Gooseberry Pie.wpd`, for example.

4. **Click Save to create the new document that contains the selected text.**

   The text you selected also remains in the original document — that is, WordPerfect saves in the new file a *copy* of the selected text.

Finding a File with a Forgotten Name

Boy, is WordPerfect ever glad that you want to know how to find your files. It has invested heavily in creating the Saint Bernard of lost and stranded files, the veritable *Rescue 911* of technology-assisted document search and rescue. It's called QuickFinder, and it's lurking almost unseen in the Save File, Save As, and Open File dialog boxes. QuickFinder is so muscle-bound that we're not even going to try to describe everything it can do. Instead, we focus on how it helps you find a file.

QuickFinder finds files by looking for certain text. If you want to find a letter to Ms. Tannenwald, for example, but you can't remember the name of the file, you just type *Tannenwald* in the right place in the QuickFinder.

It doesn't matter whether the word is even associated in the document's filename. As long as the word appears somewhere in the document, QuickFinder executes your humble request and comes marching back, proudly carrying in its teeth any and all files that have any hint of the word in them. This feature works for phrases and various word combinations, too.

Before we go any further, we want to show you how to perform a simple single-word search. Follow these steps:

1. **Choose File⇨Open.**

2. **Click the File Name box and type a word that you want to search for in the files.**

   Don't let the File Name box fool you. QuickFinder looks in the contents of documents — not in the filenames — to find files.

3. **Select the folder where you want the search to start.**

   The QuickFinder starts its search in the folder where it expects that you put your documents. It searches that folder and all the folders in it.

   To search an entire disk, click the Look In box, and choose My Computer from the list of folders. (It's not really a folder, but we won't tell if you won't.) If you don't see My Computer in this list, keep clicking the Go Back One Folder Level button until you see it. (The Go Back One Folder Level button is the one with the folder and the upward-pointing hooked arrow on it.)

   Be patient; searching your entire disk can take a long, long time, especially if your disk is large and you have a lot of files.

4. **Click the Find Now button.**

   The Find Now button becomes the Stop Find button while QuickFinder searches. As QuickFinder finds files, it lists them in the list of documents.

5. **Double-click one of these files to open it in WordPerfect.**

   Alternatively, you can just click the Close button in the Search Results dialog box and go about your business, satisfied with a Find job well done.

Sometimes a single word may not be enough when you're looking for a file. You can't just type a phrase in the Content box; QuickFinder interprets a phrase such as *Dear Elaine* (Ms. Tannenwald's first name) as a list of individual words and finds files that contain any of those words. (In this example, QuickFinder returns all files that contain either the word *Dear* or the word *Elaine* somewhere in them). That may be a few more files than you want to sift through, especially if you write a lot of letters.

If you want to search for an exact phrase, put it in quotation marks like this: "Dear Elaine." Then click the Find Now button. Now QuickFinder searches for all documents that contain the exact phrase *Dear Elaine.*

The same QuickFinder capabilities are available also in the Save File and Save As dialog boxes.

File Management, the WordPerfect Way

Basic file management — such as moving, copying, or deleting files — is usually done in Windows Explorer, outside of WordPerfect. But if you find yourself in WordPerfect's Save File or Save As dialog boxes and you need to do some housecleaning and reorganization, then you're in luck, because you can do many file management tasks directly from the dialog box.

To begin, display the Save As dialog box (choose File➪Save As) and make sure its menu is visible. If you don't have a menu displayed, click the Toggle Menu On/Off button on the top right side of the dialog box.

Creating a folder

After you click this button, follow these steps to create a folder:

1. **In the Save As dialog box, choose File➪New➪Folder.**

   A new folder, cleverly named New Folder, appears in the list of folders and files. Your folder is created in the folder whose name is in the Save In portion of the dialog box. Because New Folder probably isn't the name that you had in mind, you can change it.

   The New Folder name should be highlighted. And if you look carefully, you see that the right end of the selected text is blinking.

2. **Type the folder name that you actually want to use and press Enter.**

Then, to save a document in that new folder, you can double-click the folder name. The new folder name appears in the Save In portion of the dialog box. Type the document name in the File Name portion of the dialog box, and press Enter.

Moving a file

To move a file, follow these steps:

1. **Click the View Folders button on the Save File dialog box's toolbar.**

   The list of folders is displayed on the left side of the Save As dialog box, as shown in Figure 16-3.

2. **On the right side of the Save As dialog box, find the file that you want to move.**

View Folders

Figure 16-3:
A mini-
Windows
Explorer
packed in
the Save As
dialog box.

3. **Move around the tree view until you see the folder to which you want to move the file.**

   Don't click any folder name. If you do, the folders and files list changes, and you need to select your file again. Go back to Step 2, and do not collect $200.

   If you need to see folders that don't fit into the tree view, use the scroll bars. If you still can't find the folder that you're looking for, it may be hidden inside another folder. You can open a folder by clicking its plus sign (+). You can do all this without disturbing your file selection in the folders and files part of the dialog box.

4. **Click the file that you want to move.**

5. **Move the file.**

   To move the file with the mouse, drag it to the folder where you want it to go. To move the file with the keyboard, choose Edit⇨Cut. Then double-click the folder where you want the file to go and choose Edit⇨Paste. You see a message box, telling you that the file is being moved.

Copying a file

Pardon us if we get a little brief here — copying a file is so much like moving a file that we don't want to put you to sleep by repeating everything. Just refer to the preceding section, "Moving a file." Hold down the Ctrl key while you do the dragging. If you do things with the keyboard, choose Edit⇨Copy instead of Edit⇨Cut. The difference? The original file stays in the location from which you copied it and also appears in the new location.

Or, if you like to right-click, do so and choose Copy from the menu.

Deleting a file

As the Good Book says, there's a time for everything. A time to create and a time to save. A time to print and a time to delete. Ok, maybe those aren't the exact words, but you get the idea. But, when using WordPerfect, there will be times when you want to send a document off to Siberia or beyond.

To delete a file, follow these instructions carefully. We assume that you've already selected the file that you want to delete inside the Save As dialog box.

To delete a file, follow these steps:

1. **In the Save As dialog box, highlight the file that you want to delete.**

2. **Press the Delete key.**

   Or, if you already have your hand on the mouse, choose File⇨Delete from the Save As dialog box menu (or right-click the filename and choose Delete). WordPerfect displays a dialog box, asking whether you're sure that you want to delete the file.

3. **Confirm that you *do* want to send the file to the Recycle Bin.**

4. **Cry in anguish as you realize that you just deleted the only copy of the project justification that funds your job.**

   Actually, there is a way back. Double-click the Recycle Bin, the cute little trash-can icon with a recycle symbol on it. Find your file in that folder, and use the procedure that we talk about in the "Moving a file" section to move it back where it belongs. Alternatively, after you find your file in the Recycle Bin, you can right-click it and choose Restore from the QuickMenu that appears. The file disappears from the Recycle Bin and mysteriously reappears wherever it came from.

Chapter 17

Reveal Codes: Getting Ultimate Control Over Your Document

- -

In This Chapter

▶ Knowing what secret formatting codes are

▶ Seeing reveal codes in your document

▶ Changing and deleting codes

▶ Working with character codes

▶ Dealing with character formatting codes

▶ Undoing sentence and paragraph formatting

▶ Undoing page and document formatting

▶ Finding and replacing codes

- -

A *gent 009. Licensed to reveal.*

James Bond, 007, gets all the glory, fame, and big movie contracts, but another "double-o" agent is working behind the scenes of WordPerfect, doing the hard work of formatting your document for you. We call that undercover operative Agent 009, known throughout the spy underworld as The Revealer.

Agent 009 works beneath the surface of every WordPerfect document to keep track of all the formatting commands you've set. To perform its impressive formatting tricks, it scatters hidden and powerful codes, called *reveal codes,* throughout your document.

In most cases, you should never have to see or work with these codes; you can just let 009 do its thing. However, on rare occasions you may find yourself trying to deal with a document that won't format in a way that you want or expect. At these times, you'll have to roll up your sleeves and get total control over your document by tweaking its reveal codes.

Your silver bullet

If you're struggling with the idea of secret codes lurking about your document and formatting the text, feel free to hold off on this chapter for now. But, if you ever get into trouble and need to find out why your document is doing something you don't want it to, come back. Consider this chapter your "silver bullet" to get you out of a tight spot.

But first, get your secret decoder ring and other standard issue spy equipment. 009 is waiting . . .

What Are Reveal Codes?

Every WordPerfect document consists of *content* — the stuff you type — and *formatting instructions* — the appearance of the document and text. Normally you work only with the content and the visual results of the formatting operations. However, WordPerfect keeps track of that formatting information as a behind-the-scenes part of the document through *reveal codes*.

When you set formatting using a dialog box (such as Format➪Font) or by clicking a formatting button on a toolbar (such as the Bold button), WordPerfect shows you the results instantly in your document and also inserts reveal codes in your document that indicate the formatting you just turned on. In this way, when you open up your document later, WordPerfect will know how to format the document in the same way.

WordPerfect has three types of codes: character codes, single codes, and paired codes. We describe each type of code in gory detail later in this chapter and tell you how to spot them and what they do. This list briefly describes the codes:

- ✔ **Character codes:** These codes represent special non-alphanumeric characters, such as Tab. Some codes represent keys on the keyboard and others (such as Indent) don't.

- ✔ **Single codes:** This type of code turns on a formatting feature. The Lft Marg and Rgt Marg codes, for example, set the left and right margins, beginning at the position of the code. The formatting that the code does remains in effect for the rest of the document or until WordPerfect runs across another occurrence of the same code.

✔ **Paired codes:** We bet you guessed that this type of code comes in pairs. WordPerfect also calls these codes *revertible codes* — who knows where that little piece of jargon comes from? The first code in the pair turns a feature on, and the second one turns it off. Bold codes, for example, come in pairs: one to turn on bold and the other to turn it off. The text between the two codes is in bold.

Uncovering Reveal Codes

This code business is all very exciting, you say. So where are all these codes that have been running around in my documents? Simple: Choose View⇨ Reveal Codes (or press Alt+F3) to see the codes in your document. Figure 17-1 shows the WordPerfect window with the Reveal Codes window at the bottom.

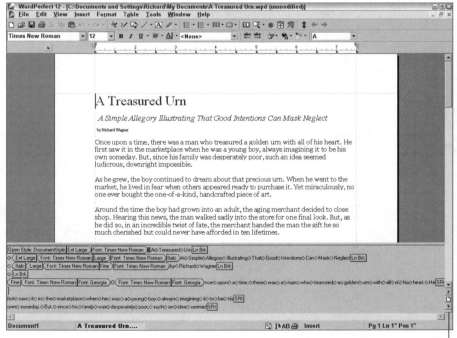

Figure 17-1:
Strange-
looking
codes are
lurking in
your
document.

Toggle off/on and resize Reveal Codes window

Exploring the Reveal Codes window

The Reveal Codes window shows the same text that you see in the regular window. Because the Reveal Codes window usually can't hold as much text as the regular window can, it shows the part around the cursor's position. The cursor appears as a red box; its location in the Reveal Codes window corresponds to its position in the regular window.

Scrolling up or down in the Reveal Codes window is awkward. You can press the navigation keys on your keyboard, such as PgUp and PgDn. Or you can move the cursor in the regular window and allow the Reveal Codes cursor to follow along.

Text in the Reveal Codes window is unformatted. Spaces appear as diamonds, and codes look like buttons. Character and single codes look like rectangular buttons, and paired codes (such as the `Italc` codes) have pointed ends, with the points of each pair pointing to each other.

You can type, edit, and perform all your usual WordPerfect activities while the Reveal Codes window is visible; some people like to leave it open all the time.

You can control the colors that WordPerfect uses for the text and background of the Reveal Codes window, how much information is shown for each code, and more. Chapter 18 shows you where to find the controls for this stuff.

Click into the gap

You can reveal your codes by using the mouse and the scroll bar. You may have noticed (we didn't, until we read the manual) a little gray lump between the top of the vertical scroll bar and the property bar, and a matching lump between the bottom of the vertical scroll bar and the application bar. It turns out that if you move your mouse pointer into one of these little lumps, the pointer turns into a double-headed arrow that points up and down.

Drag the arrow with the mouse, and the dividing line between the regular window and the Reveal Codes window appears, and you can drag the line up and down to the position you want. If you click one of those little lumps instead of dragging, you get all codes all the time. But don't panic; you can adjust how much of the window shows codes and how much shows your document the way you formatted it. Just drag the fat gray bar (it's probably just above the codes) until you see enough of your document to make you comfortable.

TIP

A note to Microsoft Word users

If you've used Microsoft Word, you might be looking like a deer staring into headlights with all this talk of secret codes. Unlike WordPerfect, Microsoft Word doesn't use codes for formatting, so you never see the WordPerfect type of x-ray view of the document.

Microsoft Word does have a Field Codes command, which provides a way to include text that's under the control of the Word program — today's date, for example, which Word can update automatically. Some WordPerfect codes do this, too, but most don't.

Adjusting the size of the window

A dividing line separates the regular window from the Reveal Codes window. Using the mouse, you can click the line and drag it up or down.

Getting rid of the Reveal Codes window

When you finish looking at your codes, you can make the Reveal Codes window go away. After all, seeing your codes leap around at the bottom of the screen is distracting. Use one of these methods to send the Reveal Codes window back into byte oblivion:

- ✔ Choose View➪Reveal Codes again.
- ✔ Press Alt+F3.
- ✔ Click the dividing line and drag it down to the application bar.
- ✔ Right-click anywhere in the Reveal Codes window and choose Hide Reveal Codes from the QuickMenu.

Cracking the Codes

Now that you know how to bring the secret WordPerfect formatting codes into the light of day, what can you do with them? In the Reveal Codes window, you can examine the WordPerfect codes, modify them, and even delete them.

Looking at codes

Some codes contain much more information than you might think. You may see a `Header A` code at the beginning of your document, for example. This code indicates that you have defined a header. To see more details about this code, use the cursor keys, or click just before the code.

The cursor appears as a little red box.

Suddenly, the code expands until it says, for example, `Header A: Every Page, Chocolate in the Workplace.` Many codes contain more information than meets the eye. Place the cursor before a code to see just what it says.

Modifying codes

To change a code, double-click it in the Reveal Codes window. This action tells WordPerfect that you want to do something to the code, and WordPerfect tries to guess what that something is. If you used a dialog box to insert the code in the first place, WordPerfect displays the same dialog box again. If you double-click a `Para Spacing` code, for example, WordPerfect pops up the Paragraph Format dialog box, which displays the values that you specified when you created the code. (This feature is rather useful.) If you change the information in the dialog box and then click OK, WordPerfect updates the code to match.

Deleting codes

The position of each code is important, and codes in the wrong place can be a headache. If you see a code that seems to have wandered off, you can rein it in. Move your cursor before it and press Delete, or move the cursor just after it and press Backspace. Or simply drag it aboveground — into the top window, where it evaporates in the warm light of day.

When the Reveal Codes window is not displayed, WordPerfect skips most codes when you press the Delete or Backspace keys so that you don't delete codes by accident. When the codes are revealed, however, WordPerfect figures that you can see what you're doing, so when you press Delete, it deletes the code to the right of the red cursor.

We recommend saving your document (press Ctrl+S) before you change any codes because it's easy to make a horrendous mess with this code stuff. If you save your document before you goof up, you can just close the messy version (press Ctrl+F4) and reopen the original (press Ctrl+O) to start fresh.

Your trusty friend Undo (Ctrl+Z) works when you make changes to reveal codes as well.

Understanding the Open Style code

At the beginning of every document, you may notice a mysterious `Open Style` code. WordPerfect doesn't allow you to delete this code. This code tells Word-Perfect that unless you insert codes to tell it otherwise, it should format the document using a style called `DocumentStyle`, which is the default format that WordPerfect uses for all new documents. (We talk all about styles in Chapter 9.)

Working with Character Codes

The most common codes in every document are carriage-return (line-ending) codes:

- ✔ **Soft return (**`SRt`**):** A return (line-ending) character that WordPerfect inserts automatically when you reach the right margin

- ✔ **Hard return (**`HRt`**):** A character that WordPerfect inserts automatically whenever you press the Enter key to signal the end of a paragraph

This list shows some other popular character codes:

- ✔ **Left tab:** This code is what you get when you press the Tab key and it moves to a left tab stop. (Chapter 7 discusses the types of tab stops.) `Right Tab`, `Center Tab`, `Dec Tab`, `. . .Left Tab`, `. . .Right Tab`, `. . .Center Tab`, and `. . .Dec Tab` are the other types of tab-character codes that WordPerfect may insert, depending on the type of tab stop to which these tabs move.

- ✔ **Shift+Tab:** Pressing these keys inserts a `Hd Back Tab` code, used mainly in hanging indents (see Chapter 7).

- ✔ **Hard page break (**`HPg`**):** The `HPg` code represents the hard page break that you produce by pressing Ctrl+Enter (or choosing Insert➪New Page).

- ✔ **Soft page break:** When WordPerfect inserts a soft page break because a page has become full, it may use the `SRt-SPg` or `HRt-SPg` code (but don't worry about the difference between the two).

- ✔ **Automatic hyphenation:** If you use WordPerfect's automatic hyphenation feature (see Chapter 8), WordPerfect sticks in two codes when it decides to hyphenate a word at the right margin. First, you see `Auto Hyphen EOL` (EOL is computerese for *end of line*); then you see `TSRt` (temporary soft return, maybe?).

Hard and soft landings

WordPerfect has two versions of many codes: one hard and one soft. This terminology has nothing to do with how well they'd serve as a pillow. No, it has to do with how seriously WordPerfect takes them.

WordPerfect inserts a soft code itself and could just as well take it right back out. WordPerfect continually shuffles soft codes around. When you edit the text in a paragraph, for example, WordPerfect changes SRt codes into spaces (and vice-versa) as necessary so that the margins are correct. But WordPerfect never deletes a HRt code, one that you added yourself.

You can delete any of these codes to get rid of the characters that they represent.

Removing and Editing Character Formatting Codes

Chapter 6 shows you how to format the characters in your documents six ways from Sunday. When you use character formatting, WordPerfect creates a flurry of secret codes. Most of the codes are paired and mark the beginning and end of the text to be formatted. This list shows some of the character-formatting codes that you may see:

- ✔ **Bold:** A pair of Bold codes encloses text in bold.
- ✔ **Italic:** Likewise, Italc codes surround text in italic.
- ✔ **Underline:** Und codes appear around underlined text.
- ✔ **Font size:** A lone Font Size code changes the font size from the code's location to the end of the document or until you get to another Font Size code. A pair of Font Size codes can also enclose text that appears in a different size.
- ✔ **Fonts:** Likewise, one Font code (or a pair of Font codes) changes the font (typeface).

Removing character formatting

To undo character formatting, just blow away the formatting codes in the Reveal Codes window. To get rid of a paired code, simply delete one of them. When one of a pair of paired codes disappears, the other does, too.

Editing formatted text

After you format your text with character formatting codes, editing can be a little tricky. If you format a heading in bold, for example, and then add a word to the end of the heading, that word may not be in bold. Why not? Because you typed the new text *after* the closing Bold code. Without using the Reveal Codes window, it's difficult to see whether your cursor is inside or outside a pair of formatting codes.

Some types of formatting are shown on the toolbar and property bar. If your cursor is in bold text, for example, the Bold button appears to be pushed in. Likewise, the Font Face and Font Size buttons on the property bar tell you the font and size, respectively, of the text at the cursor's location. But unless you study the toolbars carefully, you have to use the Reveal Codes window to understand the exact formatting state the cursor is in.

Removing Sentence and Paragraph Formatting

In Chapter 7, you fool around with the margins and tab stops in your document, as well as with some other things that affect entire paragraphs of text at a time. As you can imagine, WordPerfect inserts a secret code every time you use one of these formatting commands. This list shows some codes that you may encounter:

- ✔ **Tab set (**Tab Set**):** Contains the settings for all the tabs that you can see on the ruler. Even if you change just one stop, the Tab Set code stores the positions of all of them. These codes belong at the beginning of a paragraph — never in the middle of a line.

- ✔ **Indent (**Hd Left Ind**):** The indent character that you get when you press the F7 key.

✓ **Double indent** (Hd Left\/Right Ind)**:** The double-indent character that you get when you press Ctrl+Shift+F7 to indent from both the left and right margins.

✓ **Hanging indents** (Hd Left Ind **and** Hd Back Tab)**:** Used for hanging indents. When you create a hanging indent, WordPerfect inserts two — count 'em, two — codes. First, it inserts a Hd Left Ind code so that all the lines of the paragraph are indented. Then it inserts a Hd Back Tab code so that the first line of the paragraph is not indented. It's not elegant, but it works.

✓ **Center of left and right margin** (Hd Center on Marg)**:** Centers a line between the left and right margins.

✓ **Flush text with right margin** (Hd Flush Right)**:** Pushes your text to the right margin.

✓ **Hyphenation on or off** (Hyph:On **or** Hyph:Off)**:** Indicates that you have turned on or off the hyphenation feature.

You may see the following codes by themselves or in pairs. If you see just one, the code has set the formatting for the rest of the document or until you get to another of the same kind of code. If you see a pair of these codes, they set the formatting for the text enclosed by the pair. This list briefly describes the codes:

✓ **Left and right margins** (Lft Mar **and** Rgt Mar)**:** Set the left and right margins of your document, beginning at the position of the code. These codes belong at the beginning of a paragraph.

✓ **The** Just **family of codes:** Tell WordPerfect how to justify the text between the left and right margins.

✓ **Line spacing** (Ln Spacing)**:** Sets the spacing between lines.

You can delete any of these codes to remove unwanted formatting from your document. When formatting codes come in pairs, you can delete just one of the pair; then they both disappear.

Removing Page and Document Formatting

Most codes that affect entire pages or the entire document appear at the beginning of a document, or at least at the top of the page. That arrangement makes them a little easier to find in the Reveal Codes window. To cancel the formatting controlled by these codes, just delete the code.

This list shows the codes created by the commands we describe in Chapter 8:

- ✔ **Paper size and type** (Paper Sz **and** Paper Typ)**:** Sets the paper size and paper type for the document.

- ✔ **Top and bottom margins** (Top Mar **and** Bot Mar)**:** Sets the top and bottom margins.

- ✔ **Center of top and bottom margins** (Cntr Cur Pg)**:** Centers the current page between the top and bottom margins.

- ✔ **Widow and orphan settings** (Wid **and** Orph)**:** Tells WordPerfect how to deal with widows and orphans (at least with the types of widows and orphans we describe in Chapter 8).

- ✔ **Conditional end of page** (Condl EOP)**:** Tells WordPerfect to keep the next few lines together and not to split them with a page break.

- ✔ **Block protect** (Block Pro)**:** Encloses text that should not be split by a page break. This code should always come in pairs.

- ✔ **Page numbers** (Pg Num Pos)**:** Tells WordPerfect where to print page numbers.

- ✔ **Headers and footers** (Header A, Header B, Footer A, **and** Footer B)**:** Define what WordPerfect prints at the top and bottom of each page. When you discontinue headers, you get codes called Header A End, Header B End, Footer A End, and Footer B End. When you suppress the printing of headers or footers on a page, WordPerfect sticks a Suppress code at the top of the page.

Finding Codes

The Reveal Codes window is not a model of readability; user-friendliness is not its middle name. (Heaven knows that it's a vast improvement over the Reveal Codes windows that appeared more than a decade ago in DOS-based versions of WordPerfect, which looked like a strange form of algebra crossed with some kind of circuit diagram.)

The main difficulty in using the Reveal Codes window is finding the code that you want. Because the line endings don't correspond with those in the regular window, it can be confusing to tell where you are.

Enter the WordPerfect Edit➪Find and Replace command, which we describe in Chapter 3. In addition to using the Find and Replace dialog box to find text, you can use it to find codes.

You can tell WordPerfect to look for codes in two ways. Both methods can be useful:

- ✔ **Codes:** Tell WordPerfect the type of code to look for — a Lft Mar (left margin) code, for example. This method is useful when you want to know what the heck is going on with the margins in your document.

- ✔ **Specific codes:** Tell WordPerfect the exact code to look for (a Lft Mar code that sets the left margin to ½ inch, for example). This method is useful if you've decided to change all ½-inch margins to ¾-inch margins and aren't interested in any other margin settings. You can also automatically replace all ½-inch margin codes with ¾-inch margin codes; see "Finding specific codes" later in this chapter.

Finding all codes of one type

To find all codes of one type in your document (all the Tab Set codes, for example, regardless of the tab-stop positions that they contain), follow these steps:

1. **Move your cursor to the beginning of the document or to the beginning of the part of the document that you want to search.**

2. **If the Reveal Codes window is not already open, choose View⇨Reveal Codes.**

3. **Choose Edit⇨Find and Replace or press F2.**

   You see the Find and Replace dialog box, shown in Figure 17-2. This dialog box has its own little menu bar (described in more detail in Chapter 3).

Figure 17-2:
Finding codes starts with finding regular old text.

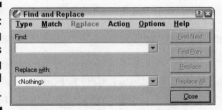

4. **Choose Match⇨Codes from this menu bar.**

   WordPerfect displays the Codes dialog box, shown in Figure 17-3. The Find Codes box lists all the secret codes that you can search for.

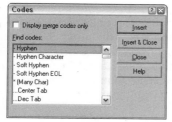

Figure 17-3:
Choosing
the code to
search for in
the text.

5. **Choose the code that you want to search for.**

   Choose the `Tab Set` code, for example.

6. **Click the Insert button in the Codes dialog box.**

   The code name appears in the Find box in the Find and Replace dialog box.

7. **Click the Close button in the Codes dialog box.**

   You've finished telling WordPerfect which code you want to look for.

8. **Click the Find Next button in the Find and Replace dialog box.**

   WordPerfect looks for the code or codes that you specified and highlights the next occurrence in the Reveal Codes window.

When you display the Find and Replace dialog box, its Find box contains text or codes — the last information that you searched for. The content of the Find box is selected, though, so as soon as you insert something new, that content replaces the former content. You can also just delete the information if you don't want to search for it again.

If WordPerfect can't find your code, it displays a small dialog box that tells you so. Click OK to make this dialog box go away. For more information about using the Find and Replace dialog box, see Chapter 3.

To search backward through your document, click the Find Prev button in the Find and Replace dialog box.

Keep in mind the following tips when searching for reveal codes:

✔ **Selecting codes:** In the Find Codes list in the Codes dialog box, the first 16 codes have names that begin with punctuation, such as `. . .Left Tab` (a tab that moves to a left tab stop with dot leaders). After these codes, the other codes are listed in alphabetical order.

To find a code in the Codes dialog box whose name begins with *T*, for example, you can click the Find Codes listing and press T on your keyboard. The list zooms down to the *T*s.

✔ **Keeping the dialog box open:** If you plan to continue looking for codes (or text) in your document, you can leave the Find and Replace dialog box open while you edit your document. This practice is faster than opening and closing the dialog box for each search, although it does clutter your screen. You can drag the title bar of the Find and Replace dialog box to move it to an out-of-the-way part of your screen. You can leave the Codes dialog box open too if you plan to look for different codes. Just skip clicking its Close button.

✔ **Finding a sequence of codes:** You can search for a sequence of codes. WordPerfect uses the two codes Hd Left Ind and Hd Back Tab, for example, to create a hanging indent. To search for this combination of codes in this order, choose Hd Left Ind in the Codes dialog box, click Insert, choose Hd Back Tab in the list, and then click the Insert button again. The two codes appear in the Find box. When you click the Find Next button in the Find and Replace dialog box, WordPerfect looks for the sequence of codes.

✔ **Finding text and code combination:** You can search for a mixture of codes and regular characters. If you want to search for a tab followed by an asterisk, for example, you can use the Codes dialog box to make [Tab (all)] appear in the Find box and then type an asterisk.

Finding specific codes

WordPerfect has another way to look for codes that contain additional information. A margin code, for example, contains information about the size of the margin that you want. A Bold code, on the other hand, contains no other information. For codes that contain additional information, you can search for all codes that have a particular setting (all Font codes that set the font to 12-point Times New Roman, for example). Follow these steps:

1. **Move your cursor to the beginning of the document or to the beginning of the part of the document that you want to search.**

2. **Choose Edit⇨Find and Replace or press F2.**

   WordPerfect displays the Find and Replace dialog box (refer to Figure 17-2).

3. **Choose Type⇨Specific Codes.**

   You see the Specific Codes dialog box.

4. **In the Specific Codes dialog box, choose the type of code for which you want to search.**

   WordPerfect lists only the types of codes that contain additional information. (To search for a code that isn't in this list, choose Match⇨Codes, described in the preceding section.)

5. Click OK in the Specific Codes dialog box.

The Specific Codes dialog box goes away, and WordPerfect changes the Find and Replace dialog box to match the type of code that you're looking for. If you choose Font as the type of code to search for, WordPerfect transforms the Find and Replace dialog box into a Find and Replace Font dialog box. The menu bar and buttons are unchanged, but rather than choose the text for which to search, WordPerfect enables you to enter the information that the code contains. The Find and Replace Font dialog box, for example, enables you to enter the font name and font style.

6. Enter the settings of the code for which you want to search.

For example, choose Times New Roman for the font name and Italics for the style.

7. Click the Find Next button to search for the next occurrence of the code.

When you search for a specific code, you can't search for a combination of codes and text or for a sequence of more than one code. (Bummer.)

If WordPerfect can't find the code, it displays a dialog box that tells you so. Click OK to make this dialog box go away. If you're sure that your code is in there somewhere, try using the Match⇨Codes method described in the preceding section.

Knowing what to do after you find your code

After you find the code you're looking for, you can delete it by pressing the Delete or Backspace key (see "Deleting codes," earlier in this chapter). If you created the code using a dialog box, you can modify the code by double-clicking it in the Reveal Codes window.

It's a good idea to use the Reveal Codes window when you're searching for codes so that you can see whether WordPerfect finds the ones you want.

Replacing Codes Automatically

Here's a fairly common scenario: You formatted your document tastefully with several fonts, including Times Roman (Tms Rmn). But you find out that the Times *New* Roman font looks much nicer when you print the document. What's the best way to change all those Font codes from Tms Rmn to Times New Roman without going nuts?

Of course you can use the Find and Replace command that we discuss in Chapter 3 (and in previous sections of this chapter). The bad news is that you can't use the Find and Replace command to replace paired codes.

For example, suppose you used pairs of `Bold` codes to make section headings in a report bold and you decide later that you want to use italic instead. You *can't* use the Find and Replace procedures described in the following section to replace all the `Bold On` codes (the ones at the beginning of the bold heading) with `Italc On` codes. This method simply doesn't work.

Probably the best way to get around this business of finding and replacing codes is to use styles, which enable you to standardize the codes that you use for various parts of your document. For more on styles, see Chapter 9.

Replacing specific codes with other codes

Although WordPerfect's Find and Replace feature shouldn't be used with paired codes, it's great for replacing character codes and single codes. You can replace all the specific codes with other codes of the same type, such as changing all `Font:Arial Regular` codes to `Font:Times New Roman Regular`. Follow these steps:

1. **Move to the beginning of your document by pressing Ctrl+Home.**

   If you want to replace the codes in only part of your document, move to the beginning of that part.

2. **Choose Edit⇨Find and Replace or press F2.**

   WordPerfect displays the Find and Replace dialog box (refer to Figure 17-2).

3. **With the cursor in the Find part of the Find and Replace dialog box, choose Type⇨Specific Codes.**

   The Specific Codes dialog box appears.

4. **Choose the type of code that you want to replace.**

   Choose `Font`, for example.

5. **Click OK to dismiss the Specific Codes dialog box.**

   Both the Find and Replace With text boxes are transformed into boxes that are appropriate for the type of code with which you are working. If you are replacing `Font` codes, for example, WordPerfect displays settings for fonts and font styles.

6. **Choose settings for the existing codes that you want to get rid of and for the new codes that you want to replace them with.**

   For example, choose Arial for the Find Font setting and Times New Roman for the Replace With setting.

7. **To find the first instance of the code that you're looking for, click Find Next.**

   Just tell WordPerfect to start looking; you won't have to tell it again.

8. **Do one of the following:**

   - To replace this code and search for other instances one by one, so that you can eyeball each occurrence before making the replacement, click Replace in the dialog box. When you click Replace, WordPerfect replaces the code in the Find box with the code in the Replace With box.

   - To skip this code, click Find Next.

   - To replace this code and all the rest of the codes of this type in your document, go wild and click Replace All.

9. **When you finish, click Close to make the Find and Replace dialog box go away.**

If you can't see your codes, choose View⇨Reveal Codes in the WordPerfect window to open the Reveal Codes window (or press Alt+F3).

Replacing codes with other codes

You can replace one type of code with another — Hd Left Ind codes (indents) with Hd Left Tab codes (regular ol' tabs), for example. You can't use this method to insert codes that require additional information. You can't replace all your Bold codes with Font codes, for example, because Font codes require additional information (the name and style of the font). You can, however, replace combinations of codes and text with other combinations of code and text.

Unfortunately, you can't replace codes such as Bold On and Bold Off with other paired codes such as Italc On and Italc Off.

If you want to replace a character code or a single code, follow these steps:

1. **Move to the beginning of your document by pressing Ctrl+Home.**

2. **Choose Edit⇨Find and Replace or press F2.**

   You see the Find and Replace dialog box (refer to Figure 17-2).

3. **With your cursor in the Find part of the dialog box, choose Match⇨ Codes.**

   You see the Codes dialog box (refer to Figure 17-3).

4. **In the Codes dialog box, select the type of code that you want to replace, and then click Insert.**

   Choose `Hd Left Ind`, for example.

5. **Move your cursor to the Replace With text box.**

6. **Back in the Codes dialog box, choose the code that you want to replace the old codes with, and then click Insert.**

   Choose `Hd Left Tab`, for example.

7. **Click the Close button in the Codes dialog box.**

8. **To replace codes one at a time, click the Find Next button in the Find and Replace dialog box, followed by Replace.**

   Or click Replace All to go for the gold.

9. **Click the Close button when you finish replacing codes.**

Deleting all the codes

You can use the Find and Replace dialog box to get rid of all codes of one type in your document (all `Font` codes, for example). Use the preceding steps to tell WordPerfect which codes you want to find but, instead of putting anything in the Replace With box, leave it empty. This tells WordPerfect to remove the codes without replacing them with anything.

Dealing with mysterious codes

If you encounter a code that you've never seen and that isn't described in this chapter, stay calm and take a deep breath. You can always delete it, after all. But before you do that, try to find out what it is by moving the mouse cursor over it. A little yellow box pops up and gives you a hint, giving the code a more complete (though perhaps no less cryptic) English name. If the hint isn't enough, double-click the code. Depending on the code, you'll probably see a dialog box that inserts the code. You can click the Help button in the dialog box or press the F1 key to get help about the formatting feature associated with the reveal code.

Part VI
The Part of Tens

The 5th Wave   By Rich Tennant

"Ms. Lamont, how long have you been sending out bills listing charges for 'Freight', 'Handling', and 'Sales Tax' as 'This', 'That', and 'The Other Thing'?"

In this part . . .

*N*othing puts a smile on a person's face like the
number 10 does. Why else does David Letterman
have his *Top Ten List*? Or Agatha Christie have her *Ten Little
Indians*? Or the Christmas holiday have the *Ten Days of
Christmas* song? (Okay, we know it is really *Twelve Days
of Christmas*, but, please, who'd *really* want 11 pipers piping
and 12 maids a-milking anyway?)

Because *ten* makes people happy, we'd like to comply by
offering you tips, ideas, and recommendations about how
to maximize your use of WordPerfect Office — all neatly
packaged into groups of tens.

Chapter 18

Ten Ways to Tweak WordPerfect

*Y*ou know how software can be — badly behaved, saving files in the wrong folders, displaying incomprehensible things on your screen, and being generally rude. It's time for some lessons in deportment. You can teach WordPerfect to behave more like the kind of gentleman or lady with whom you'd like to be seen.

It's pretty nifty that WordPerfect allows you to customize so much about the way it works. In this chapter, you find out how to display information about your documents, how to zoom in on the text of your document, how to control which buttons appear on toolbars, how to control where WordPerfect stores things (in which folders on your hard drive), and how to set other preferences.

If you're happy with WordPerfect just the way it is, you can skip this chapter. Leaving WordPerfect alone is not such a bad idea. One advantage of this approach is that your WordPerfect will work just like everyone else's (unless they've customized *their* copies), making it easier to get help from your WordPerfect-savvy friends.

Changing Workspaces

Two-faced people are those who behave differently, depending on the situation they find themselves in or the people they're around. Although being two-faced is a character flaw for people, WordPerfect's Workspace Manager makes a virtue out of its flexibility to be different things to different people.

Workspace Manager, which you can find on the WordPerfect Tools menu, allows you to switch between four workspaces:

- ✓ **WordPerfect Office mode:** The default WordPerfect workspace and the one we've been using throughout this book. Basically, we recommend using this workspace unless you have a compelling reason to use one of the other three.

- ✓ **Microsoft Word mode:** Designed for people who switched to WordPerfect from Microsoft Word. When you use this workspace, WordPerfect changes its menu terminology and placement and toolbar buttons to reflect the standard Microsoft Word interface. It's not 100 percent identical, but it is helpful if you're accustomed to Word's way of doing things. (See Chapter 14 for more on emulating Microsoft Word in WordPerfect.)

- ✓ **WordPerfect Classic mode:** The workspace for people who want to relive the glory days of WordPerfect 5.1 for DOS (see Figure 18-1). Frankly, this workspace is probably going to appeal to you only if the following scenarios describe your life:

  - You have Culture Club, Simple Minds, and Duran Duran CDs filling your CD case.

  - You rent *The Breakfast Club* and *The Wedding Singer* from the video store each Friday.

  - You proudly wear your Dukakis or Bush in '88 button on your Izod shirt every day in the office.

Otherwise, we suspect most everyone else would rather enjoy the more visual workspaces that Windows applications provide.

Even if you use the WordPerfect Classic workspace, you aren't in a true DOS environment. You still have access to the normal top-level menu and application bar in WordPerfect and can easily switch to other Windows applications.

- ✓ **WordPerfect Legal mode:** Tailored for people working in law offices, unfortunates being sued by their money-hungry neighbors, characters in a Grisham novel, or anyone else who needs to use WordPerfect for creating legal documents. WordPerfect Legal mode is essentially the default WordPerfect Office workspace with the Legal toolbar simply made visible.

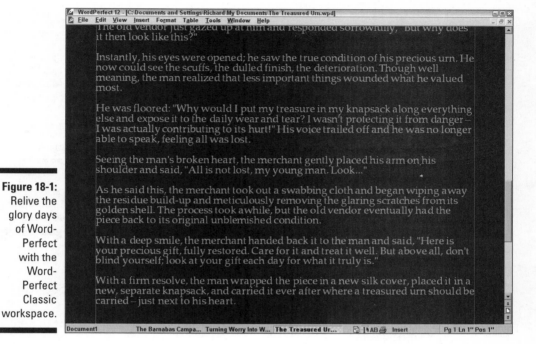

Figure 18-1:
Relive the
glory days
of Word-
Perfect
with the
Word-
Perfect
Classic
workspace.

To switch between workspaces, follow these steps:

1. **Choose Tools⇨Workspace Manager.**

   WordPerfect displays the Workspace Manager dialog box, as shown in Figure 18-2.

Figure 18-2:
Workspace
Manager
enables
Word-
Perfect
to change
faces.

2. **Choose the desired mode.**

3. **Click OK.**

   WordPerfect switches workspaces based on your selection.

Setting Your Favorite Font

Have you ever been annoyed at WordPerfect for suggesting the same font whenever you create a new document? We have. Enough with Times New Roman, already — we're in the mood for Arial!

You can use templates (see Chapter 12), or you can tell WordPerfect the name of your favorite font. If you choose the latter route, WordPerfect uses this font for all new documents (based on the selected printer) unless you select another one. To do so, follow these steps:

1. **Choose File➪Document➪Default Font.**

   WordPerfect, ever ready to pop open another dialog box, displays the Document Default Font dialog box.

2. **Choose your favorite font, size, and style.**

3. **Click the Settings button, then click Set Face and Point Size as Default for All Documents.**

   Otherwise, these steps set the font for the current document only.

4. **Click OK.**

   If you use several printers, display the Print dialog box, click the Details tab, and choose a printer. Then click the Default Font button and set the font in the Printer Default Font dialog box.

Tweaking Your WordPerfect Settings

The process of teaching WordPerfect how to behave is generally simple: You tell WordPerfect your preferences, and it whips itself into shape. Wouldn't it be nice if everyone worked this way (especially your teenager)? To inform WordPerfect of your ideas, choose Tools➪Settings, which displays the Settings dialog box, shown in Figure 18-3.

Figure 18-3:
Your
gateway to
individual
expression.

Instead of the dull, boring boxes and buttons that you see in most dialog boxes, this one has nifty little icons for the different types of preferences that you can express:

- ✔ **Display:** What WordPerfect displays on-screen, including what the ruler includes; how the Reveal Codes window looks; and whether you want to see symbols where your spaces, tabs, and returns are. We describe these settings in detail later in this chapter.

- ✔ **Environment:** Miscellaneous stuff that didn't fit into any of the other categories of preferences.

- ✔ **Files:** Where WordPerfect stores your documents, templates, macros, and other files; and whether you want it to keep backups of your files. This stuff is described later in this chapter.

- ✔ **Summary:** How document summaries work and when you want to see them (if ever).

- ✔ **Convert:** Some advanced settings that tell WordPerfect how to convert ASCII-delimited text files, WordPerfect 4.2, DCA, and DisplayWrite documents.

- ✔ **Application bar:** What information to display, in addition to the font and general appearance that you prefer. Read on for more information.

- ✔ **Customize:** How you want the keyboard, toolbars, property bars, and menu bars to work. This is discussed later in this chapter, although we refuse to go into detail.

To use the Settings dialog box to express your preferences, click the icon of your choice; it displays one or more dialog boxes. When you dismiss the dialog box(es), you return to the Settings dialog box. When you finish fooling with WordPerfect's innards, click the Close button in the Settings dialog box.

Changing too many things at the same time can be a bad idea. When you're fooling around with settings, make one or two changes and then close all the dialog boxes. Look around in WordPerfect to see what you have done. Otherwise, you might find it difficult to remember how to reverse a change you just made.

Choosing Which Hidden Symbols Appear and Other Display Settings

If you don't particularly like the way WordPerfect displays something — the shadow cursor, for instance, or the Reveal Codes window, or the symbols WordPerfect displays in your document when you choose View➪Show ¶ — you may be able to change WordPerfect's behavior. All the settings that control such appearances are in the Display Settings dialog box. To display this dialog box, follow these steps:

1. **Choose Tools➪Settings to display the Settings dialog box.**

2. **Click the Display icon to see the Display Settings dialog box.**

WordPerfect displays a tab at the top of the dialog box for each type of display setting. If you click the Document, Symbols, View/Zoom, Reveal Codes, Ruler, or Merge tab, the rest of the dialog box changes to show settings that pertain to that subject.

A faster way to display the Display Settings dialog box is to right-click the scroll bar on the right side of your document window and choose Settings from the QuickMenu.

The display settings that we most often find ourselves changing are the settings on the Symbols tab. These settings determine which symbols you see when you choose View➪Show ¶. (The symbols tend to encompass invisible characters that control the way your text is laid out: spaces, tabs, indent characters, and characters for line justification such as centering.) You can turn off the display of certain characters by choosing View➪Show ¶ and following these steps:

1. **Choose Tools➪Settings.**

2. **Click the Display icon to see the Display Settings dialog box.**

3. **Click the Symbols tab.**

4. **Click to remove the check marks next to items for which you don't want to see symbols.**

5. **Click OK and then click the Close button in the Settings dialog box.**

You can also use the Reveal Codes window to see all your codes — not just the spaces, tabs, indents, and returns. Refer to Chapter 17 for details.

Telling WordPerfect about Folders and Backups

To tell WordPerfect where you want to store your documents in general (you can always choose different folders for some documents), as well as when to make automatic backups of your documents, follow these steps:

1. Choose Tools➪Settings, and then click the Files icon.

WordPerfect displays the File Settings dialog box. The Document tab is selected, so the dialog box shows the settings that have to do with documents and backups.

2. To indicate where you want your documents to go, enter a folder name in the Default Document Folder box.

Initially, the box reads `C:\Documents and Settings\<Your Name>\My Documents`. The name you enter must be a complete path name, which begins with the hard drive letter (such as `C:`), lists any folders containing your chosen folder, separated by backwards slashes (\), and ends with your chosen folder. For instance, you might enter `C:\Letters` to create a letter folder. Or you might add a folder in My Documents like this: `C:\Documents and Settings\<Your Name>\My Documents\ Letters`, for example. (If the folder that you type doesn't exist yet, Windows asks whether you want to create it.) If you don't understand path names, you can click the little button with the file folder on it to browse to the folder that you want instead of typing its path.

3. Leave this setting as-is: Use Default Extension on Open and Save.

We strongly recommend you leave this setting check marked and set to `.wpd`. The check mark enables you to simply type the name of a file and omit the extension when you save a document. The `.wpd` setting causes WordPerfect to make sure the file ends in the standard WordPerfect file extension, `.wpd`.

If you uncheck this option and don't manually add the file extension to your document, Windows won't know the file you saved is a WordPerfect document, and you can't open the document directly from Windows Explorer by double-clicking it.

4. To change how often WordPerfect makes a backup copy of your open documents, alter the time for the setting currently labeled Timed Document Backup Every 10 Minutes.

Make sure that the check mark for this setting is present. (If it isn't, click the check box.) This setting tells WordPerfect to save copies of all your open documents every so often. If the power goes out or you kick the computer's plug out of the outlet, this option is a godsend. Right after this list, you find out how to get these files back.

Also, we recommend increasing the frequency of the timed backups to one to two minutes. With today's fast PCs, the constant saving in the background won't slow you down and will help ensure that you lose very little if something should go wrong.

5. **To keep yourself from accidentally replacing good files with bad ones, choose Save Original Document as a Backup at Each Save.**

   If this option is selected, every time you save a document, WordPerfect renames, rather than deletes, the previously saved version. It renames these backup documents using the .bak file extension.

   If you mess up a document irretrievably and then compound your error by saving it, this setting prevents WordPerfect from deleting the preceding version of the document. You can close the document without saving it again and then open the .bak version of the document.

6. **If you use templates, but don't keep them in WordPerfect's default template location, click the Template tab at the top of the File Settings dialog box.**

   The default template location is

   ```
   C:\Documents and Settings\<Your Name>\Application Data\
   Corel\PerfectExpert\12\Custom WP Templates
   ```

   You can change the folder in which WordPerfect looks for your templates by choosing the Default Template Folder option. See Chapter 12 for a description of using templates.

7. **If you use graphics, macros, spreadsheet files, or database files in your documents, and you don't keep these items in the usual default folders, you may click the Graphic, Merge/Macro, or Spreadsheet/Database tab to change the default folders to more convenient ones.**

   You're probably better off leaving these settings alone, though.

8. **Click OK and then click Close to get rid of all these dialog boxes.**

   WordPerfect puts your changes into effect (invisibly).

If WordPerfect or Windows crashes and you use timed backups as described in the preceding section, listen up. The next time you run WordPerfect, it notifies you if timed backup files are lying around. If you had several documents open, you may have several of those files.

WordPerfect displays a Timed Backup dialog box with the message that a Document1 backup file exists. (Unfortunately, WordPerfect doesn't remember the name of the file that this is a copy of, so it calls it `Document1`.) You have these three choices:

- ✔ **Open:** This option, which is your best choice, opens the backup file in WordPerfect. You may want to open the copy that you saved in the regular way, compare it with the backup, and see which version you want to keep. If you want to save the file, choose File➪Save or File➪Save As to save it under a more meaningful name than `Document1` (say, something more like the original file's name) in a specific folder. If you don't want to save the file, choose File➪Close.

- ✔ **Rename:** This option tells WordPerfect to store the backup files in an out-of-the-way place (usually in your `C:\Documents and Settings\ <Your Name>\Application Data\Corel\WordPerfect\12\Backup` folder) with a name that you specify.

- ✔ **Delete:** Choose this option if you're sure that you don't want the backup file. It's hard to imagine why you'd want to choose this option, though. Why not open the backup file, just to be sure?

More Useful Environment Settings

The environment settings enable you set configure the overall WordPerfect interface. You use them, for example, to tell WordPerfect how to select words and (using one of our favorite features) that you want it to open documents automatically. Figure 18-4 shows the environment settings that you can control.

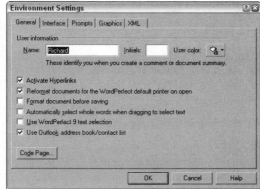

Figure 18-4:
The settings in the Environment Settings dialog box tell Word-Perfect how to work.

Picking up where you left off

The Interface tab of the Environment Settings dialog box gives you a neat way to pick up where you left off in yesterday's editing session. You save the entire workspace, including multiple documents and cursor positions, and they're restored the next time you open WordPerfect.

To turn on WordPerfect's workspace-saving feature, follow these steps:

1. **Choose Tools⇨Settings.**

2. **Click the Environment icon.**

   The Environment Settings dialog box appears (refer to Figure 18-4).

3. **Click the Interface tab.**

4. **In the Save Workspace section, change the setting to Always.**

   If you prefer, you can set the Save Workspace setting to Prompt on Exit, which means that WordPerfect will ask you each time whether you want to save your workspace.

5. **Click OK to close the dialog box.**

6. **Click Close when you're finished with all your settings.**

From now on, WordPerfect always opens the documents that you had open when you last closed WordPerfect. In each document, the cursor will be where it was when you closed WordPerfect.

Another way to pick up where you left off

Another way to resume editing where you left off is to tell WordPerfect to create a special bookmark, called a QuickMark, at the spot where your cursor is when you save a document. Follow these steps:

1. **Choose Tools⇨Bookmark.**

   You see the Bookmark dialog box, with two check boxes at the bottom.

2. **Make sure that the Set QuickMark on File Save box is checked. (If it isn't, click it.)**

   As the name implies, every time you save a document, WordPerfect silently creates a

bookmark (called QuickMark) at the place you were typing when you saved the document. This is not tremendously useful unless you also complete Step 3.

3. **Make sure the Go to QuickMark on File Open box is checked. (If it isn't, click it.)**

4. **Click Close.**

   Every time you open your document, you'll be right back where you were when you saved it. This convenient feature applies also to any new documents you make.

Selecting less than an entire word

You may have noticed that WordPerfect assumes that when you're selecting text with the mouse, you want entire words. So the selection often jumps to include the entire word when you really wanted only part of it. For most of us most of the time, this feature is useful — but it may drive some of you bonkers. Here's how to turn it off:

1. **Choose Tools⇨Settings.**

2. **Click the Environment icon.**

   You see the General tab of the Environment Settings dialog box.

3. **Click to clear the Automatically Select Whole Words When Dragging to Select Text check box.**

4. **Click OK.**

Customizing Toolbars and Property Bars

Do you perform tasks that require you to navigate through menus? You can often do the job more quickly using a toolbar button instead. But what if you can't find a toolbar button for your task? You have two options:

✔ Add a toolbar that contains the button you need.

✔ Add a new button to one of the existing toolbars.

WordPerfect gives you several ways to add or remove various toolbars from the WordPerfect window:

✔ Choose View⇨Toolbars.

✔ Right-click any toolbar.

✔ Choose Tools⇨Settings, then click the Customize icon.

A list of available toolbars appears:

✔ WordPerfect 12, the default toolbar

✔ WordPerfect 11, for WordPerfect 11 compatibility

✔ WordPerfect 10, for WordPerfect 10 compatibility

✔ WordPerfect 9, for WordPerfect 9 compatibility

- WordPerfect 8, for WordPerfect 8 compatibility
- WordPerfect 7, for WordPerfect 9 compatibility
- Draw Shapes, includes drawing tools
- Font, provides font-related commands
- Format, display general formatting commands
- Graphics, provides graphics features
- Hyperlink Tools, for creating and working with hyperlinks
- Legal, features designed for legal-related documents
- Macro Tools, for recording and programming macros (advanced)
- Microsoft Word 2002, simulates the Microsoft Word 2002 toolbar
- Microsoft Word 97, simulates the Microsoft Word 97 toolbar
- Microsoft Word Compatibility, functionality for converting to Microsoft Word format
- Navigation, for navigating bookmarks within a document
- Outline Tools, for outlining
- Page, provides page-related functionality
- Print Preview, options associated with previewing a document before printing
- Reference, provides commands related to tables of contents, indexes, etc.
- Shipping Macros, several handy utility macros that can save you time
- Tables, shows table-related functions
- Template, displays commands related to customizing templates (advanced)
- Visual Basic, for programming Visual Basic macros (advanced)
- XML, for creating and working with XML documents (advanced)

To add a particular toolbar, click to add a check mark before its name. (Click to delete the check mark in front of the name of any toolbar you want to remove.) For instance, if you draw shapes frequently, you might add the Draw Shapes toolbar. Because you can't tell in advance exactly what buttons a toolbar has, you may have to try a few before you find the exact button you need.

To add a button to a toolbar, do the following:

1. **Choose Tools⇨Settings, and then click the Customize icon in the Settings dialog box that appears.**

   The Customize Settings dialog box appears, with the Toolbars tab displayed.

2. **In the list of available toolbars, click the name (not the check box) of the toolbar you want to modify, and then click the Edit button.**

   If you would rather create a new custom toolbar, click the Create button instead of the Edit button. Type a name for your toolbar in the Create Toolbar dialog box that appears, and then click OK. The Toolbar Editor dialog box appears, with the Features tab displayed.

3. **Click the Feature Categories box (or the down arrow next to it), and in the list that drops down, click any category that seems likely to contain the function you want.**

4. **Examine the Features list box for the feature you need. If you find the feature, click it. If not, go back to Step 3 and try another category.**

   As you click features, a short feature description appears near the bottom of the Toolbar Editor dialog box.

5. **Click Add Button to add the feature to the toolbar, and then click OK to return to the Customize Settings dialog box.**

6. **Make sure that a check mark appears next to your chosen toolbar (if not, click the toolbar's check box).**

7. **Click Close to return to the Customize dialog box, and then Close in that dialog box.**

If you need to remove a button from a toolbar, your only option is to reset that toolbar to its initial state. Repeat Steps 1 and 2 in the preceding instructions, but in Step 2 click Reset instead of Edit (or click Delete if the toolbar is your own invention). Click Yes when the warning appears.

To customize a property bar, use the preceding steps, but just before doing Step 2, click the Property Bar tab of the Customize Settings dialog box. (Remember, a property bar appears automatically while you're working on something such as a table.)

Moving and Morphing Toolbars

Toolbars sometimes take up valuable real estate in your WordPerfect window. If you'd like that extra space for your document text, try dragging your toolbars somewhere else. Move your mouse until the pointer is over the blank, gray area at the far right of the toolbar, where the pointer turns into a four-headed arrow. Click and drag with your mouse, and you'll find that you're dragging an outline of the toolbar.

When you first drag the outline away from the top of the window, the outline gets chunkier. This shape indicates that the toolbar has morphed (reshaped itself) into its *palette* form. In that form, it floats free of your WordPerfect window. Release the mouse button now to turn the toolbar into a palette. You can drag it around anywhere on your screen by the bar on its top or change its dimensions by dragging any corner.

If you don't want a palette, continue dragging the chunky outline to the bottom (or side) of your window. When the outline thins and expands again to the width (or height) of the window, release the mouse button. The toolbar now sits nicely at the bottom or along the side of the window. To restore a toolbar to its original position, just drag it back to its original position under the menu bar.

Assigning Different Meanings to Keys

WordPerfect has been around for a long time. (The first versions of WordPerfect weren't even for PCs!) As the world of software settled on certain standards for what all the keys on the keyboard should mean, the folks at WordPerfect were in a quandary. Older versions of WordPerfect had always used the F3 key to display on-line Help, for example, and WordPerfect users the world over were used to it. Now the world of software agrees that F1 — not F3 — is the key to use. What to do?

The answer: Wimp out and try to please everyone. WordPerfect gives you the opportunity to tell it which set of keyboard meanings you want to use: the old-fashioned WordPerfect meanings (WPDOS) or the newfangled standard meanings (WPWin). These sets of meanings are stored as keyboard definitions.

Keyboard definitions don't usually affect most of the keys on the keyboard. The Q key on your keyboard types a *Q* on your screen, regardless of which keyboard definition you use (unless you create your own definition and get perverse). But the keyboard definition controls the meanings of the function keys and what keys do when you hold down Ctrl and Alt.

As we mention in the introduction, all the instructions in this book assume that you are a hip, modern, 21st century kind of person and that you're using the newfangled standard meanings of the keys (the WPWin keyboard definitions). The following steps show how you can check this out:

1. **Choose Tools⇨Settings.**

2. **Click the Customize icon.**

3. **Click the Keyboards tab.**

    WordPerfect displays the Keyboard Settings dialog box. Eight keyboards are listed in all. The one that's highlighted is the one that you're using.

4. **Click the Close button in both open dialog boxes.**

Most people use the WPWin 12 keyboard because it makes the keys use the Windows-standard meanings, such as F1 for help, Ctrl+C for copy, and Ctrl+V for paste.

Here are some reasons to use the old-fashioned WPDOS-compatible keyboard:

- You've upgraded from an older version of WordPerfect and don't want to learn any new habits. (Who does?)

- You work in an office with lots of people who use the old-fashioned WPDOS keyboard, and you want to be able to swap WordPerfect techniques with them.

If you're migrating to WordPerfect from Microsoft Word and have a particular affection for the way Word did things, you can select the MS Word 2002 keyboard. (See Chapter 14 for more on how to emulate Microsoft Word in WordPerfect.)

Reading and Recording Information about Your Documents

If it's important to your business to record exactly when a document was created and edited, by whom, for which client, and so on, you can enter information about your document in the Summary page of the Properties dialog box. To display this dialog box, choose File➪Properties. There's more to the dialog box than can be displayed at one time, so use the little scroll bar to slide down to see the rest.

The information that you enter in the document summary is stored along with your document. You can view or edit it at any time by choosing File➪ Properties. You can print it by choosing Options➪Print Summary in the Properties dialog box.

Even if you don't want to tell WordPerfect a great deal about your document, WordPerfect has a lot it would like to share with you. Click the Information tab of the Properties dialog box, and WordPerfect gives you some interesting statistics about your document: the number of characters, words, lines, paragraphs, and so on.

WordPerfect enables *you* to choose which blanks appear in the Summary page of the Properties dialog box. To change the facts included in all summaries that you create, click the Setup button in the Summary page. WordPerfect displays the Document Summary Setup dialog box and enables you to choose among a long list of possible facts about a document, including Authorization, Checked By, Document Number, Project, Status, and Version Number. Does this sound official, or what?

Chapter 19

Ten Really Good Editing Suggestions

Moses may have had the definitive Ten Commandments, but in our own modest way, we have a little something to offer you as well: our own Ten Really Good Suggestions for Using WordPerfect. Don't worry, lightning won't strike if you don't use them, but we think you'll be glad you did.

Don't Fight WordPerfect — Work with It

When you're hurrying to get a job completed, the natural tendency is to simply dash off and write a document in a quick-and-dirty fashion just to get it done. However, when you do this, you can develop bad habits that end up taking more time than if you had just done a little preparation at the outset.

Therefore, our first Really Good Suggestion is that when you create a document, don't fight with WordPerfect; instead, let WordPerfect help. If you want multiple columns, use the WordPerfect columns feature. If you want wide margins, tell WordPerfect to widen them by dragging the margin guidelines around or by using the Format⇨Margins command (see Figure 19-1). Don't fight WordPerfect by skipping all that and just using extra hard returns, spaces, or tabs to put the text where you want it. This method always means extra work later when you edit your text.

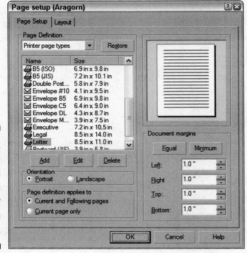

Figure 19-1:
Use Word-Perfect's built-in functionality to set up your page.

The WordPerfect word-wrap feature, for example, enables it to begin a new line whenever it sees you getting perilously close to the right margin. In the mind of WordPerfect (such as it is), a bunch of text that ends when you press the Enter key is a paragraph, so type your paragraphs like that and let WordPerfect do the rest of the work. Don't press Enter until you get to the end of a paragraph.

For more on the evils of the Enter key, see Chapter 1.

Don't Use Extra Spaces or Tabs

In high school, your typing teacher taught you to type two spaces after each period. Other than that, you should never type more than one space consecutively (with rare exceptions). If you want to move across the line and leave some white space, use tabs. (See Chapter 7 to find out how to set tab stops and use different types of tabs.)

In the world of typesetting, which includes proportionally spaced fonts, typing only one space after each period is considered good form. Somehow, after the text is typeset, it looks fine. But we can understand if your ingrained two-spaces habit is too hard to break. WordPerfect is willing to help you out. Choose Tools⇨QuickCorrect and click the Format-As-You-Go tab. You see a group of End of Sentence Corrections options, including one called Change Two Spaces to One Space Between Sentences. If you check it, WordPerfect deals with all this space nonsense for you.

Incidentally, if you're using tabs to create something that looks like a table, adjust the tab stops so that you use only one tab for each column. This technique enables you to press Tab just once between entries (see Chapter 7). Better yet, use the WordPerfect table feature (see Chapter 13).

Don't Keep Pressing Enter to Begin a New Page

If you decide to begin a new page manually (that is, before filling the current page), tell WordPerfect so in no uncertain terms: Click where you want the page break and then press Ctrl+Enter. Don't pussyfoot around the issue by pressing Enter repeatedly until you fill the current page with blank lines. This technique is yet another example of the first commandment in action — if you want a page break, say so. (Chapter 8 explains why the Ctrl+Enter method works best.)

Don't Number Your Pages Manually

WordPerfect can number your pages for you and place the page numbers at the left, center, or right of either the top or bottom of the page. What more could you ask? So don't type page numbers yourself; they become a mess if you edit your document and the page breaks move around. Chapter 8 tells you how to number your pages and print other information in headers and footers.

Backing Out of Edit ⇨ Find and Replace

WordPerfect's find-and-replace feature (see Chapter 3) has awesome power, either to make lots of wonderful updates throughout your document or to trash it big time. What if you want to replace Smith with Smythe, for example, but you type a space by mistake in the Find box just before you click Replace All? Poof — all the spaces in your document are replaced by Smythe. Your important letter has just been transformed into performance art.

Never fear: Simply use good ole' Undo by clicking the Undo button on the toolbar. Undo will reverse your changes so fast Smythe won't even be able to get a chance to enjoy his new environs in your document. Or, as a last-ditch alternative, simply close the document without saving changes. Then reopen it again.

Make Frequent Timed Backups

We recommend making timed backups (see Chapter 18) every one or two minutes, much more frequently than the default ten-minute setting, as shown in Figure 19-2 (accessible by choosing Tools⇨Settings⇨Files). Do you really want to risk losing eight or nine minutes or so of your work?

Figure 19-2:
Never lose your document due to power outages or a bratty nephew who likes to press your PC's reset button.

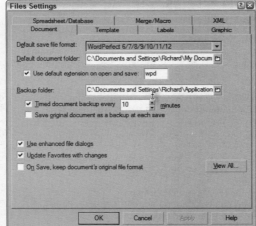

Okay, we admit that we're usually so busy Web browsing or checking our e-mail every other moment that those extra minutes often may not matter much. But we up the frequency anyway for those rare occasions when we're actually highly productive.

Save Early and Often

WordPerfect creates backup versions of your document, but it's a good habit to save early and often on your own as well. You never know what potential disaster awaits you while you're working to put that finishing touch on your document: space aliens frying your city's electrical grid; your bratty nephew sticking a screwdriver through your PC's front cover; or your outraged co-worker throwing a triple-shot cappuccino at your monitor (should've gotten her decaf!). Be prepared for calamity. Every time you squirm around in your chair, scratch your foot, or take a sip of coffee, press Ctrl+S to save your document. 'Nuff said.

Save Periodic Versions of Your Document

When you're working on an important document in which you're making multiple edits, it's a good idea to choose File⇨Save As periodically and give the latest version a new name. If so, you can revert to an older document if you change your mind on any particular change you made. We recommend a tried-and-true file naming method: successive numbering. For example, we start with `EverestTrip1.wpd` and later save it as `EverestTrip2.wpd`, and so on. Then, when we finish and save our final version of the document, we simply leave off the number, saving the file as `EverestTrip.wpd`.

Create a Halfway House for Semi-Abandoned Text

When you decide to remove a section of text from your document, you may want to copy it and paste it to a separate file in case you ever need to use it later or decide to add it back into your document. For example, if we're working on that `EverestTrip.wpd` document, we have an `EverestTrip-Fodder.wpd` file that acts as our halfway house for semi-abandoned text. Maintaining a document like this is much better than being forced to rewrite a paragraph that you decided to delete on a whim. Heck, if nothing else, it's fun to go back to the document later and laugh (or shudder) at what you *almost* added to your important document.

Back Up Your Work

Saving is good, but saving your documents on your hard drive doesn't help if your hard disk crashes. We strongly recommend making periodic backups of your important documents onto a floppy disk, CD, or USB portable device, whichever option is most convenient for you.

Index

FOR DUMMIES®

The easy way to get more done and have more fun

PERSONAL FINANCE & BUSINESS

0-7645-2431-3

0-7645-5331-3

0-7645-5307-0

Also available:

Accounting For Dummies
(0-7645-5314-3)

Business Plans Kit For Dummies
(0-7645-5365-8)

Managing For Dummies
(1-5688-4858-7)

Mutual Funds For Dummies
(0-7645-5329-1)

QuickBooks All-in-One Desk Reference For Dummies
(0-7645-1963-8)

Resumes For Dummies
(0-7645-5471-9)

Small Business Kit For Dummies
(0-7645-5093-4)

Starting an eBay Business For Dummies
(0-7645-1547-0)

Taxes For Dummies 2003
(0-7645-5475-1)

HOME, GARDEN, FOOD & WINE

0-7645-5295-3

0-7645-5130-2

0-7645-5250-3

Also available:

Bartending For Dummies
(0-7645-5051-9)

Christmas Cooking For Dummies
(0-7645-5407-7)

Cookies For Dummies
(0-7645-5390-9)

Diabetes Cookbook For Dummies
(0-7645-5230-9)

Grilling For Dummies
(0-7645-5076-4)

Home Maintenance For Dummies
(0-7645-5215-5)

Slow Cookers For Dummies
(0-7645-5240-6)

Wine For Dummies
(0-7645-5114-0)

FITNESS, SPORTS, HOBBIES & PETS

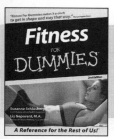
0-7645-5167-1

0-7645-5146-9

0-7645-5106-X

Also available:

Cats For Dummies
(0-7645-5275-9)

Chess For Dummies
(0-7645-5003-9)

Dog Training For Dummies
(0-7645-5286-4)

Labrador Retrievers For Dummies
(0-7645-5281-3)

Martial Arts For Dummies
(0-7645-5358-5)

Piano For Dummies
(0-7645-5105-1)

Pilates For Dummies
(0-7645-5397-6)

Power Yoga For Dummies
(0-7645-5342-9)

Puppies For Dummies
(0-7645-5255-4)

Quilting For Dummies
(0-7645-5118-3)

Rock Guitar For Dummies
(0-7645-5356-9)

Weight Training For Dummies
(0-7645-5168-X)

Available wherever books are sold.
Go to www.dummies.com or call 1-877-762-2974 to order direct

WILEY

FOR DUMMIES®

A world of resources to help you grow

TRAVEL

0-7645-5453-0

0-7645-5438-7

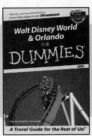
0-7645-5444-1

Also available:

America's National Parks For Dummies
(0-7645-6204-5)

Caribbean For Dummies
(0-7645-5445-X)

Cruise Vacations For Dummies 2003
(0-7645-5459-X)

Europe For Dummies
(0-7645-5456-5)

Ireland For Dummies
(0-7645-6199-5)

France For Dummies
(0-7645-6292-4)

Las Vegas For Dummies
(0-7645-5448-4)

London For Dummies
(0-7645-5416-6)

Mexico's Beach Resorts For Dummies
(0-7645-6262-2)

Paris For Dummies
(0-7645-5494-8)

RV Vacations For Dummies
(0-7645-5443-3)

EDUCATION & TEST PREPARATION

0-7645-5194-9

0-7645-5325-9

0-7645-5249-X

Also available:

The ACT For Dummies
(0-7645-5210-4)

Chemistry For Dummies
(0-7645-5430-1)

English Grammar For Dummies
(0-7645-5322-4)

French For Dummies
(0-7645-5193-0)

GMAT For Dummies
(0-7645-5251-1)

Inglés Para Dummies
(0-7645-5427-1)

Italian For Dummies
(0-7645-5196-5)

Research Papers For Dummies
(0-7645-5426-3)

SAT I For Dummies
(0-7645-5472-7)

U.S. History For Dummies
(0-7645-5249-X)

World History For Dummies
(0-7645-5242-2)

HEALTH, SELF-HELP & SPIRITUALITY

0-7645-5154-X

0-7645-5302-X

0-7645-5418-2

Also available:

The Bible For Dummies
(0-7645-5296-1)

Controlling Cholesterol For Dummies
(0-7645-5440-9)

Dating For Dummies
(0-7645-5072-1)

Dieting For Dummies
(0-7645-5126-4)

High Blood Pressure For Dummies
(0-7645-5424-7)

Judaism For Dummies
(0-7645-5299-6)

Menopause For Dummies
(0-7645-5458-1)

Nutrition For Dummies
(0-7645-5180-9)

Potty Training For Dummies
(0-7645-5417-4)

Pregnancy For Dummies
(0-7645-5074-8)

Rekindling Romance For Dummies
(0-7645-5303-8)

Religion For Dummies
(0-7645-5264-3)

Available wherever books are sold. Go to www.dummies.com or call 1-877-762-2974 to order direct

FOR DUMMIES®

Plain-English solutions for everyday challenges

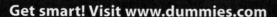